KS3 Maths Progress

Confidence • Fluency • Problem-solving • Progression

δ ONE

Series editors:

Dr Naomi Norman • Katherine Pate

PEARSON

Published by Pearson Education Limited, Edinburgh Gate, Harlow, Essex, CM20 2JE.

www.pearsonschoolsandfecolleges.co.uk

Text © Pearson Education Limited 2014
Typeset by Tech-Set Ltd, Gateshead
Original illustrations © Pearson Education Limited 2014
Cover illustration by Robert Samuel Hanson
Index by Wendy Simpson

The rights of Sharon Bolger, Jack Barraclough, Lynn Byrd, Andrew Edmondson, Catherine Murphy and Katherine Pate to be identified as authors of this work have been asserted by them in accordance with the Copyright, Designs and Patents Act 1988.

First published 2014

17 16 15 14
10 9 8 7 6 5 4 3 2 1

British Library Cataloguing in Publication Data
A catalogue record for this book is available from the British Library

ISBN 978 1 447 962311

Printed in Italy by Lego S.p.A

Acknowledgements
The publisher would like to thank the following for their kind permission to reproduce their photographs:

DK Images: William Reavell 192; Fotolia.com: agsandrew 59, Brian Jackson 141, Grasko 37, James Thew 244, kbuntu 11, Tan Kian Khoon 92, 131, Tyler Olson 35; Getty Images: Agence Zoom / Alexis Boichard 133, National Geographic / Brian J.Skerry 14, Vladimir Rys Photography 41; Masterfile UK Ltd: 207; Pearson Education Ltd: Lord and Leverett 215, Oxford Designers & Illustrators Ltd 1; Plainpicture Ltd: Mira 39; Science Photo Library Ltd: Detlev van Ravenswaay 29, Peter Menzel 242; Shutterstock.com: 5AM Images 113, Anton Balazh 61, bikeriderlondon 183, Four Oaks 240, gwb 181, Johan Swanepoel 212, Stephen VanHorn 87, Warren Goldswain 6; Veer / Corbis: Alexey Stiop 110, arekmalang 137, Baloncici 159, CandyBoxImages 210, cbrignell 218, Comaniciu Dan Dumitru 65, Corepics 139, Eyesee 116, Gabriel Blaj 135, Imager 221, Ivonne 186, j. sierpniowka 188, kuzma 107, leeser 167, majaPHOTO 144, Monkey Business Images 89, Norbert Suto 235, pixelsaway 56, QQ7 237, solarseven 165, stefano lunardi 4, stillfx 84, suljo 67, trekandscout 81, Tristan3D 162, Tritooth 190

All other images © Pearson Education

Every effort has been made to trace the copyright holders and we apologise in advance for any unintentional omissions. We would be pleased to insert the appropriate acknowledgement in any subsequent edition of this publication.

CONTENTS

Unit 8 Multiplicative reasoning

Unit 9 Perimeter, area and volume

Unit 10 Sequences and graphs

KS3 Maths Progress

Confidence • Fluency • Problem-solving • Progression

Pedagogy at the heart – This new course is built around a unique pedagogy that's been created by leading mathematics educational researchers and Key Stage 3 teachers. The result is an innovative learning structure based around 10 key principles designed to nurture confidence and raise achievement.

Pedagogy – our 10 key principles

- Fluency
- Mathematical Reasoning
- Multiplicative Reasoning
- Problem Solving
- Progression
- Concrete-Pictorial - Abstract (CPA)
- Relevance
- Modelling
- Reflection (metacognition)
- Linking

Progression to Key Stage 4 – In line with the 2014 National Curriculum, there is a strong focus on fluency, problem-solving and progression to help prepare your students' progress through their studies.

Stretch, challenge and support – Catering for students of all abilities, these Student Books are structured to deliver engaging and accessible content across three differentiated tiers, each offering a wealth of worked examples and questions, supported by key points, literacy and strategy hints, and clearly defined objectives.

Within each unit:

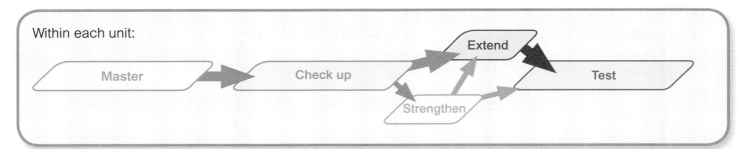

Master → Check up → Extend → Strengthen → Test

Differentiated for students of all abilities:

Alpha	Pi	Theta	Delta
Tier Access	Tier 1	Tier 2	Tier 3

Progress with confidence!

This innovative Key Stage 3 Maths course embeds a modern pedagogical approach around our trusted suite of digital and print resources, to create confident and numerate students ready to progress further.

Help at the front-of-class – **ActiveTeach Presentation** is our tried and tested service that makes all of the Student Books available for display on a whiteboard. The books are supplemented with a range of videos and animations that present mathematical concepts along a concrete - pictorial - abstract pathway, allowing your class to progress their conceptual understanding at the right speed.

Learning beyond the classroom – Focussing on online homework, **ActiveCourse** offers students unprecedented extra practice (with automarking) and a chance to reflect on their learning with the confidence-checker. Powerful reporting tools can be used to track student progression and confidence levels.

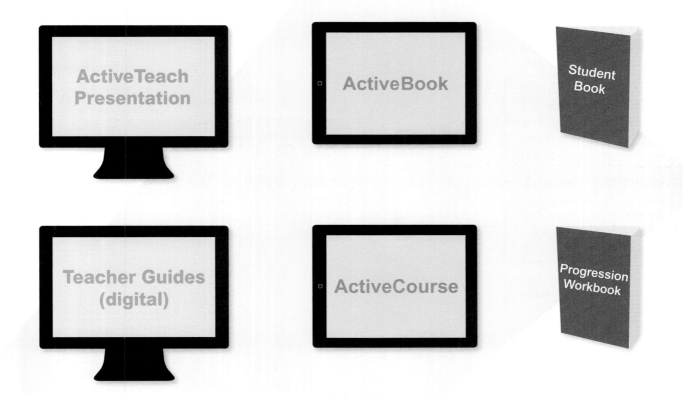

Easy to plan, teach and assess – Downloadable **Teacher Guides** provide assistance with planning through the Schemes of Work. Lesson plans link both front-of-class **ActiveTeach Presentation** and **ActiveCourse** and provide help with reporting, functionality and progression. Both **Teacher Guides** and **ActiveTeach Presentation** contain the **answers** to the Student Book exercises.

Teacher Guides include **Class Progression Charts** and **Student Progression Charts** to support formative and summative assessment through the course.

Practice to progress – KS3 Maths Progress has an extensive range of practice across a range of topics and abilities. From the **Student Books** to write-in **Progression Workbooks** through to **ActiveCourse**, there is plenty of practice available in a variety of formats whether for in the classroom or for learning at home independently.

> **For more information, visit**
> **www.pearsonschools.co.uk/ks3mathsprogress**

Welcome to KS3 Maths Progress student books!

Confidence · Fluency · Problem-solving · Progression

Starting a new course is exciting! We believe you will have fun with maths, at the same time nurturing your confidence and raising your achievement.

Here's how:

Extend helps you to apply the maths you know to some different situations. *Strengthen* and *Extend* both include *Enrichment* or *Investigations*.

At the end of the *Master* lessons, take a *Check up* test to help you decide to *Strengthen*, or *Extend* your learning. You may be able to mark this test yourself.

Choose only the topics in *Strengthen* that you need a bit more practice with. You'll find more hints here to lead you through specific questions. Then move on to *Extend*.

When you have finished the whole unit, a *Unit test* helps you see how much progress you are making.

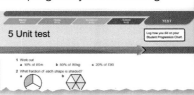

Clear *Objectives,* showing what you will cover in each lesson, are followed by a *Confidence* panel to boost your understanding and engage your interest.

Have a look at *Why Learn This?* This shows you how maths is useful in everyday life.

Improve your *Fluency* – practise answering questions using maths you already know.

The first questions are *Warm up.* Here you can show what you already know about this topic or related ones…

…before moving on to further questions, with *Worked examples* and *Hints* for help when you need it.

Your teacher has access to Answers in either ActiveTeach Presentation or the Teacher Guides.

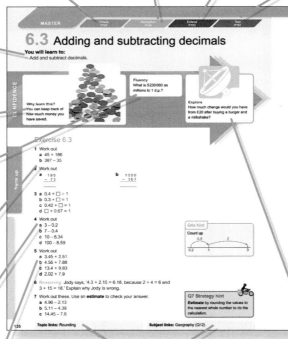

Topic links show you how the maths in a lesson is connected to other mathematical topics. Use the *Subject links* to find out where you might use the maths you have learned here in your other lessons, such as science, geography and computing .

Explore a real-life problem by discussing and having a go. By the end of the lesson you'll have gained the skills you need to start finding a solution to the question using maths.

STEM and Finance lessons

Context lessons expand on *Real, STEM* and *Finance* maths. Finance questions are related to money. STEM stands for Science, Technology, Engineering and Maths. You can find out how charities use maths in their fundraising, how engineers monitor water flow in rivers, and why diamonds sparkle (among other things!)

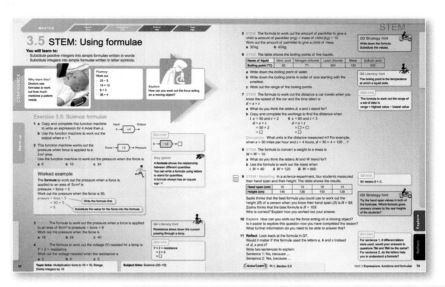

Some questions are tagged as *Finance* or *STEM*. These questions show how the real world relies on maths. Follow these up with whole lessons that focus on how maths is used in the fields of finance, science and technology.

As well as hints that help you with specific questions, you'll find *Literacy hints* (to explain some unfamiliar terms) and *Strategy hints* (to help with working out).

You can improve your ability to use maths in everyday situations by tackling *Modelling, Reasoning, Problem-solving* and *Real* questions. *Discussions* prompt you to explain your reasoning or explore new ideas with a partner.

At the end of each lesson, you get a chance to *Reflect* on how confident you feel about the topic.

Your teacher may give you a Student Progression Chart to help you see your progression through the units.

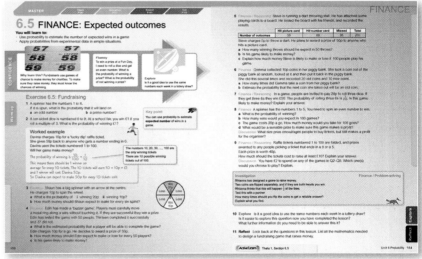

Further support

You can easily access extra resources that tie in to each lesson – look for the ActiveLearn icon on the lesson pages for ActiveCourse online homework links. These are clearly mapped to lessons and provide fun, interactive exercises linked to helpful worked examples and videos.

The Progression Workbooks, full of extra practice for key questions will help you reinforce your learning and track your own progress.

Enjoy!

1.1 Two-way tables and bar charts

You will learn to:
- Use two-way tables
- Interpret and draw dual bar charts and compound bar charts.

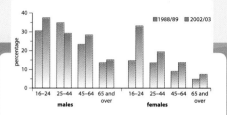

Why learn this?
Tables and charts are used by the Office of National Statistics to show how data compares.

Fluency
What are the next two numbers?
- 0, 5, 10, 15...
- 20, 22, 24, 26...
- 0, 50, 100, 150...

Explore
What information does the Office for National Statistics display using dual bar charts?

CONFIDENCE

Exercise 1.1

Warm up

1 Chris drew this bar chart to show his classmates' favourite cold drinks.
   a How many students like squash best?
   b Four students prefer which drink?
   c How many more students prefer fizzy drinks to juice?
   d How many students are in Chris's class?

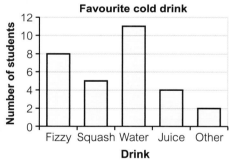

Favourite cold drink

2 Alan and Yolanda complete record sheets for their weekend press-ups.

Name: Alan	Name: Yolanda
Press-ups	Press-ups
Sat 20	Sat 20
Sun 22	Sun 15

   a Copy and complete this **two-way table**.

	Sat	**Sun**	**Total**
Alan			
Yolanda			
Total			

Key point
A **two-way table** splits data into groups in rows across the table and in columns down the table. You can calculate the totals across and down.

   b Write Alan's data in the top row. Work out the total.
   c Write Yolanda's data in the second row.
   d Work out the total of each column.
   e Add the row totals together. Check by adding the column totals together.

Subject links: Geography (Q8)

3 The gadgets owned by some Year 7 students are recorded.
smartphone, tablet, laptop, mp3, smartphone, mp3, tablet, smartphone,
smartphone, tablet, laptop, mp3, smartphone, mp3, tablet, mp3,
smartphone, smartphone

a Copy and complete the **frequency** table for this data.

Digital gadget	Frequency
mp3 player	
smartphone	
tablet	
laptop	

b Copy and complete the **frequency diagram**.

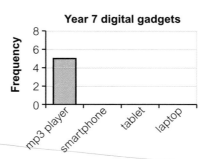

4 The frequency table shows some recycling by the Sohal and Jenkins families for a month.

	Cans	Glass bottles	Plastic bottles	Cardboard boxes	Newspapers and magazines
Sohal	45	50	45	20	30
Jenkins	35	20	65	50	5

a Copy and complete the dual bar chart.

b How many cans did the Jenkins family recycle?

c Which item was recycled most by the Sohal's?

d How many glass and plastic bottles were recycled altogether?

e Which family recycled more?

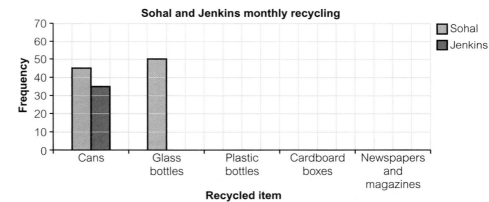

5 The **compound bar chart** shows the photos Giselle uploaded to different websites.

a **i** How many photos of herself did Giselle upload to Facebook?

   ii How many photos of places did Giselle upload to Facebook?

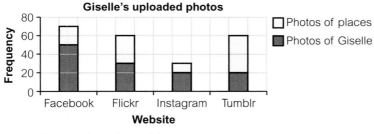

b Copy and complete the table.

	Facebook	Flickr	Instagram	Tumblr
Photos of Giselle				
Photos of places				

c Did Giselle upload more photos of herself than of places? Explain your answer.

6 Students from three different schools were asked which charity they would prefer to raise money for. The tally chart shows the results.

	Oxfam	Save the Children	RSPCA	Help the Aged
St Mary	卌	卌 l	卌 l	lll
Chilbrook	ll	卌 llll	卌 ll	llll
Oakmead	lll	llll	卌 卌	lll

a Copy and complete the compound bar chart.

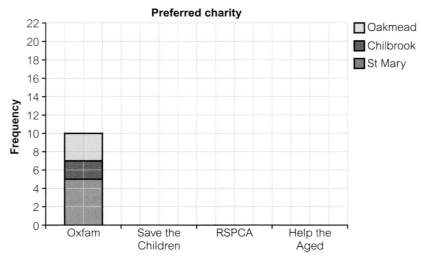

b How many students at Chilbrook answered the questionnaire?
c At which school did the RSPCA receive the most votes?
d Which charity received the most votes overall?

7 STEM Hugh counted the butterflies and bees that were attracted to different colours of flowers in his garden.

	White	Yellow	Red	Blue	Green
Bees	7	15	2	18	1
Butterflies	7	10	8	3	3

a How many butterflies and bees visited blue flowers?
b Which are the most attractive colours for bees?
c Hugh says, 'Bees and butterflies are equally attracted to white.'
   Is he correct? Explain your answer.
d Write a sentence about how bees and butterflies

   i differ in their colour preferences

   ii are similar in their colour preferences.

8 Explore What information does the Office for National Statistics display using dual bar charts?
Look back at the maths you have learned in this lesson. How can you use it to answer this question?

9 Reflect In this lesson you compared data using dual bar charts and compound bar charts. Which type of chart did you find easier to interpret? Why?
When would it be more useful to use a compound bar chart?
When would it be more useful to use a dual bar chart?

1.2 Averages and range

You will learn to:
* Choose the most appropriate average for a set of data
* Find the mode, median, mean and range for a set of data
* Compare sets of data using averages and the range.

Why learn this?
Personal fitness trainers use statistics to track the progress of their clients.

Fluency
1, 2, 2, 3, 7
* What is the mode?
* What is the range?
* What is the median?

Explore
How would you compare fitness before and after a 6-week training programme?

Exercise 1.2

1 Two players scored these points in a table-tennis tournament.
   Sara   12, 11, 10, 9, 10   **Jamil**   2, 12, 6, 0, 8, 10
   For each player, work out the
   a mode   **b** median   **c** mean   **d** range.

2 A group of people are asked their favourite sport.
   The frequency diagram shows the results.
   What is the mode?

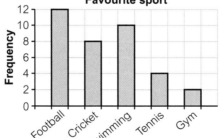

Favourite sport

3 Two football clubs scored these goals in a tournament:
   Wanderers   6, 0, 6, 0, 0, 1, 7   **Rangers**   2, 1, 0, 1, 2, 1, 2, 2
   a Work out the range for each team.
      Which team is more consistent?
   b Work out the median for each team.

Q2 hint

Which bar shows the 'most common' sport?

Key point

The **average** gives a typical value for a set of data. The mode, median and mean are different ways of describing the average.

Q3 hint

The closer the results are to one another, the more *consistent* they are. The smaller the range, the more consistent the values.

Worked example

The table shows the number of players injured in rugby matches. Work out the mean.

Injuries	Frequency	Total number of injuries
0	8	8 × 0 = 0
1	4	4 × 1 = 4
2	6	6 × 2 = 12
3	2	2 × 3 = 6
Total	20	22

Mean = 22 ÷ 20 = 1.1

Add a column to work out the total number of injuries.

6 players had 2 injuries. 6 × 2 = 12 injuries altogether.

Work out the total frequency number of rugby players and the total number of injuries.

Mean = total number of injuries ÷ number of players.

Warm up

4 The table shows the number of goals scored in netball matches in one season. Work out the mean.

Goals scored	Frequency
0	4
1	8
2	5
3	3

5 The table shows the number of fouls in hockey games. Work out the mean.

Fouls	Frequency
0	4
1	9
2	5
3	0
4	2

6 Joel recorded the transfer fees paid for new players in his favourite two football clubs. He used the data to work out these **statistics**.

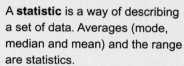

	Range	Mean (£1000s)
Sheffield Wednesday	£650 000	£315 000
Doncaster Rovers	£1 050 000	£285 000

Write two sentences comparing the fees paid by the two clubs.

Q6 Literacy hint

A **statistic** is a way of describing a set of data. Averages (mode, median and mean) and the range are statistics.

7 Reasoning Here are the finishing times, in minutes, of all the runners in a cross-country race.
17, 20, 18, 24, 16, 20, 21, 18, 21, 100
  a Which is an **extreme value**?
  b Work out the mean, median and mode.
  c Which average best describes the runners' times?
  Discussion Which of the mean, median and mode is affected most by an extreme value?

Key point

An **extreme value** is one that is much bigger or smaller than the other values.

8 The table shows how far, in metres, different remote control toys can go before losing signal.

Q8 hint

Which toy was most consistent? Which had the greatest range?

Helicopter	20	20.5	19	21	18	19.5	18
Plane	19	17.5	20	18	18.5	19.5	19.5
Dog	19.5	19	20.5	16	18	20	17.5

Use the ranges and medians to write two sentences comparing the performance of the different toys.

9 **Explore** How would you compare fitness before and after a 6-week training programme?
Is it easier to explore this question now you have completed the lesson?
What further information do you need to be able to answer this?

10 **Reflect** You often see the word 'average' in headlines:
    Average screen size of TVs grows again
      The changing face of the average American
Think carefully about your understanding of mean, median and mode.
Which type of average do you think each headline refers to and why?

Q10 Strategy hint

It may help you to write definitions in your own words.

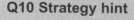

1.3 Grouped data

You will learn to:
- Group discrete and continuous data
- Draw and interpret grouped frequency diagrams.

Why learn this?
Grouping people's ages helps to show the age distribution in the UK.

Fluency
12, 20, 9, 19
- Which of these numbers are contained in the class 10–19?
- How can you tell the mode from a frequency diagram?

Explore
Estimate the percentage of the population that is eligible to vote.

Exercise 1.3

1 Write these values into a grouped frequency table like this:
7, 3, 8, 11, 2, 21, 15, 12, 4, 20, 13, 2, 15, 12, 4, 17

Class	Tally	Frequency
1–5		
6–10		

2 **Real** Harry measured the pulse rate (beats per minute) of some classmates.

Pulse rate	Frequency
70–79	1
80–89	8
90–99	7
100–109	3

a How many students had a pulse rate between 80 and 89?
b How many students had a pulse rate between 90 and 109?
c What is the **modal class**?

3 Is each set of data **discrete** or **continuous**?
a The maximum daily temperatures in May.
b The numbers of songs on some mp3 players.
c The masses of a batch of bread loaves.
d The data in Q2.
e Shoe sizes

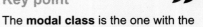

Key point
The **modal class** is the one with the highest frequency.

Key point
Discrete data can only take particular values. For example, dress sizes can only be even numbers. For discrete data you can use groups like 1–10, 11–20 …
Continuous data is measured and can take any value. For example, length, mass and capacity. For continuous data there are no gaps between the groups.

4 A researcher measured the wingspans of some long-eared bats.
18 cm, 28 cm, 25 cm, 8 cm, 19 cm, 22 cm, 11 cm, 24 cm, 5 cm, 13 cm,
23 cm, 23 cm

a Copy and complete the grouped frequency table for the data.
Make the **classes** have equal widths.

b What is the modal class?

Wingspan, w (cm)	Frequency
$0 \leqslant w < 10$	
$10 \leqslant w < \square$	
$\square \leqslant w < \square$	

> **Key point**
>
> Continuous data is grouped into
> continuous **class intervals**.
> The class interval 140 cm $\leqslant h <$ 150 cm
> includes all heights h between 140 cm
> and 150 cm.
> The $\leqslant$ symbol means that 140 cm is
> included.
> The $<$ symbol means that 150 cm is
> not included.
> The width of this class is 10 cm.

Investigation   Problem-solving

The data shows the times, in minutes, that some students spent vigorously exercising in a day.
90, 15, 10, 0, 5, 0, 10, 20, 25, 50, 0, 0, 15, 8, 50, 45, 20, 30, 17, 10, 30, 70, 45, 25, 20

a **i** Make a frequency table for the data. Use 5 equal class intervals.
  ii Draw a frequency diagram for the data.
b Repeat part **a**. This time use 10 equal class intervals.
c Which diagram do you think shows the data best? Explain your answer.

Discussion Explain your choice of intervals.

---

5 Carla measured the heights, h cm, of some students in her class.
The grouped frequency table shows her results.

Height, h (cm)	Frequency
$120 \leqslant h < 130$	1
$130 \leqslant h < 140$	4
$140 \leqslant h < 150$	6
$150 \leqslant h < 160$	5
$160 \leqslant h < 170$	2

> **Q5 hint**
>
> For continuous data, there are no
> spaces between the bars.

a Copy and complete the frequency
diagram.
b Which is the modal class?
c How many students are at least
150 cm tall?

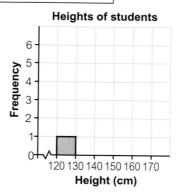

Heights of students

6 **Explore** Estimate the percentage of the population that is eligible
to vote.
Look back at the maths you have learned in this lesson.
How can you use it to answer the question?

7 **Reflect** Look back at the investigation. When do you think it is
sensible to use grouped data? When would using grouped data look
confusing?
Do you think it's always important to have equal class intervals for
grouped data? Why or why not?

1.4 More graphs

You will learn to:
- Interpret and draw line graphs
- Recognise when a graph is misleading.

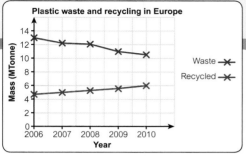

Plastic waste and recycling in Europe

Waste —✕—
Recycled —✕—

Why learn this?
Line graphs can be used to predict future outcomes.

Fluency
Which graph shows the temperatures:
- increasing
- decreasing
- staying the same?

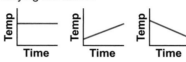

Explore
How can line graphs show the worst and best scenarios?

Exercise 1.4

1 The line graph shows how the volume of air in a scuba tank changed during a dive.
  a How much air was in the tank
    i at the start of the dive
    ii after 20 minutes?
  b How long did it take for volume of air to drop to 7 litres?
  c How much air did the diver use during the last 20 minutes of the dive?
  d When was the diver the most active during the dive? Explain your answer.

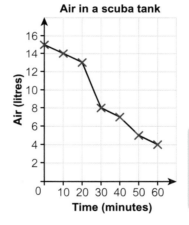

Air in a scuba tank

Key point
When a line graph shows changes over time, put time on the horizontal axis.

2 Modelling The table shows the daily maximum wind speed in knots in the Hebrides in one week.

Day	Mon	Tue	Wed	Thu	Fri	Sat	Sun
Speed (knots)	31	33	41	41	42	57	60

  a Copy the axes. Plot the points using crosses. Join the points with a ruler.
  b Callum says this is a good model for predicting the wind speed for the next few months. Explain why he is wrong.

  Discussion Does every point on the line graph mean something?

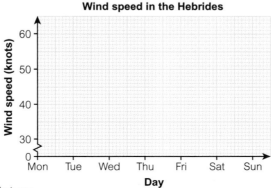

Wind speed in the Hebrides

Q2 Literacy hint
A 'knot' is a unit of speed used on ships and aircraft.

Q2a hint
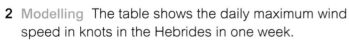
The zig-zag shows there's a break in the axis scale.

Q2b hint
'Explain' means write a sentence:
This is not a good model because…

3 Real The graph shows the predicted and recorded tide heights at Lowestoft during a winter storm in 2013.

a   **i** What time was the highest recorded tide?

   ii What height was the highest recorded tide?

   iii How much higher was the recorded tide than the predicted tide at 4 pm?

b   What time is the lowest recorded tide?

c   Write a sentence to compare

   i the predicted and recorded tide times

   ii the predicted and recorded heights.

Tide heights at Lowestoft

(Graph: Height (m) on vertical axis, Time on horizontal axis from 8 am to 8 pm; two lines labelled Recorded and Predicted.)

Q3 hint

Were the predicted high and low tide times correct?

4 Real The table gives the mean monthly temperatures (°C) in Canberra and London over one year.

	Jan	Feb	Mar	Apr	May	Jun	Jul	Aug	Sep	Oct	Nov	Dec
Canberra	20	21	17	13	9	6	5	7	9	12	15	18
London	10	4	4	6	8	12	15	17	17	14	10	7

a   Draw a line graph to show both sets of temperatures.
   Put the months on the horizontal axis.
   Choose a suitable scale for the vertical axis.

b   Which are the coldest three months in

   i Canberra

   ii London?

c   Write two sentences about your graph, comparing the temperatures in Canberra and London.
   You could use some of these words: warmer, colder, maximum, minimum, range.

Q4c hint

Compare maximum, minimum and range.

5 Reasoning Apasra drew these two line graphs to show the sales of digital tablets and personal computers.

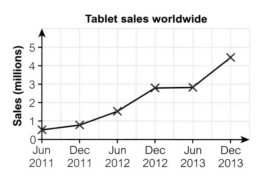

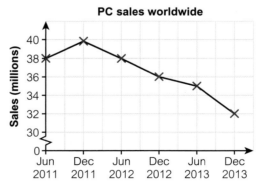

She wrote this newspaper headline:
'Massive rise in tablet sales. Epic decline in PC sales.'

a   Explain why Apasra's line graphs are misleading.

b   Draw the PC sales graph using the axis for the tablet sales graph.

c   Write a more accurate newspaper headline.

Q5a hint

Look at the vertical scale of each graph.

6 The bar chart and table show the CD sales of music singles between 1997 and 2003 in the UK.

Year	Sales, millions
1997	78
1998	74
1999	71
2000	56
2001	51
2002	44
2003	31

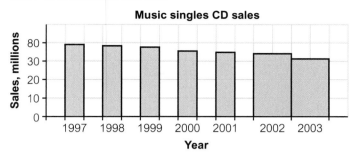

Music singles CD sales

a Give two reasons why the bar chart is misleading.
b Draw an accurate bar chart.

Q6b hint

Do you need to start the sales axis at 0?

7 The table shows the weather for Lerwick, Scotland.

	Jan	Feb	Mar	Apr	May	Jun	Jul	Aug	Sep	Oct	Nov	Dec
Max temp, °C	5	5	6	8	11	13	14	14	13	10	8	6
Rainfall, mm	109	97	69	68	52	55	72	71	87	104	111	118

Copy these axes.

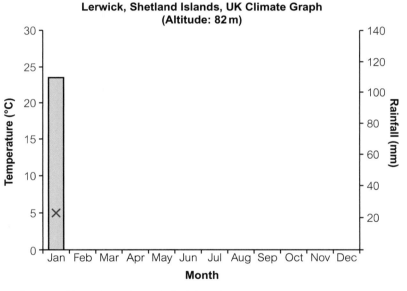

Lerwick, Shetland Islands, UK Climate Graph (Altitude: 82 m)

Q7 hint

Plot the temperature in the middle of each month.

a Draw a bar chart for rainfall (mm).
b On the same graph, draw a line graph for maximum temperature (°C).
c Write two sentences describing how the weather changed during the year.

8 **Explore** How can line graphs show the worst and best scenarios? Is it easier to explore this question now you have completed the lesson?
What further information do you need to be able to answer this?

9 **Reflect** List five ways that graphs can mislead you.
You could begin with 'It is misleading when different scales are ...'

1.5 Pie charts

You will learn to:
- Draw and interpret pie charts.

CONFIDENCE

Why learn this?
Pie charts can show who receives portions of income.

Fluency
- How many degrees are there in a circle?

- What fraction is blue?

Explore
How much do bands get paid?

Exercise 1.5

Warm up

1 Work out the fraction of each amount.

  a $\frac{1}{2}$ of 60   **b** $\frac{1}{4}$ of 32   **c** $\frac{1}{8}$ of 16

  d $\frac{1}{3}$ of 120   **e** $\frac{1}{4}$ of 360   **f** $\frac{1}{8}$ of 260

2 Use a ruler and protractor to draw these angles.
  a 60°   **b** 135°

3 The **pie chart** shows the favourite musical instruments of some Year 7 students.

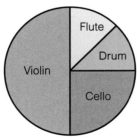

> **Key point**
>
> A **pie chart** is a circle divided into slices called **sectors**.
> The whole circle represents a set of data.
> Each sector represents a fraction of the data.

  a Which is the most popular instrument? How do you know?

  b What fraction of students prefer the

    i cello

    ii flute?

  c There are 32 students altogether.
    Copy and complete this frequency table.

Instrument	Frequency
Violin	
Flute	
Cello	
Drum	

> **Q3c hint**
>
> Work out a fraction of 32 for each instrument.

Topic Links: Fractions, Drawing angles

Worked example

Draw a pie chart to show this data about the tracks on a classical CD.

Track	Frequency
Opera	6
Orchestra	4
Piano	2

Total number of tracks = 6 + 4 + 2 = 12

> The total number of tracks is the total frequency.

÷ 12 (12 tracks is 360° / 1 track is 30°) ÷ 12

> Work out the angle for one track.

Opera × 6 (1 track is 30° / 6 tracks are 180°) × 6

> Work out the angle for each type of music.

Orchestra 4 × 30° = 120°

Piano 2 × 30° = 60°

> Check that the angles add up to 360°.

Check: 180° + 120° + 60° = 360°

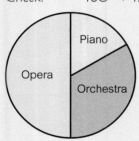

Tracks on CD

> Draw the pie chart. Label each sector or make a key (you do not have to label the angles).
> Give your pie chart a title.

---

4 The table shows the number of boys, girls and teachers in a school orchestra.

Musician	Frequency	Angle
Boys	12	
Girls	9	
Teachers	3	

a Work out the total number of musicians.

b Copy and complete: one musician is 360° ÷ □ = □°

c Work out the angle for boys, girls and teachers. Check that the angles add up to 360°.

d Draw a pie chart.

> **Q4d hint**
>
> Draw a circle. Draw in a radius. Then use a protractor to draw the angles. Label the sectors.

5 The table shows the percentages of sales in a bakery in one month.

a What angle in a whole circle represents

i 40%

ii 30%

iii 10%?

b Draw a pie chart of the data.

Item	Percentage
bread	40%
cakes	10%
pies	30%
pastries	20%

6 A travel company asked 180 people where they went for their
holidays. The table shows their answers.

   a When you divide a circle into equal sectors to show 180 people,
   how many degrees represent one person?

   b Work out the angles for 15, 30, 45 and 90 people.

   c Draw a pie chart to show the holiday data.

Holiday	Frequency
England	90
Scotland	30
Ireland	15
Wales	45
Total	**180**

7 **Problem-solving** The pie charts show a rock band's
income in 2004 and 2014.

   a In 2004, $\frac{1}{3}$ of income was from concerts.
   How much did the band earn from concerts in 2004?

   b How much did the band earn from CDs in 2014?

   c Hedda says, 'The pie charts show that the band
   earned more from CDs in 2004 than in 2014.'
   Explain why she is wrong.

   d Copy and complete the two-way table to show the
   income.

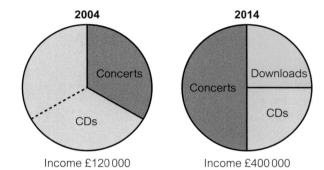

2004 — Concerts, CDs

2014 — Downloads, Concerts, CDs

Income £120 000   Income £400 000

	Concerts	CDs	Downloads
2004			
2014			

Q7 Strategy hint

Show working to explain
why Hedda is wrong.

Investigation   **Problem-solving**

1 Use a spreadsheet to draw a pie chart for this data on the top popular music.
   Pop 27%, Rock 20%, RnB 15%, Classical 8%, Dance 5% Country 4%, Other 21%

   a Input the data.

   b Select the cells containing the data.

   c Click the **Insert tab** on the top menu and select **Pie**.

   d Try 2D and 3D charts.

   e Give your pie chart a title.

2 Save your pie chart, then move the Classical, Dance and Country to the 'Other' section.
   Create and save a new pie chart. Which pie chart is easier to read?

Discussion What do you think is the maximum number of sectors for a pie chart to be able to read it clearly? Why?

3 Create and save a new pie chart showing 'Pop' and 'Other'.

Discussion Is two sectors enough for a pie chart? Explain your answer.

---

8 **Explore** How much do bands get paid?
   Is it easier to explore this question now you have completed the
   lesson? What further information do you need to be able to answer
   this?

9 **Reflect** Tomar says that fractions help you to interpret pie charts
   (like in Q3).
   What other areas of mathematics help you to interpret pie charts?
   What maths skills do you need to draw pie charts?

1.6 STEM: Scatter graphs and correlation

You will learn to:

- Interpret and draw scatter graphs
- Describe the correlation between two sets of data
- Draw a line of best fit and use it to estimate values.

Why learn this?
Biologists and ecologists collect data about plants and animals. This helps us understand how habitats are changing and the impact we have on the natural world.

Fluency
Look at these coordinate axes. What does one small square represent
- on the horizontal axis
- on the vertical axis?

Explore
How can a biologist work out whether water pollution in a river has any effect on the growth of plants and wildlife?

Exercise 1.6

1 What are the coordinates of points A, B, C and D?

2 Copy the coordinate grid from Q1.
Plot these points. A (8, 4) B (5, 0) C (3, 10) D (7, 1)

Key point

A **scatter graph** shows two sets of data on the same graph.
The shape of a scatter graph shows if there is a relationship or **correlation** between two sets of data.

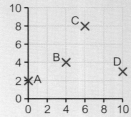
Positive correlation

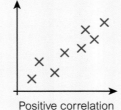
Negative correlation

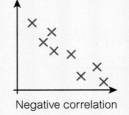
No correlation

3 STEM / Reasoning This **scatter graph** shows the heights of 20 trees in a conservation area, and the diameter of their trunks 1 m above the ground.

a Describe the **correlation** shown by this scatter graph.

b Write down the height of the tree that had a trunk diameter of 6 cm.

c Write down the trunk diameter of the trees that had a height of 26 m.

d Nisha believes that one of the points has been plotted incorrectly. Which point do you think this is? Give a reason for your answer.

Discussion Can you suggest another reason why one of the data points might not be in line with the others?

Tree sizes

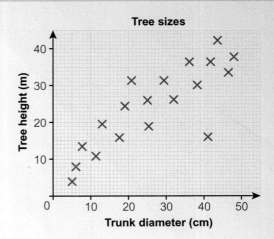

4 STEM / Reasoning This table shows the gestation period and litter size for 12 mammals.

Mammal	Baboon	Dog	Goat	Hamster	Hedgehog	Raccoon	Squirrel	Tiger
Gestation period (days)	180	62	150	16	34	64	38	104
Average litter size	1	4	2	6.3	4.6	3.5	3	3

a Copy these axes onto graph paper.
Draw a scatter graph to show this information.

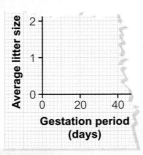

Q4a hint

Remember to give your scatter graph a **title**.

b Describe the correlation between gestation period and litter size.
c Choose two words from the cloud to complete this sentence:
Mammals with _____ gestation periods tend to have _____ offspring in each litter.

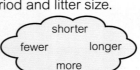

shorter
fewer   longer
more

Q4 Literacy hint

The gestation period for a mammal is the length of time it takes a foetus to grow from fertilisation to birth.

Worked example

The scatter graph shows the body length and wingspan of 10 peregrine falcons.
a Draw a line of best fit on the scatter graph.

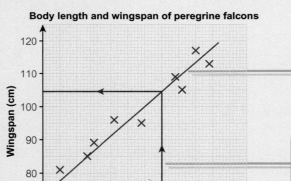

Body length and wingspan of peregrine falcons

Use a transparent ruler to draw your **line of best fit**. Try it in different positions until you have roughly the same number of points on each side of the line. The line can pass through some of the points.

Draw a line from 50 cm body length to the line of best fit. Draw a line across and read off the wingspan.

b Use your line of best fit to estimate the wingspan of a peregrine falcon with a body length of 50 cm.

104 cm

Key point

A **line of best fit** shows the relationship between two sets of data. There should be the same number of crosses on each side of the line. There may also be crosses on the line.

5 STEM / Real This table shows the age and shell size of 8 Dungeness crabs.

Shell size (mm)	152	150	140	133	156	138	142	155
Age (years)	3.3	3.0	2.4	2.3	3.3	2.5	2.7	3.4

a Draw a scatter graph for this data.
Use axes like these.

b Describe the correlation between shell size and age.

c Draw a line of best fit on your scatter graph.
In California, fishermen are not allowed to catch Dungeness crabs with a shell size smaller than 146 mm.

d Use your line of best fit to estimate the minimum age of a Dungeness crab which can be legally caught in California.

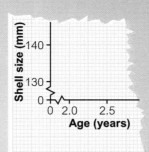

Q5a hint

Read the scales carefully and work out what each small subdivision represents.

6 STEM / Reasoning This table shows the number of plaice recorded at 12 different points in the Barents Sea, and the sea temperature at each point.

Temperature (°C)	1.6	2.4	2.9	0.4	1.2	0.2	1.0	0.6	2.2	2.9	1.7	2.6
Number of fish	135	70	30	225	145	290	160	250	130	45	100	75

a Draw a scatter graph for this data.

b Describe the correlation between number of fish and sea temperature.

c Draw a line of best fit on your scatter graph.

d Use your line of best fit to estimate the number of fish where the sea temperature is 2.1°C.

e Climate scientists estimate that average sea temperatures have increased by approximately 0.2°C. Use your graph to discuss how this could affect the population of plaice in the Barents sea.

Q6a Strategy hint

Use one large grid square to represent 50 fish.

7 Explore How can a biologist work out whether water pollution in a river has any effect on the growth of plants and wildlife?
Is it easier to explore this question now you have completed the lesson?
What further information do you need to be able to answer this?

8 Reflect What are the limitations of the data given in Q6?
Think about your answer to Q6e.
How confident are you in your statement?
What additional data would you need to improve your confidence?

Explore

Reflect

1 Check up

Log how you did on your
Student Progression Chart.

Averages and range

 1 The frequency table shows the number of children in the families of some Year 7 students.

Work out the mean number of children per family.

Children	Frequency
1	9
2	7
3	3
4	1

 2 Hayley recorded the distances, in km, pupils live from Primary school.
0.5, 1, 1, 1, 2, 2, 7, 3, 0.5, 2

  a **i** Find the median distance.

    ii Work out the mean distance.

    iii Work out the range.

  b Hayley says, 'The median is the best average to use for this data.'
Is she correct? Explain your answer.

  c Hayley also recorded distances, in km, from Secondary school. She calculated the same statistics.

Median	Mean	Range
3 km	3.63 km	11 km

Choose the correct word to complete this statement.
Students live closer to _____ school, on average.

Primary
Secondary

Charts and tables

3 80 boys and 60 girls choose their favourite topics in maths.
The pie chart shows the results for boys.

  a Which is the boys' favourite topic?

  b Copy and complete the two-way table.

	Number	Algebra	Statistics	Geometry
Boys				
Girls	20	10	20	10

  c Draw a pie chart for the girls.

  d Draw a dual bar chart for the data.

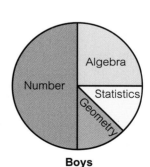

Boys

4 This frequency diagram shows the heights of wheat stalks.

  a What is the modal class?

  b How many stalks are in the class $120 \leqslant h < 125$?

  c How many stalks are at least 120 cm tall?

  d Marcia says, 'This graph shows there are more than double the number of stalks in class $125 \leqslant h < 130$ than in $120 \leqslant h < 125$.'
Explain why she is wrong.

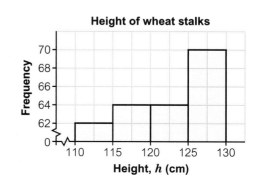

Height of wheat stalks

5 The bar chart shows the medals received by four countries at the 2012 Olympics.

a Which country won most silver medals?

b How many more gold medals did Kazakhstan win than Iran?

c A quarter of the medals won by one country were bronze. Which country?

d Which kind of medal was won by these countries the most?

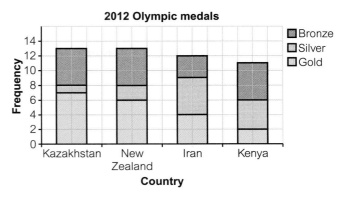

2012 Olympic medals

Line graphs, scatter graphs and correlation

6 The line graphs show the depth of snow at two ski resorts at the end of each month.

a What was the depth of snow at Winter Park in April?

b Which ski resort had snow earliest?

c In which months did Winter Park have more snow than Avoriaz?

d At which ski resort did the snow start melting first? How can you tell?

e What was the difference in depth of snow between the two resorts in February?

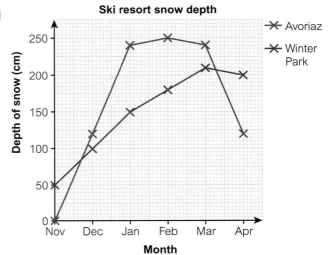

Ski resort snow depth

7 The scatter graph shows the fuel consumption of some second-hand cars of different masses.

a Describe the correlation between fuel consumption and mass.

b What is the missing word in this sentence.
The greater the mass of the car, the _____ the fuel consumption.

c Use the red line of best fit to estimate

  i the fuel consumption of a car of mass 1000 kg

  ii the mass of a car with a fuel consumption of 20 mpg.

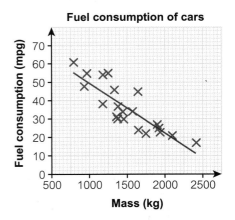

Fuel consumption of cars

8 How sure are you of your answers? Were you mostly

 Just guessing 😐 **Feeling doubtful** 🙂 **Confident**

What next? Use your results to decide whether to strengthen or extend your learning.

Challenge

9 a Write down three numbers whose range is 2.

b Write down three numbers whose median is 8.

c Write down three numbers whose mean is 5.

10 a The numbers 4, 2, 7, □ have a mode of 2. What is the missing number?

b The numbers 4, 2, 5, □ have a mean of 4. What is the missing number?

c The numbers 20, 70, 10, □ have a range of 80. What is the missing number?

d The numbers 8, 4, 6, □ have a median of 5. Write down a possible value of the missing number.

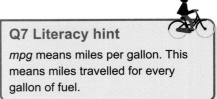

Q7 Literacy hint

mpg means miles per gallon. This means miles travelled for every gallon of fuel.

Reflect

Master
P1

Check
P17

STRENGTHEN

Extend
P23

Test
P27

1 Strengthen

You will:

• Strengthen your understanding with practice.

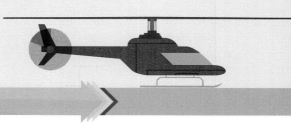

Averages and range

1 Here are marks for three rounds of a quiz.
Jo: 6, 5, 7   Karl: 12, 1, 6

   a Whose results are the more consistent?

   b Work out the range for Jo and for Karl.

   c Write the missing word from this sentence.
Choose from 'greater' or 'smaller'.
The _____ the range, the more consistent the results.

   d Who would you like on your team, Jo or Karl? Explain why.

 2 Fiona recorded the number of times she used her smartphone each hour one Sunday evening:
3, 0, 1, 2, 7

   a **i** Work out the mean.

      ii Work out the range.

   b Work out the mean and range for Monday evening:
2, 1, 1, 2, 3

   c Write down the missing word for each sentence. Choose from 'more' or 'less'.
On average, Fiona used her smartphone _____ on Sunday.
The data for Sunday is _____ consistent than the data for Monday.

3 You can tell the mass of a bowling ball in kg by its colour.

   a Copy this frequency table.

Mass (kg)	Frequency	Total mass (kg)
2	3	3 × 2 = 6
3		
4		
5		
Total		

   b Fill in the row for each mass. The first one has been done for you.

   c **i** Work out the total in the last row.

      ii What is the total mass of the balls?

      iii How many balls are there?

   d Work out the mean mass of these bowling balls.

Q1a hint

Whose results are more or less the same every time?

Q2ai hint

Work out the total. Divide the total by the number of values.

Q3b hint

3 balls at 2 kg each = 6 kg

Q3d hint

Mean = Total mass
  ÷ Total number of balls

Charts and tables

1 The table shows some dentist appointments on one day.

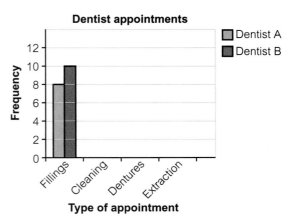

Dentist appointments

Type of appointment	Fillings	Cleaning	Dentures	Extraction
Dentist A	8	11	5	3
Dentist B	10	4	1	3

The blue bar shows Dentist A had 8 appointments for fillings.

a How many appointments did Dentist B have for fillings?

b Copy and complete the dual bar chart for the data.

Q1b hint

Look at one type of appointment at a time. Draw the blue bar (Dentist A) and then the orange bar (Dentist B) touching it.

2 Ollie asked some Year 7 students what they like reading most.

	Fiction	Graphic novels	Non-fiction	Magazines
Boys		7	6	5
Girls		5	4	6

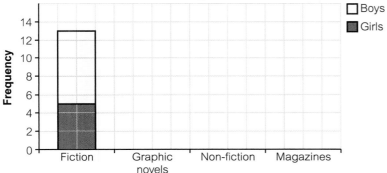

Year 7 reading choices

He started to draw a compound bar chart for the data.

a How many girls prefer fiction?

b How many boys prefer fiction?

c Copy and complete the bar chart.

Q2b hint

Look at the Frequency axis. Count up from the top of the orange part to find the height of the yellow part.

Q2b hint

Draw the yellow bars (girls) first. Then draw the green bars (boys) on top.

3 The pie charts show how Dana and Karen spent their birthday money.

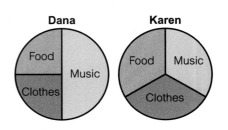

a Who spent the bigger proportion of birthday money on clothes?

b What fraction of her birthday money did Dana spend on music?

c Dana had £40 for her birthday. How much did she spend on music?

d What fraction of her birthday money did Karen spend on food?

e Karen had £30 for her birthday. How much did she spend on food?

f Copy and complete the table to show the amounts Dana and Karen spent on music, clothes and food.

	Music	Clothes	Food
Dana			
Karen			

Q3a hint

Which colour shows clothes? Who has the bigger sector for clothes?

4 This table shows the O'Brien family recycling.

Item	Frequency	Sector angle
Newspapers	5	
Cans	4	
Bottles	10	
Cardboard	1	

a How many items did they recycle altogether?

b This circle is divided into 20 equal sectors.
Work out the angle of one sector.

c How many sectors of the circle would you shade for cardboard?

d How many sectors of the circle would you shade for cans?

e What is the sector angle for cans?

f Copy and complete the table of sector angles.
Check they add up to 360°.

g Draw a pie chart to show the O'Brien family's recycling.

O'Brien family recycling

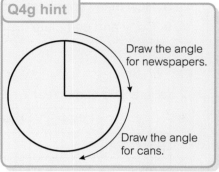

Q4g hint

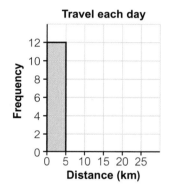

Draw the angle for newspapers.

Draw the angle for cans.

5 Darren recorded the distance, d km, he travelled each day.
0, 0, 0, 1, 1, 2, 2, 2, 2, 3, 3, 4, 5, 7, 7, 8, 9, 9, 10, 12, 12, 15, 18, 19, 21, 23

Distance, d (km)	Tally	Frequency
$0 \leqslant d < 5$	卌 卌 ‖	12
$5 \leqslant d < 10$		
$10 \leqslant d < 15$		
$15 \leqslant d < 20$		
$20 \leqslant d < 25$		

a Copy and complete the tally chart.

b Which is the modal class?

c Copy and complete the frequency diagram for this data.

Travel each day

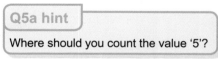

Q5a hint

Where should you count the value '5'?

Line graphs, scatter graphs and correlation

1 Leo recorded his best javelin throw at a competition each year.
He drew two graphs to show his results.

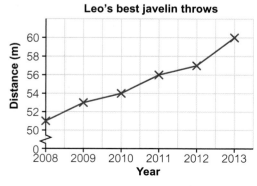

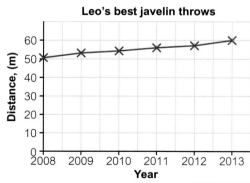

Which graph makes Leo look better? Why?

Q1 hint

Leo looks better in graph ☐ because...

Topic links: Using formulae, Conversions

2 The line graph shows the money, in £, John gave to two charities.

a How much was given to each charity in January?

b In which month was £50 given to Oxfam?

c In which month was more money given to the RSPCA than Oxfam?

d How much more money was given to Oxfam than the RSPCA in May?

e Fill in the missing word. Choose from: 'increased', 'decreased'.

   i Between April and June, the amount donated to the RSPCA ___.

   ii Between April and June, the amount donated to Oxfam ___.

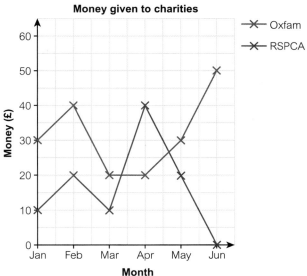

Money given to charities

3 A group of students took tests in French reading and writing.

The table shows their results.

Student	Dave	Sierra	Vicky	Will	Lila	Paul	Raj	Gavin	Chris
Reading	4	2	5	6	7	7	8	10	10
Writing	6	3	4	6	8	5	7	10	9

a Copy the axes. Plot a point for each student.

b What is the missing word from this sentence? Choose from: 'positive', 'negative', 'no'.
There is _____ correlation between the students' reading and writing results.

c Draw a straight line of best fit.

d Use your line of best fit to estimate

   i the reading score of a student who scored 4 on the writing test.

   ii the writing score of a student who scored 8 on the reading test.

> **Q2c hint**
> Where is the red point higher than the blue point?

> **Q2d hint**
> Work out the difference between the two amounts.

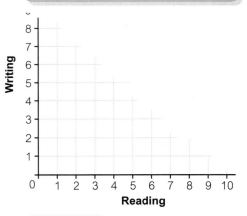

Enrichment

1 Gabby and her friend Rebecca travel by bus to Rochdale.
Gabby gets on at Rawtenstall, and Rebecca gets on at Rising Bridge.

a How much longer is Rebecca on the bus than Gabby?

b How much time are they on the bus together?

Bus timetable for route 464						
Accrington	1133	1148	1203	1218	1233	1248
Rising Bridge	1141	1156	1211	1226	1241	1256
Rawtenstall	1202	1217	1232	1247	1302	1317
Waterfoot	1207	1222	1237	1252	1307	1322
Rochdale	1248	1303	1318	1333	1348	1403

> **Q3b hint**
> Positive correlation: looking from (0, 0), the points go 'uphill': the values are increasing.
> Negative correlation: looking from (0, 0), the points go 'downhill': the values are decreasing.
> No correlation: the points are not close to a straight line, uphill or downhill

2 Reflect For these strengthen lessons, copy and complete these sentences:

I found questions _____ easiest. They were on _____ (list the topics)

I found questions _____ most difficult. I still need help with _____ (list the topics)

1 Extend

You will:
• Extend your understanding with problem-solving.

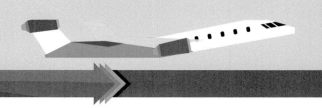

1 The tables show the goals scored by Arsenal and Newcastle United during the same period.

Arsenal	
Goals	**Frequency**
0	4
1	4
2	7
3	4
4	1

Newcastle United	
Goals	**Frequency**
0	7
1	5
2	4
3	2
4	1
5	1

Which team scored the most goals, on average?

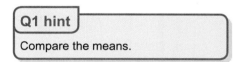

Q1 hint

Compare the means.

2 **Problem-solving** These compound bar charts show the percentage of medals won by The Netherlands and Poland in the 2012 Olympics.
   a Which country won the higher percentage of Gold medals?
   b What percentage of The Netherlands' medals were Silver?
   c The Netherlands won 20 medals altogether.
      Poland won 10 medals.
      How many Bronze medals did Poland win?
   d How many Silver medals did The Netherlands win?
   e Draw a two-way table to show the numbers of medals won by each country.

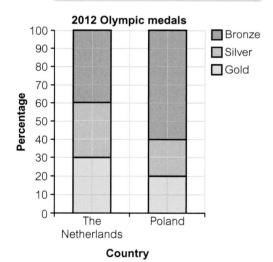

3 A station manager recorded the number of minutes late for all trains in one hour.
   18, 1, 0, 3, 2, 11, 4, 9, 42, 11, 12, 0, 0, 23, 25, 2, 15, 13
   a Design a grouped frequency table for the data.
      The classes in your table must have equal widths.
      Write the inequality for each class.
   b Write a sentence about the lateness of the trains.

4 Reasoning The line graph shows the number of full-time and part-time workers in the USA.

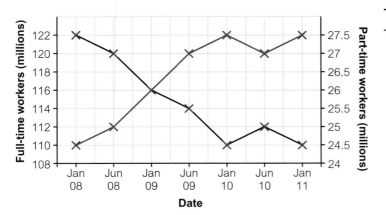

a How many part-time workers were there in June 2010?

b How many full-time workers were there in January 2011?

c A magazine used this caption with the graph:
'Fall in full-time jobs matched by rise in part-time jobs.'
Explain why the caption is wrong.

Discussion Does the point where the graphs cross mean anything?

Q4 hint

Read the values on each graph.

5 a Here are the masses, in kg, of the rowers in the 2012 Oxford University rowing team.
77.8, 82.4, 91.6, 93.6, 91.2, 94.6, 79.6, 96.8

 i What is their median mass?

 ii Work out the range.

 iii Calculate their mean mass.

b The table below shows some statistics about the masses of the 2012 Cambridge University rowers.

Mean	Median	Range
96.3	94.5	17.8

Write two sentences comparing the masses of the rowing teams.

c **Reasoning** The cox is an extra member of the rowing team.
The Oxford cox has a mass of 49.6 kg.

 i Which statistic does this extra value change the most?

 ii What is the most suitable average to use for the mass of the team?

6 Reasoning The chart shows the number of generators hired out each day by a company.

  a What is the modal number of generators hired per day?

  b On how many days were more than 2 generators hired out?

  c Draw a frequency table for the data in the chart.

  d Work out the mean number of generators hired per day.

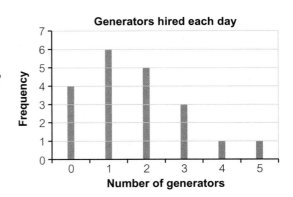

Generators hired each day

7 Real The emergency response times, t minutes, for ambulances in a town were recorded for a week.
8.2, 4.2, 16.1, 5.3, 7.3, 9.6, 6.9, 19.3, 12.7,
13.6, 4.9, 6.1, 5.8, 7.3, 3.5, 8.8, 11.1

a Tally the times into a grouped frequency table.
   Use 5 equal classes.
b What is the modal class?

Time, t minutes	Frequency
$0 \leqslant t < 4$	
$4 \leqslant t < \square$	

c **Reasoning** The government target is to respond within 8 minutes.
   i How many ambulances achieved this target?
   ii How many did not?
d Draw a frequency diagram for the data.
e Here are the first few emergency response times for the next week.
   4.2, 7.8, 5.1, 6.0, 9.7, 7.3, 8.4, 8.9
   i What is unusual about this data? Give a possible reason for it.
   ii Work out the mode, median and mean for this data.
   iii **Reasoning** Which one of these three averages best represents the data?

8 STEM / Reasoning The pie charts show the electricity generated by renewable technology in France in 2010 and Germany in 2011.

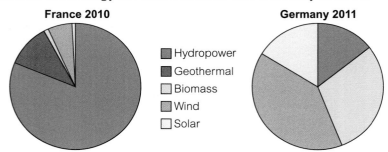

France 2010 **Germany 2011**

- Hydropower
- Geothermal
- Biomass
- Wind
- Solar

a Estimate the fractions generated by
   i hydropower in France   ii biomass in Germany.
b The total renewable electricity generated in France was 4468 GWh.
   Estimate the electricity generated by hydropower.
c The total renewable electricity generated in Germany was 123 000 GWh.
   Estimate the electricity generated by biomass.
d Write one or two sentences describing the main differences in the way France and Germany generate electricity using renewable technology.

9 Problem-solving For his geography project, Lee asked shoppers in the town centre how far they had travelled to the shops that day.

Distance travelled, d (miles)	Frequency
$0 \leqslant d < 3$	9
$3 \leqslant d < 6$	5
$6 \leqslant d < 9$	4
$9 \leqslant d < 12$	2

a Draw a pie chart to show his data.
b Complete these sentences from Lee's report.
   i The modal distance travelled to the shops is _____.
   ii Fewer than half the shoppers had travelled less than _____.
   iii Just over 25% of shoppers had travelled more than _____.

> **Q9 hint**
> The pie chart will have 4 sectors.
> Work out the total frequency first.

Topic links: Percentages, Fractions, Drawing angles, Measures, Money

Subject links: PE (Q1, 2, 5), Science (Q8), Geography (Q9)

10 The table shows the heights, h cm, of a class of Year 7 students.

	$135 \leqslant h < 140$	$140 \leqslant h < 145$	$145 \leqslant h < 150$	$150 \leqslant h < 155$	$155 \leqslant h < 160$	Total
Boy	3	7	3	4	0	
Girls	2	2	6	4	1	
Total						

a Copy and complete the table.
b How many girls are shorter than 150 cm?
c How many students are at least 145 cm tall?
d Compare the average height of girls and boys.

Investigation   Reasoning

1 Work out the mean of these numbers: 2, 2, 2, 6, 8
2 a Add 1 to each of the numbers and work out their mean again.   **b** How has the mean changed?
3 a Multiply each of the numbers in part **1** by 3 and work out their mean again.   **b** How has the mean changed?
4 a What do you think would happen to the mean if you divided the numbers in part **1** by 2?   **b** Try it and see if
   your prediction is correct.

Worked example

Find the mean of 100, 97, 98, 105, 103 using an **assumed mean**.

$$100, 97, 98, 105, 103$$
Differences from 100 $0 \quad -3 \quad -2 \quad +5 \quad +3 \quad = 3$
$$3 \div 5 = 0.6$$
100 + 0.6 = 100.6

> Add the mean difference to the assumed mean.

> The values are all close to 100, so assume the mean is 100. Work out the differences from 100.

> **Add** up the 5 differences and **divide** by 5 to find the mean difference.

Key point

The **assumed mean** is a sensible estimate for the mean.

---

11 **Finance / Reasoning** A consumer watchdog recorded the prices a supermarket charged for a box of cereal each week. Here are the results.
£2.90, £3.50, £3.00, £3.20, £3.70
Use an assumed mean of £3 to calculate the mean price.

12 **Problem-solving** Lars and 9 other students measured their left- and right-hand grip strength.

Student	Lars	Dana	Phil	Esther	Jane	Marcus	Derek	Jack	Mason	Rafiq
Left-hand strength (kg)	25	17	34	20	24	48	32	41	33	26
Right-hand strength (kg)	27	14	31	16	22	50	36	39	38	25

Lars did hand exercises for the next 6 months. At the end of each month, he recorded the strength of his right hand. The results are shown below.

Month	Mar	Apr	May	Jun	Jul	Aug
Right-hand strength (kg)	26	28	28	30	35	37

a Draw a suitable graph for each table of data.
b Use your graphs to estimate the strength of Lars' left hand at the end of August.

> **Q12b hint**
> Draw a line of best fit and use it to make an estimate.

13 **Reflect** List all the different ways you have learned for displaying data.
Which way to display data do you find:
• Easiest to read and understand? Why?
• Hardest to read and understand? Why?
• Easiest to draw? Why?
• Hardest to draw? Why?

Reflect

Master
P1
Check
P17
Strengthen
P19
Extend
P23
TEST

1 Unit test

Log how you did on your Student Progression Chart.

1 The table shows the sizes of parcels delivered by a postman and a courier on Monday.

	Small	Medium	Large
Postman	15	10	5
Courier	10	15	20

a How many parcels were delivered by the postman on Monday?
b How many large parcels were delivered in total?
c How many parcels were delivered altogether?
d The compound bar chart shows the deliveries made on Tuesday.
   i How many large parcels were delivered by the courier on Tuesday?
   ii How many more small parcels did the postman deliver on Tuesday than on Monday?
   iii How many medium parcels were delivered on both days altogether?

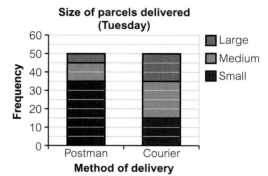

Size of parcels delivered (Tuesday)

2 The frequency table shows the accidents in one month on a busy road before speed cameras were fitted.
a What is the modal number of accidents?
b Work out the mean number of accidents.
c The average number of accidents after speed cameras were fitted is shown here.

Mode	Mean
0	1.2

Accidents	Frequency
0	10
1	12
2	9
3	6
4	3

Write a sentence comparing the number of accidents before and after speed cameras were fitted.

3 The table shows dogs' favourite treats.

Draw a pie chart for the data.

Treat	Frequency
Biscuits	3
Bones	4
Rawhide	6
Chicken	5

4 Zakira recorded the distance, in km, she walked each day.
7, 4, 2, 6, 4, 31, 5
Which average should she use to describe the data?
Explain your answer.

5 Two pans of hot water were left to cool to room temperature.
One pan had a lid. The graph shows the recorded temperatures.
a What was the temperature of the water in the pan with the lid after 20 minutes?
b What was room temperature?
c Compare the times it took the pans to reach room temperature.
d What was the difference in the temperatures after 30 minutes?

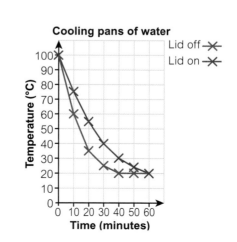

Cooling pans of water

10 The table shows the heights, h cm, of a class of Year 7 students.

	$135 \leqslant h < 140$	$140 \leqslant h < 145$	$145 \leqslant h < 150$	$150 \leqslant h < 155$	$155 \leqslant h < 160$	Total
Boy	3	7	3	4	0	
Girls	2	2	6	4	1	
Total						

   a Copy and complete the table.   **b** How many girls are shorter than 150 cm?

   c How many students are at least 145 cm tall?   **d** Compare the average height of girls and boys.

Investigation   **Reasoning**

1 Work out the mean of these numbers: 2, 2, 2, 6, 8

2 a Add 1 to each of the numbers and work out their mean again.   **b** How has the mean changed?

3 a Multiply each of the numbers in part **1** by 3 and work out their mean again.   **b** How has the mean changed?

4 a What do you think would happen to the mean if you divided the numbers in part **1** by 2?   **b** Try it and see if your prediction is correct.

Worked example

Find the mean of 100, 97, 98, 105, 103 using an **assumed mean**.

                         100, 97, 98, 105, 103

Differences from 100   0 −3 −2 +5 +3   = 3

                                   3 ÷ 5 = 0.6

100 + 0.6 = 100.6

> Add the mean difference to the assumed mean.

> The values are all close to 100, so assume the mean is 100. Work out the differences from 100.

> **Add** up the 5 differences and **divide** by 5 to find the mean difference.

Key point

The **assumed mean** is a sensible estimate for the mean.

---

11 **Finance / Reasoning** A consumer watchdog recorded the prices a supermarket charged for a box of cereal each week. Here are the results.

£2.90, £3.50, £3.00, £3.20, £3.70

Use an assumed mean of £3 to calculate the mean price.

12 **Problem-solving** Lars and 9 other students measured their left- and right-hand grip strength.

Student	Lars	Dana	Phil	Esther	Jane	Marcus	Derek	Jack	Mason	Rafiq
Left-hand strength (kg)	25	17	34	20	24	48	32	41	33	26
Right-hand strength (kg)	27	14	31	16	22	50	36	39	38	25

Lars did hand exercises for the next 6 months. At the end of each month, he recorded the strength of his right hand. The results are shown below.

Month	Mar	Apr	May	Jun	Jul	Aug
Right-hand strength (kg)	26	28	28	30	35	37

   a Draw a suitable graph for each table of data.

   b Use your graphs to estimate the strength of Lars' left hand at the end of August.

Q12b hint

Draw a line of best fit and use it to make an estimate.

13 **Reflect** List all the different ways you have learned for displaying data. Which way to display data do you find:

   • Easiest to read and understand? Why?

   • Hardest to read and understand? Why?

   • Easiest to draw? Why?

   • Hardest to draw? Why?

Reflect

1 Unit test

Log how you did on your Student Progression Chart.

1 The table shows the sizes of parcels delivered by a postman and a courier on Monday.

	Small	Medium	Large
Postman	15	10	5
Courier	10	15	20

a How many parcels were delivered by the postman on Monday?
b How many large parcels were delivered in total?
c How many parcels were delivered altogether?
d The compound bar chart shows the deliveries made on Tuesday.
  i How many large parcels were delivered by the courier on Tuesday?
  ii How many more small parcels did the postman deliver on Tuesday than on Monday?
  iii How many medium parcels were delivered on both days altogether?

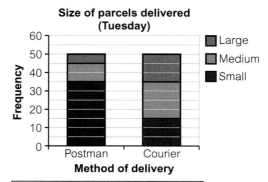

2 The frequency table shows the accidents in one month on a busy road before speed cameras were fitted.

Accidents	Frequency
0	10
1	12
2	9
3	6
4	3

a What is the modal number of accidents?
b Work out the mean number of accidents.
c The average number of accidents after speed cameras were fitted is shown here.

Mode	Mean
0	1.2

Write a sentence comparing the number of accidents before and after speed cameras were fitted.

3 The table shows dogs' favourite treats.

Draw a pie chart for the data.

Treat	Frequency
Biscuits	3
Bones	4
Rawhide	6
Chicken	5

4 Zakira recorded the distance, in km, she walked each day.
7, 4, 2, 6, 4, 31, 5
Which average should she use to describe the data?
Explain your answer.

5 Two pans of hot water were left to cool to room temperature.
One pan had a lid. The graph shows the recorded temperatures.
a What was the temperature of the water in the pan with the lid after 20 minutes?
b What was room temperature?
c Compare the times it took the pans to reach room temperature.
d What was the difference in the temperatures after 30 minutes?

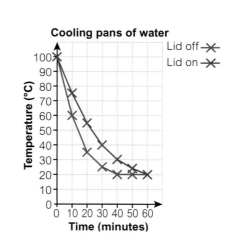

6 The table shows the distances jumped in the men's large hill ski jumping individual qualifying round at the Sochi Winter Olympics.

Distance (m)	131	130	130	129	128	127	127	126	126	125

Work out the mean distance jumped.

7 Here are the masses of some calves on a farm:
37 kg, 58 kg, 49 kg, 42 kg, 38 kg, 57 kg, 44 kg, 40 kg, 51 kg, 48 kg, 38 kg, 40 kg, 46 kg, 50 kg, 41 kg

a Copy and complete the tally chart for the data.

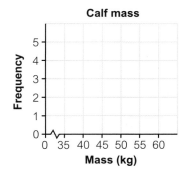

Calf mass

Mass, m (kg)	Tally	Frequency
$35 \leqslant m < 40$		
$40 \leqslant m < 45$		
$45 \leqslant m < 50$		
$50 \leqslant m < 55$		
$55 \leqslant m < 60$		

b What is the modal class?
c Copy and complete the frequency diagram for the data.

8 The table shows the wingspan and leg length, in cm, of some peregrine falcons.

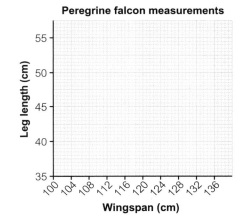

Peregrine falcon measurements

Wingspan (cm)	102	120	117	112	132	111	126	118	121	107
Leg length (cm)	40	47	45	44	54	45	50	43	50	47

a Draw a scatter graph for the data using these axes.
b Describe the correlation between wingspan and leg length.
c Draw a line of best fit.
d Use your line of best fit to estimate
  i the leg length of a falcon with a wingspan of 124 cm
  ii the wingspan of a falcon with leg length 45 cm.

Challenge

9 The table shows the music albums sold monthly by two bands.

	Jan	Feb	Mar	Apr	May	Jun	Jul	Aug
The Breakers	1200	1300	1350	1500	1700	1750	1700	1600
Tempest	500	550	500	600	700	850	850	950

a Draw a misleading line graph that suggests The Breakers are improving sales quicker than Tempest.
b Draw a misleading bar chart that suggests that Tempest is improving sales quicker than The Breakers.

> **Q9 hint**
> You can decide the scale, where the scale starts and how much data to show.

10 Reflect Think back to when you have struggled to answer a question in a maths test.
a Write two words that describe how you felt.
b Write two things you could do when you struggle to answer a question in a maths test.
c Imagine you have another maths test and you do those two things you wrote in your answer to part **b**. Would you feel the same as you answered in part **a**? Explain.

Reflect

2.1 Factors, primes and multiples

You will learn to:
- Understand the difference between multiples, factors and primes
- Find all the factor pairs of any whole number
- Find the HCF and LCM of two numbers.

CONFIDENCE

Why learn this?
Astronomers use the LCM to work out when planets are going to be in line.

Fluency
What are the missing numbers?
- $6 \times \square = 36$
- $\square \times 4 = 36$
- $12 \times \square = 36$
- $\square \times 18 = 36$
- $1 \times \square = 36$

Explore
How many rows of bricks and how many rows of breeze blocks would you need to make walls the same height?

Exercise 2.1

1 Look at these numbers.
   2, 3, 4, 5, 8, 12, 15, 18, 20, 24, 30
   Which are
   a **multiples** of 3   b multiples of 5   c **factors** of 40?

Q1 hint

A **multiple** of 3 is a number in the 3 times table.
A **factor** of 10 is a whole number that divides exactly into 10.

2 Look at these numbers.
   4, 6, 8, 12, 16, 18, 20, 24, 28, 30, 32, 36
   a Which are multiples of
      i 4   ii 6   iii 4 and 6?
   b Copy and complete this **Venn diagram**.
      Write each number in the correct section.

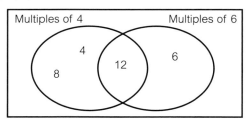

Multiples of 4   Multiples of 6

4   12   6

8

Warm up

Q2b Literacy hint

A **Venn diagram** shows sets of items.

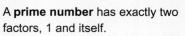

3 Here is a list of numbers.
   2, 3, 6, 9, 11, 14, 17, 21, 25
   Which are **prime numbers**?
   Discussion Is a prime number always an odd number? Is an odd number always a prime number?

4 a Write down all the factors of 28.
   b Write down all the **prime factors** of 28.

Key point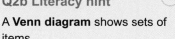

A **prime number** has exactly two factors, 1 and itself.

Key point

A **prime factor** is a factor of a number that is also a prime number.

Subject links: Technology (Q13, Q15)

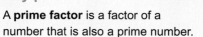

Worked example

Find all the factors of 72.

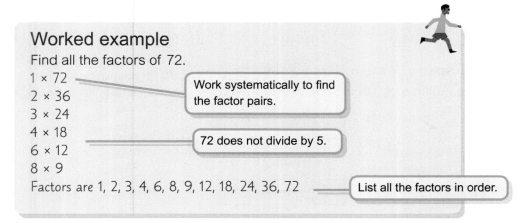

1 × 72 — Work systematically to find the factor pairs.
2 × 36
3 × 24
4 × 18 — 72 does not divide by 5.
6 × 12
8 × 9

Factors are 1, 2, 3, 4, 6, 8, 9, 12, 18, 24, 36, 72 — List all the factors in order.

5 Find all the factors of
   a 48   **b** 56   **c** 104   **d** 100   **e** 36

   Discussion What type of number has an odd number of factors?

6 Problem-solving Hayley finds all the factors of a number.
   This is her list.

   1, 2, 3, 4, ☐, 9, 12, 13, ☐, ☐, 36, 39, ☐, 78, ☐, 156, 234, 468
   What are the missing numbers?

7 **a** Write down all the factors of 8.
   b Write down all the factors of 12.
   c Write down the common factors of 8 and 12.
   d What is the **highest common factor** of 8 and 12?

8 **a** Copy and complete this Venn diagram to show the factors of 15 and 18.

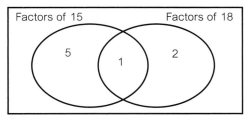

   b What is the HCF of 15 and 18?

9 Find the HCF of each pair of numbers.
   a 6 and 9   **b** 20 and 24   **c** 6 and 18
   Discussion Is the HCF always one of the numbers?

10 Problem-solving / Reasoning In this number wheel, the HCF of opposite numbers is equal to the number in the middle.
   Use the numbers from the cloud to copy and complete the wheel.
   Explain how you worked out your answers.

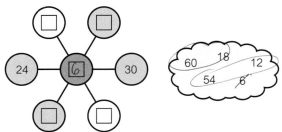

> **Q7c Literacy hint**
>
> What factors do 8 and 12 have in common?

> **Key point**
>
> The **highest common factor (HCF)** of two numbers is the largest number that is a factor of both numbers.

11 a List the first 10 multiples of 3.

b List the first 6 multiples of 5.

c Write down the common multiples of 3 and 5.

d What is the **lowest common multiple** of 3 and 5?

Key point

The **lowest common multiple** (**LCM**) of two numbers is the smallest number that is a multiple of both numbers.

12 Reasoning The diagram shows four numbers linked by lines.

a Work out the LCM of each pair of linked numbers.

b Which pair of numbers has the smallest LCM? Explain why.

c Which pairs of numbers have the same LCM? Explain why.

13 STEM The diagram shows two cogs. The larger cog has 12 teeth and the smaller cog has 8 teeth.

The cogs start to turn with the red dots next to each other.

What is the smallest number of turns each cog must make before the red dots are next to each other again?

14 Problem-solving Sita draws this Venn diagram to work out the LCM of two numbers.

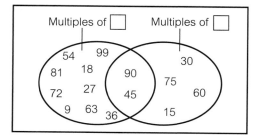

Copy and complete Sita's statement.

The LCM of ☐ and ☐ is ☐

Investigation   Problem-solving

A red light flashes every 6 seconds.

A blue light flashes every 8 seconds.

Work with a partner to answer these questions.

1 Both lights flash at the same time. How many seconds until they flash at the same time again?

2 Explain how you can work out all the times when the lights flash together.

3 A purple light flashes every 7 seconds and a yellow light flashes every 9 seconds.
Which pair of lights will flash together most within 1 minute?

---

15 Explore How many rows of bricks and how many rows of breeze blocks would you need to make walls the same height?
Is it easier to explore this question now you have completed the lesson? What further information do you need to be able to answer this?

16 Reflect Write your own short definition for each of these mathematical words:

highest   lowest   common   factor   multiple

Now use your definitions to write (in your own words) the meaning of:

highest common factor   lowest common multiple

Active Learn   Delta 1, Section 2.1

2.2 Using negative numbers

(core) incl. larger no's + decimals

You will learn to:
- Add, subtract, multiply and divide positive and negative numbers.

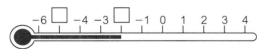

Why learn this?
The number line extends equally in the positive and negative directions – infinitely.

Fluency
Which is colder?
- 3°C or −2°C
- −4°C or −1°C

Explore
What is the difference between the average temperatures on different planets in the solar system?

Warm up

Exercise 2.2

1 What are the missing numbers on the thermometer?

−6 ☐ −4 −3 ☐ −1 0 1 2 3 4

2 a The temperature is 6°C. It gets 8 degrees colder.
   What is the new temperature?
 b The temperature is −7°C. It gets 5 degrees warmer.
   What is the new temperature?

3 Which sign, < or >, goes between each pair of numbers?
 a 3 ☐ −2   **b** −4 ☐ −1   **c** 5 ☐ −8   **d** −10 ☐ −11

4 Use this number line to work out

−10 −9 −8 −7 −6 −5 −4 −3 −2 −1 0 1 2 3 4 5 6 7 8 9 10

 a 7 − 12   **b** −9 + 15   **c** −2 − 7   **d** −10 + 8

5 a Copy and complete these patterns.

i 2 + 3 = 5	**ii** 2 − 3 = −1
2 + 2 = ☐	2 − 2 = ☐
2 + 1 = ☐	2 − 1 = ☐
2 + 0 = ☐	2 − 0 = ☐
2 + −1 = ☐	2 − −1 = ☐
2 + −2 = ☐	2 − −2 = ☐
2 + −3 = ☐	2 − −3 = ☐

 b Reasoning Which sign, + or −, is missing from each statement?
   i 2 + −3 is the same as 2 ☐ 3.
   ii 2 − −3 is the same as 2 ☐ 3.

 c Copy and complete these rules
   replace + + with +   replace + − with ☐
   replace − + with ☐   replace − − with ☐

Q5b hint
Numbers without a sign in front of them are positive.
2 − 3 is 2 − +3

6 Work out

a $8 + -6$ **b** $-4 + 9$ **c** $-12 + -3$ **d** $-3 - -7$

Q6a hint

$8 + -6 = 8 - 6 = \square$

7 STEM The table shows the melting point and boiling point of four compounds.

   a What is the difference between the melting point and the boiling point of

     i nitric acid

     ii sulfur dioxide?

   b Work out the range of the melting point temperatures.

   c Work out the range of the boiling point temperatures.

Compound	Melting point (°C)	Boiling point (°C)
nitric acid	−42	83
nitrogen chloride	−40	71
nitrogen oxide	−163	−152
sulfur dioxide	−75	−10

8 Problem-solving Here are some number cards.

$\boxed{-5}$ $\boxed{3}$ $\boxed{-7}$ $\boxed{9}$ $\boxed{-4}$

   a Which cards make the calculation $\boxed{} + \boxed{} =$

     i with the greatest possible answer

     ii with the smallest possible answer?

   b Which cards make the calculation $\boxed{} - \boxed{} =$

     i with the greatest possible answer

     ii with the smallest possible answer?

9 a Copy and complete these patterns.

     i $2 \times 3 = 6$ **ii** $-2 \times 3 = -6$

         $2 \times 2 = 4$ $-2 \times 2 = -4$

         $2 \times 1 = \square$ $-2 \times 1 = \square$

         $2 \times 0 = \square$ $-2 \times 0 = \square$

         $2 \times -1 = \square$ $-2 \times -1 = \square$

         $2 \times -2 = \square$ $-2 \times -2 = \square$

         $2 \times -3 = \square$ $-2 \times -3 = \square$

Q9a hint

$2 \times 3 = 6$			$-2 \times 3 = -6$		
2	2	2	−2	−2	−2

   b Reasoning Copy and complete these rules.

     positive × positive = positive   positive × negative = _____

     negative × positive = _____   negative × negative = _____

10 Work out

   a 4×-5 **b** -7×2 **c** -6×-5 **d** 3×-6

   e -4×-4 **f** $-3 \times 2 \times 4$ **g** $5 \times -3 \times -2$ **h** $-7 \times -3 \times -10$

11 Problem-solving Juan writes this question to go with the calculation $3 \times -15 = -45$.

   Anna and John are divers. Anna dives 3 times as deep as John. John dives 15 m below sea level. How deep does Anna dive?

   Write a question to go with this calculation: $4 \times -25 = -100$

Q11 hint

The question could be about money, temperature, distance below sea level or ground level, etc.

12 Copy and complete these number facts.

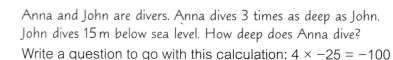

   a $8 \times -2 = -16$ **b** $-8 \times 2 = -16$ **c** $-8 \times -2 = 16$

       $-16 \div -2 = 8$ $-16 \div 2 = \square$ $16 \div -2 = \square$

       $-16 \div 8 = \square$ $-16 \div -8 = \square$ $16 \div -8 = \square$

13 Work out

   a $20 \div -5$ **b** $-12 \div 2$ **c** $-16 \div -4$ **d** $30 \div -6$

   e $-24 \div 4$ **f** $-36 \div -12$ **g** $5 \div -5$ **h** $-7 \div -7$

Key point

Division is the inverse of multiplication.

Multiplication is the inverse of division.

positive ÷ positive = positive

positive ÷ negative = negative

negative ÷ positive = negative

negative ÷ negative = positive

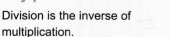

Topic links: Range, Mean   **Subject links:** Science (Q7), Geography (Q15)

14 Problem-solving Here are some number cards.

 −5 3 −7 9 −4

Which cards make the calculation ⬚ × ⬚ =

1·3

a with the greatest possible answer
b with the smallest possible answer?

15 Real / Reasoning The table shows the average minimum temperature in 10 cities in January.

City	Budapest	Canberra	Ellsworth	Harare	Imst	Madrid	Nuuk	Oslo	Ottawa	Stanley
Temperature (°C)	−4	13	−18	17	−6	3	−11	−7	−14	7

a Work out the range in temperatures.
b Work out the mean temperature.
Plymouth has a minimum temperature of 5 °C.
Bucharest has a minimum temperature of −5 °C.
These two cities are added to the list.
c How do these two temperatures affect the range you found in part **a**?
d How do these two temperatures affect the mean you found in part **b**?

1·3

Investigation Reasoning

Here is part of a number grid.

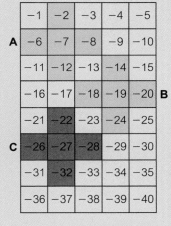

1 A cross of five numbers is shaded green (A).
   Copy and complete these calculations for the green cross:
   left + right = −6 + −8 = ⬚
   top + bottom = −2 + −12 = ⬚
   2 × centre = 2 × −7 = ⬚
2 What do you notice about your three answers to part **1**?
3 Do the same for the cross of numbers shaded
   a blue (B)   b red (C).
4 What do you notice about your answers to part **3**?
5 Does this pattern work for any cross on this grid?
6 Investigate crosses of five squares on different number grids.
   For example, rows of 6, 9, 12 etc.
7 What do you notice about your answers?
8 What happens if you make crosses in a grid with a top row −6 to −1?
9 What about −7 to −1?

---

16 Explore What is the difference between the average temperatures on different planets in the solar system?
Is it easier to explore this question now you have completed the lesson?
What further information do you need to be able to answer this?

17 Reflect Mihir and Zane discuss what is different or the same about negative and positive numbers.
Mihir says, 'Negative numbers get smaller the further you get from zero, but positive numbers get bigger.'
Zane says, 'When you multiply two negative numbers you get a positive answer and when you multiply two positive numbers, you get a positive number answer as well.'
Look back at what you have learned in this lesson about negative numbers.
What else is different about working with positive and negative numbers?
What else is the same?

2.3 Multiplying and dividing

You will learn to:
- Use mental and written strategies for multiplication
- Divide a 3-digit integer by a single or 2-digit integer.

Why learn this?
If you estimate the total cost of a day out, you can make sure you take enough money to pay.

Fluency
Round these numbers to the nearest 10.
- 23
- 69
- 471
- 395

Explore
Estimate the cost of a day out.

Exercise 2.3

1 Work out
  a $4 \times 7 + 9$ **b** $10 - 14 \div 7$ **c** $5 \times 7 - 4 \times 8$

2 Work out
  a $135 \div 3$ **b** $312 \div 6$ **c** $1952 \div 8$

3 Work out
  a 20×50 **b** 22×23 **c** 46×13

4 a Estimate the answer to each of these by rounding to the nearest 10.
  i $23 \times 37 \approx 20 \times \square = \square$
  ii 18×72
  iii 39×64
  b Work out the accurate answers to the calculations in part **a**. Use your estimates to check your answers.

5 Work out
  a 24×8 **b** 12×16 **c** 6×32 **d** 3×64
  Discussion What do you notice about your answers? Why has this happened?

6 Problem-solving / Reasoning In these number wheels, opposite numbers multiply to give the number in the middle. Copy and complete the number wheels.

a
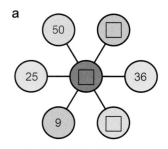

b
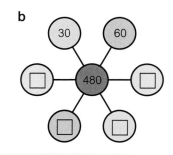

Q1 hint
Use the priority of operations to do calculations:
- Brackets
- Indices or powers
- Multiplication and Division
- Addition and Subtraction

Q4 Literacy hint
In maths, **estimation** means using rounded values to do the calculation. $\approx$ means 'is approximately equal to'.

Topic links: Mean, Area

1-2 as on

Worked example

Work out 326 ÷ 14 using long division.
Estimate the answer first.

Estimate: 326 ÷ 14 is roughly 330 ÷ 15 = 22

$$
\begin{array}{r}
2... \\
14\overline{)326} \\
-28 \quad 2 \times 14 = 28 \\
\hline
46
\end{array}
$$

> 2 × 14 = 28. So 14 goes into 32 twice. 6 − 0 = 6, so bring down 6.

Key point

You can divide a 3-digit number by a 2-digit number using long division.

$$
\begin{array}{r}
23 \\
14\overline{)326} \\
-28 \quad 2 \times 14 = 28 \\
\hline
46 \\
-42 \quad 3 \times 14 = 42 \\
\hline
4
\end{array}
$$

> Try multiplying 14 by different numbers to get close to 46. 3 × 14 = 42

> 4 is less than 14, so the remainder is 4.

326 ÷ 14 = 23 remainder 4

Check: 23 remainder 4 is close to 22 ✓

> Check your answer.

1-2

7 Work out
   a 756 ÷ 12   **b** 832 ÷ 26   **c** 925 ÷ 37   **d** 966 ÷ 42

Q7 hint

Estimate first. Use your estimate to check your answer.

8 Work out
   a 999 ÷ 14   **b** 485 ÷ 21   **c** 432 ÷ 17   **d** 836 ÷ 48

9 These are the ages of 14 members of a dance club.

16	18	15	15	20	19	24
12	25	13	24	22	21	22

Work out the mean age.

10 a Copy and complete the workings for 3 ÷ 5.

$$
\begin{array}{r}
0.\square \\
5\overline{)3.^30}
\end{array}
$$

Q10b i, ii hint

Write in the decimal point and some zeros.

   b Work out
   i $8\overline{)5.000}$ **ii** $4\overline{)7}$ **iii** $5\overline{)14}$

11 Explore Estimate the cost of a day out.
Is it easier to explore this question now you have completed the lesson?
What further information do you need to be able to answer this?

12 Reflect Adele and Fiona are discussing division.
Adele says, 'Division means sharing between people.'
Fiona says, 'Division means grouping into multiples.'
Look at your division answers in this lesson. Who do you agree with?
Write down what division means to you.

Explore

Reflect

2.4 Squares and square roots

You will learn to:
- Use index notation for squares and square roots
- Calculate with squares and square roots.

Why learn this?
Square numbers are used to work out the projectile of a football, or the equivalence of mass and energy, or the area you need to tile.

Fluency
Work out
- 5 × 5
- 8 × 8
- 0.3 × 3
- 0.3 × 0.3
- 0.5 × 5
- 0.5 × 0.5

Explore
What is the best way to arrange 8000 seats into square blocks for a music concert?

Exercise 2.4

1 Which numbers from this list can be arranged as dots in a square?

2   4   8   12   16   20   24   36   42   49   55

2 Work out
a −2 × −2   **b** −4 × −4   **c** −9 × −9

3 Work out the area of each square.

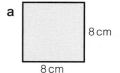
a 8 cm × 8 cm

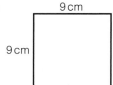
b 9 cm × 9 cm

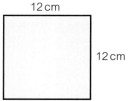
c 12 cm × 12 cm

Discussion How do you find the area of a square using the length of one side?

4 a Copy and complete this table of square numbers from 1 to 15.

1^2	2^2	3^2	4^2	5^2	6^2	7^2	8^2	9^2	10^2	11^2	12^2	13^2	14^2	15^2
1	4													

b Use your table in part **a** to write down the answers to these.
  i $\sqrt{64}$ **ii** $\sqrt{121}$ **iv** $\sqrt{169}$ **iii** $\sqrt{225}$

Discussion Is there another **square root** of 64, 121, 169, 225?

5 a Copy and complete.
  i 4 × 4 = ☐   **ii** 7 × 7 = ☐
     −4 × −4 = ☐   −7 × −7 = ☐
     so, $\sqrt{16}$ = ☐ or ☐   so, $\sqrt{49}$ = ☐ or ☐

b Write down both answers to each of these.
  i $\sqrt{25}$ **ii** $\sqrt{81}$ **iii** $\sqrt{9}$

Discussion Can square numbers be positive or negative?

Key point
To find the square of a number you multiply it by itself.
$3 \times 3 = 3^2 = 9$
3^2 means '3 squared'.

Key point
The inverse of square is **square root**.
$3^2 = 3 \times 3 = 9$, so the square root of $9 = \sqrt{9} = 3$

Topic links: Area, Range

6 Reasoning The area of a square is $100 \, cm^2$.

Amisha says 'The side length of the square could be 10 cm or −10 cm.'

Ishan says 'The side length of the square can only be 10 cm.'

Who is correct? Explain your answer.

7 Check each of these calculations is correct by using the inverse operation.

    a $14^2 = 196$ **b** $2.5^2 = 6.25$ **c** $\sqrt{2116} = 46$ **d** $\sqrt{12.96} = 3.6$

Q7 hint

a Work out $\sqrt{196}$.

c Work out 46^2.

Worked example

Work out an estimate of $\sqrt{55}$.

$\sqrt{49} = 7$ and $\sqrt{64} = 8$

$\sqrt{55}$ lies between 7 and 8

Estimate is 7.4

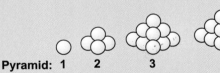

55 is between 49 and 64

55 is closer to 49 than 64, so estimate just less than 7.5

8 a Work out an estimate for these square roots.

    i $\sqrt{20}$ **ii** $\sqrt{5}$ **iii** $\sqrt{79}$ **iv** $\sqrt{90}$

  b Check your estimates by working out the accurate square roots on a calculator.

Q8a hint

Use your table from Q4 to help you.

9 a Work out

    i 2^2 **ii** 20^2 **iii** 200^2 **iv** 0.2^2

  Discussion What do you notice about your answers to part **a**?

  b Work out

    i 50^2 **ii** 900^2 **iii** 4000^2 **iv** 0.6^2

10 Work out

    a $\sqrt{36}$ **b** $\sqrt{9} \times \sqrt{4}$ **c** $\sqrt{324}$ **d** $\sqrt{784}$

  Discussion What do you notice about your answers to parts **a** and **b**?

Investigation   Reasoning

The diagram shows four pyramids made from balls.

Pyramid: 1   2   3   4

1 Copy and complete this table

Pyramid	1	2	3	4
Number of balls	$1^2 = 1$	$1^2 + 2^2 = \square$		

2 How many balls will be in

    a pyramid 5   **b** pyramid 6?

3 Explain how you can work out the number of balls in pyramid 12 without working out the number of balls in pyramids 1 to 11 first.

---

11 Explore What is the best way to arrange 8000 seats into square blocks for a music concert?

Is it easier to explore this question now you have completed the lesson?

What further information do you need to be able to answer this?

12 Reflect Think about the *square* of 100 and the *square root* of 100.

Which is 10 and which is 10 000? Make sure you know the difference between these two terms.

Write down a definition in your own words to help you remember.

Explore

Reflect

2.5 More powers and roots

You will learn to:
- Carry out calculations involving squares, cubes, square roots and cube roots
- Use factorising to work out square roots and cube roots
- Solve word problems using square roots and cube roots.

CONFIDENCE

Why learn this?
Scientists can use square roots to estimate how long an object takes to fall.

Fluency
Work out
- 5^2
- $\sqrt{36}$

Explore
For how long are you falling in a bungee jump from the Sidu River Bridge in China?

Exercise 2.5

Warm up

1 Work out
  a $5 \times 5 \times 5$ **b** $3 \times 3 \times 3$
  c $-1 \times -1 \times -1$ **d** $-4 \times -4 \times -4$

2 Work out
  a $7 + 5 \times 9$ **b** $14 - \frac{8}{2}$ **c** $3 \times 4 + 7 \times 5$ **d** $\frac{45}{5} - \frac{30}{5}$

3 Write these calculations using **index notation**.
  a $3 \times 3 \times 3 \times 3 = 3^\square$ **b** $2 \times 2 \times 2 \times 2 \times 2$ **c** $7 \times 7 \times 7$

4 Match each cube number in the cloud to a number written in index notation in the other cloud.

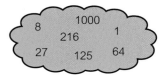

8 1000 1 216 27 125 64

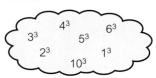

4^3 6^3 3^3 5^3 2^3 1^3 10^3

5 Work out these **powers** of 10.
  a 10^3 **b** 10^5 **c** 10^4 **d** 10^6

6 Work out
  a $\sqrt[3]{27}$ **b** $\sqrt{125}$ **c** $\sqrt[3]{1000}$
  d $\sqrt[3]{1}$ **e** $\sqrt[3]{-8}$ **f** $\sqrt[3]{-64}$

7 Work out the missing numbers.
  a $\sqrt[3]{216} = \sqrt[3]{8} \times \sqrt[3]{27} = 2 \times \square = \square$
  b $\sqrt[3]{8000} = \sqrt[3]{64} \times \sqrt[3]{125} = \square \times \square = \square$
  c $\sqrt[3]{1728} = \sqrt[3]{27} \times \sqrt[3]{64} = \square \times \square = \square$

Key point

You can use **index notation** to write a number to a **power** or **index**. The power tells you how many times the number is multiplied by itself.
$2^3 = 2 \times 2 \times 2$
2^3 is '2 to the power 3'.
3 is the power.

Key point

To find the cube of a number, multiply it by itself and then multiply by the number again.
2 cubed = $2 \times 2 \times 2$

Key point

The inverse of cube is **cube root**.
$2^3 = 8$, so the cube root of 8 is $\sqrt[3]{8} = 2$.

Q6e hint

$\square \times \square \times \square = 8$
$\square \times \square \times \square = -8$

Topic links: Area   **Subject links:** Science (Q12)

8 Work out

a $4^2 - 12$ **b** $3 + 9^2$ **c** $4 \times 3^2 + 5$

d $\dfrac{6^2}{4} - 15$ **e** $\sqrt{49} + 5 \times 8$ **f** $\dfrac{\sqrt{100}}{2} + 10^2$

9 Work out

a 3×2^3 **b** $10^3 \times 5$ **c** $\dfrac{10^3}{500}$

d $\dfrac{40}{2^3}$ **e** $4 \times \sqrt[3]{64}$ **f** $\dfrac{24}{\sqrt[3]{8}}$

(handwritten: others in 1–5)

10 Work out

a $50 - 3^3$ **b** $4^3 + 6^2$ **c** $6 \times 2^3 - 18$

d $4 \times \sqrt[3]{1000} - 35$ **e** $\dfrac{20}{\sqrt[3]{125}} - 2^2$

11 Use a calculator to work out

a $7^3 + 27$ **b** $2 \times 8^3 - 624$ **c** $6 \times 10^3 - 4 \times 9^3$

d $4 \times \sqrt[3]{729} + 4$ **e** $\dfrac{\sqrt[3]{1728}}{6} - 2$ **f** $4 \times \sqrt[3]{216} - 5^2$

Q11 hint

Use the $\sqrt[3]{}$ and x^y buttons on your calculator.

12 STEM / Modelling You can estimate the time it will take an object to fall using this flowchart.

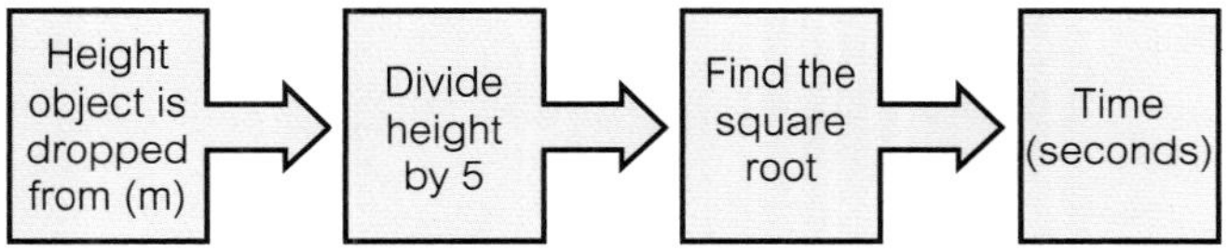

| Height object is dropped from (m) | → | Divide height by 5 | → | Find the square root | → | Time (seconds) |

Work out the time it will take a ball to drop from these heights.

a 80 m **b** 125 m **c** 405 m

13 Problem-solving / Reasoning One number is missing from this list.

$\sqrt{49} \times 40$ *(280)* 30^2 *(900)* 10×5^2 *(250)* $\dfrac{800^2}{1000}$ *(160)* $\square$

The range of the numbers is 800.

a Work out the missing number.

b Is there only one possible answer to part **a**? Explain why.

(handwritten right margin:)
160 000 ÷ 1000
160 + 800 = 960
900 − 800 = 100

14 Work out *(handwritten: 8 × 3√3)*

a $\sqrt[3]{8}$ *(2)* **b** $8\sqrt{27}$ **c** $8\sqrt[3]{8 \times 27}$ *(8 × 2 × 3 = 48)*

What do you notice?

15 Problem-solving Work out $\sqrt[3]{512}$.

Q15 hint

Work out which two cube numbers multiply to give 512.

16 Problem-solving $13\,824 = 8 \times 27 \times 64$

Use this fact to work out $\sqrt[3]{13\,824}$.

17 Explore For how long are you falling in a bungee jump from the Sidu River Bridge in China?
Is it easier to explore this question now you have completed the lesson?
What further information do you need to be able to answer this?

18 Reflect The $\sqrt{}$ root symbol began as the letter *r* in the 16th Century. You could remember *r* for root! List the mathematics notation used in this lesson, and ways you might remember it.

Q18 hint

'Notation' means the signs and symbols you use.

2.6 Calculations

You will learn to:
- Estimate answers to complex calculations
- Carry out calculations involving brackets.

Why learn this?
Brackets help to split a calculation up into separate parts. For example, when working out the speed of a car.

Fluency
Which of these numbers are
- square numbers
- cube numbers
- neither?

81 10 27 125 15 64 9 24

Explore
How can you calculate all the numbers from 1 to 20 using only the number 4?

CONFIDENCE

Warm up

Exercise 2.6

1 Round each number to the nearest whole number.
  a 6.7   **b** 3.2   **c** 9.1   **d** 5.5

2 Round each number to the nearest 10.
  a 27   **b** 43   **c** 75   **d** 56

3 Work out
  a $5 + 3 \times 8$ **b** $\frac{18}{3} - 10$ **c** $7 \times 2 + \frac{20}{5}$
  d $5^2 + 6$ **e** $3^3 - 3$ **f** $4^2 + 2^3$

4 Write these values in **ascending** order.
  $\sqrt{9} + 12$ $\sqrt[3]{64} - 8$ $\sqrt{36} - \sqrt[3]{27}$

> **Q4 Literacy hint**
> Numbers in **ascending** order go from smallest to largest.

5 a Estimate the answer to each calculation.
    i $22 + 5.2 \times 41 \approx 20 + 5 \times \square = \square$ **ii** $65 \times 32 - 24 \times 73$
    iii $9.2 \times 4.6 \times 1.8 - 48.9$ **iv** $32.5 - \frac{51}{4.7}$
    v $\frac{46.7}{6.15} + 3.2 \times 4.9$ **vi** $\frac{63}{8.1} - \frac{29}{8.7}$

> **Q5a hint**
> Round numbers less than 10 to the nearest whole number. Round larger numbers to the nearest 10.

  b Use a calculator to work out the accurate answers to the calculations in part **a**.
    Use your estimates to check your answer.

6 Problem-solving Su wants to order this take-away meal.
She has £25.
Does she have enough?

Satay chicken	£4.80	Boiled rice	2 × £1.10
Crispy duck	£6.10	Chow mein	2 × £2.90
Thai beef	£5.20	Spring rolls	3 × £1.85

Topic links: Area   **Subject links:** Science (Q8)

Worked example

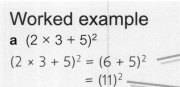

a $(2 \times 3 + 5)^2$

$(2 \times 3 + 5)^2 = (6 + 5)^2$

$\qquad\qquad = (11)^2$

$\qquad\qquad = 121$

> Work out the value inside the brackets first. Start with $2 \times 3 = 6$

> Now add the 6 and 5.

> Finally work out 11^2.

b $\sqrt{27 - \dfrac{6}{3}}$

$\sqrt{27 - \dfrac{6}{3}} = \sqrt{27 - 2}$

$\qquad\qquad = \sqrt{25}$

$\qquad\qquad = 5$

> The square root sign acts like brackets. Work out the value inside it first.

> Now work out $27 - 2$.

> Finally work out the square root of 25.

Key point

The priority of operations is
- Brackets
- Indices or Powers
- Mutiplication and Division
- Addition and Subtraction

---

7 Work out

a $4(6 - 1)$

b $(10 - 8)^2$

c $(1 + 2 \times 4)^2$

d $(\frac{28}{4} - 4)^2$

e $\sqrt{21 - 5}$

f $(-2)^3$

g $\sqrt{50 + 2 \times 7}$

h $\sqrt{\dfrac{12}{4} + 6}$

> **Q7f hint**
>
> $-2 \times -2 \times -2$

8 **Real / Modelling** Sally works out the speed of a zorb at the bottom of slopes of different heights. She uses the rule

$$\text{speed} = \sqrt{12 \times \text{height of slope}}$$

Speed is measured in metres per second.

Height is measured in metres.

Work out the speed of the zorb when the height of the slope is

a 5 m **b** 35 m **c** 57 m

height

> **Q8a hint**
>
> $\text{speed} = \sqrt{20 \times 5} = \square$

Investigation **Problem-solving**

The diagram shows two squares.

1 Work out the area of each square.

2 Work out the total area of the two squares.

3 Sita writes: $3^2 + 4^2 = (3 + 4)^2$

Is Sita correct? Explain.

4 Is Sita's statement true for different size squares?

3 cm 4 cm

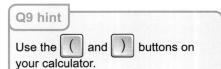

---

9 Work out these calculations. Check your answers using a calculator.

a $3 \times (\sqrt{81} - 7)$

b $(2^2 + \sqrt{9})^2$

c $10^2 - (45 + \sqrt{25})$

d $(5 \times 6 - 26)^3$

e $5^3 + (4 - 2)^3$

f $2 \times 3^3 + 10$

> **Q9 hint**
>
> Use the (and) buttons on your calculator.

10 Work out

a $\dfrac{8 + 22}{7 - 2}$

b $\dfrac{6 + 4^2}{2}$

c $\dfrac{3^3 - 3^2}{2 \times 3}$

d $\dfrac{\sqrt{81}}{12 - 9}$

e $\dfrac{\sqrt{144} - 2}{5}$

f $\dfrac{6^2 - 6}{\sqrt[3]{27}}$

Q10 hint

The dividing line of the fraction acts like a bracket.

$\dfrac{8 + 22}{7 - 2} = (8 + 22) \div (7 - 2)$

11 Problem-solving

a Match each calculation card with the correct answer card.
   Check your answers using a calculator.

| $\sqrt{3^3 + 3^2}$ | $13 - (\sqrt[3]{125} + 3)$ | $8 \times (11 - \sqrt[3]{1000})$ | $\sqrt[3]{40 + 24}$ |

| 4 | 5 | 6 | 7 | 8 |

b There is one answer card left over. Write a calculation card to go with this answer card.
   The calculation must include a cube root or a square root.

12 Work out

a $3 \times (7 + 8)^2$

b $3^2 \times (7 + 8)$

c $(3 \times (7 + 8))^2$

13 Write these numbers in descending order.

| $\sqrt{25} + 2^2$ | 3×2^2 | $2^3 - 1$ | $\sqrt{64} + \sqrt[3]{8}$ | $\sqrt{5^2 - 4^2}$ |

14 Reasoning Rewrite each calculation using only the brackets that are needed.

a $(3 \times (2 \times 5)^2)$

b $(3 \times (2 \times 5))$

15 Explore How can you calculate all the numbers from 1 to 20 using only the number 4?
   Look back at the maths you have learned in this lesson.
   How can you use it to answer this question?

16 Reflect In this lesson you were asked to estimate.
   Suzie says, 'Estimating is the same as guessing.'
   Do you agree with Suzie?
   Write down a definition of how you 'estimate' in maths.
   How might estimating be used in other subjects and in everyday life?

2 Check up

Log how you did on your Student Progression Chart.

Working with numbers

1 **a** Write down all the factors of 12.
  b Write down all the factors of 18.
  c Which of the factors of 12 are prime numbers?
  d What is the highest common factor of 12 and 18?

2 What is the lowest common multiple of 6 and 8?

3 Work out
  a $612 \div 18$ **b** $837 \div 16$

4 Work out
  a $12 - -4$ **b** $3 + -7$ **c** $-2 + 8$
  d $-15 + -4$ **e** $-2 - -5$ **f** $-8 - -12$

5 Work out
  a 6×-3 **b** -9×4 **c** -8×-7
  d $20 \div -5$ **e** $-28 \div 7$ **f** $-15 \div -5$

6 Work out an estimate for these calculations.
  a $31 + 2.9 \times 28$ **b** $10 + 31 \div 11$

Powers and roots

7 Work out
  a 10^4 **b** 2^3
  c 7^2 **d** $\sqrt{36}$
  e $\sqrt[3]{125}$ **f** $\sqrt{64}$
  g $\sqrt[3]{-125}$

8 Write down two square roots of 81.

9 Write down an estimate for $\sqrt{38}$.

10 Work out
  a 10×3^3 **b** $\dfrac{8^2}{2}$

11 Work out
  a $8 \times 2^3 - 4$ **b** $\dfrac{80}{2^3} - 2^2$

  c $10 \times \sqrt[3]{27} - 14$ **d** $\dfrac{\sqrt[3]{125}}{5} + 7 \times 5$

12 $576 = 16 \times 36$

  Use this fact to work out $\sqrt{576}$.

13 $3375 = 27 \times 125$

  Use this fact to work out $\sqrt[3]{3375}$.

Working with brackets

14 Work out

    a $7(6 - 2)$ **b** $(3 \times 2 + 4)^2$

    c $\sqrt{50 - 14}$ **d** $2 \times (\sqrt{4} + 9)$

    e $(3^2 - \sqrt{16})^2$ **f** $4^3 - (8 - 5)^3$

15 Work out

    a $28.3 - \dfrac{58}{6.1}$ **b** $\dfrac{34}{7.2} - \dfrac{37}{8.7}$

16 Work out

    a $\dfrac{45 - 5}{2 + 6}$ **b** $\dfrac{36 - 8}{2^2}$

    c $\dfrac{\sqrt{100}}{12 - 7}$ **d** $\dfrac{\sqrt[3]{125} + 13}{3^2}$

17 Work out

    a $(3 + 1) \times 5^2$

    b $(3 + 1)^2 \times 5$

    c $((3 + 1) \times 5)^2$

18 How sure are you of your answers? Were you mostly

    😠 **Just guessing**   😐 **Feeling doubtful**   🙂 **Confident**

    What next? Use your results to decide whether to strengthen or extend your learning.

Challenge

19 a Work out the HCF of 48 and 56.

    b Write down three other pairs of numbers that have the same HCF as your answer to part **a**.

20 In this spider diagram, the four calculations give the answer in the middle.

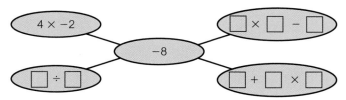

    Work out three possible sets of missing values.

21 Here are some number cards.

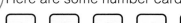

    What number cards can you use so that

$$\left(\square + \square \right)^2 + \left(\square - \square \right)^3 =$$

    a has the biggest possible answer

    b has the smallest possible answer?

Master
P29

Check
P44

STRENGTHEN

Extend
P50

Test
P54

2 Strengthen

You will:

• Strengthen your understanding with practice.

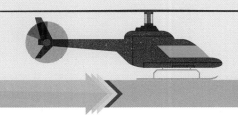

Working with numbers

1 List all the numbers from 1 to 30.
Cross out 1   Cross out all the multiples of 2 (apart from 2)
Cross out all the multiples of 3 (apart from 3)   Continue like this.
The numbers left should all be **prime**.
Check that they are.

Q1 hint

A **prime number** only divides exactly
by 1 and itself.
1 is not a prime number.

2 Steve is finding the **common factors** of 16 and 20.

a Copy and complete his working.

Factors of 16: 1, 2, ..., ..., ...
Factors of 20: 1, 2, ..., ..., ..., ...
Common factors: 1, ..., ...

b What is the highest common factor of 16 and 20?

Q2a hint

Circle the numbers that are the same
in both lists. These are the **common
factors**.

3 Find the highest common factor of 24 and 30.

Q3 hint

Follow the same steps as Q2.

4 a Copy and complete this list of multiples of 3 that are less than 40.
3, 6, 9, ..., ..., ..., ..., ..., ..., ..., ..., ..., ...,

b Copy and complete this list of multiples of 4 that are less than 40.
4, 8, 12, ..., ..., ..., ..., ..., ...,

c Write down the **common multiples** of 3 and 4 that are less than 40.

d Write down the lowest common multiple of 3 and 4.

Q4c hint

Circle the numbers that are the same
in both lists. These are the **common
multiples**.

5 Find the lowest common multiple of 6 and 10.

6 a Copy and complete this list of the first nine multiples of 24.

$1 \times 24 = 24$ $4 \times 24 = \square$ $7 \times 24 = \square$
$2 \times 24 = 48$ $5 \times 24 = \square$ $8 \times 24 = \square$
$3 \times 24 = 72$ $6 \times 24 = \square$ $9 \times 24 = \square$

Q5 hint

Follow the same steps as Q4.

b Copy and complete this long division calculation to work out $912 \div 24$.

```
        3 □
   24)9 1 2
     - 7 2     3 × 24 = 72
      1 9 2
     - 1 9 2   □ × 24 = 192
          0
```

Q6b hint

Use the 24 times-table you calculated
in part **a** to help you.

7 Work out $690 \div 15$

```
   15)6 9 0
```

Q7 hint

Write out the first 9 multiples of 15
first.

8 Shannon works out 622 ÷ 12 like this.

```
        51
  12 ) 622
     −  60      (12 × 5 = 60)
        22
     −  12      (12 × 1 = 12)
        10
```

622 ÷ 12 = 51 remainder 10

She checks her answer using a bar model.
Use Shannon's method to work out
967 ÷ 15. Check your answer.

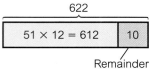

Remainder

9 Work out 449 ÷ 14

10 Eleri sets out her additions and subtractions with negative numbers like this.

7 ⊕⊖4 = 7 ⊖ 4 = 3   (replace + − with −)
9 ⊖⊖6 = 9 ⊕ 6 = 15   (replace − − with +)

Work out these. Set out your work like Eleri.

a 4 + −2   **b** 10 − −5   **c** −10 + −6

d −9 − −10   **e** −8 − 7   **f** −3 − 11

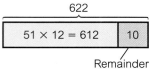

> **Q10a hint**
>
> Circle the two signs in the middle.
> Replace different signs with −.
> Replace the same signs with +.

> **Q10e hint**
>
> Start at −8, count back 7.

11 Eleri sets out her multiplications and divisions with negative numbers like this.

6 × −2   numbers: 6 × 2 = 12, ⊕ × ⊖ ⟶ ⊖   answer: −12
−16 ÷ −4 ... numbers: 16 ÷ 4 = 4, ⊖ ÷ ⊖ ⟶ ⊕   answer: 4

Work out these. Set out your work like Eleri.

a 7 × −4   **b** −8 × 3   **c** −4 × −5

d 8 ÷ −2   **e** −30 ÷ 6   **f** −12 ÷ −4

> **Q11a hint**
>
> Different signs → negative answer
> Same signs → positive answer

12 Estimate the answer to each calculation.

a $\dfrac{73}{8.7}$ **b** $\dfrac{52}{6.9}$ **c** $19.2 - \dfrac{61}{8.8}$ **d** $\dfrac{29}{6.4} + \dfrac{38}{5.1}$

> **Q12a hint**
>
> Round the 'bottom' number.
> 8.7 ≈ 9
> Then round the 'top' number to a multiple of 9.

Powers and roots

1 Work out the missing numbers

a $8^2 = 8 \times \square = \square$ **b** $3^3 = 3 \times \square \times \square = \square$

c $\square^{\square} = 7 \times 7 = \square$ **d** $\square^{\square} = 5 \times 5 \times 5 = \square$

e $\square^{\square} = 9 \times \square = \square$ **f** $\square^{\square} = 2 \times \square \times \square = \square$

> **Q1 hint**
>
> $4^3 \leftarrow$ index
> The index tells you how many 4s are multiplied together.
> $4^3 = 4 \times 4 \times 4$

2 a Copy and complete this number line.

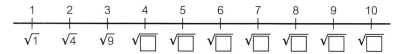

b Use the number line to estimate a value for these square roots.

   i $\sqrt{45}$ **ii** $\sqrt{18}$ **iii** $\sqrt{95}$

> **Q2b hint**
>
>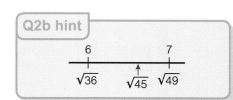

3 Work out these calculations.

   a $5 \times 2^3 = 5 \times \square \times \square \times \square = \square$

   b $3^2 \times 6$

   c $\dfrac{4^2}{2}$

   d $\dfrac{250}{5^3}$

Q3a hint

Work out numbers with an index before multiplication or division.

4 Work out these calculations.
Parts **a** and **c** have been started for you.

   a $13 + 3^3 = 13 + 3 \times \square \times \square = \square$

   b $4 \times 3^2 - 22$

   c $\dfrac{16}{2^3} + 4^2 = \dfrac{16}{\square} + \square \times \square = \square + \square \times \square = \square$

   d $8 \times \sqrt[3]{64} - 12$

   e $\dfrac{\sqrt[3]{27}}{3} + 4 \times 9$

   f $\dfrac{45}{\sqrt[3]{125}} - 5^2$

Q4 hint

Work out multiplication or division before addition or subtraction.

Q4d hint

Work out $\sqrt[3]{64}$ first. Then do the multiplication. Finally the subtraction.

5 a Copy and complete these square roots.

    $\sqrt{4} = 2$ $\sqrt{9} = 3$ $\sqrt{16} = \square$ $\sqrt{25} = \square$

    $\sqrt{36} = \square$ $\sqrt{49} = \square$ $\sqrt{64} = \square$ $\sqrt{81} = \square$

  b Complete the workings to calculate $\sqrt{729}$.
Use the fact that $729 = 9 \times 81$.

    $729 = 9 \times 81$
    $\sqrt{729} = \sqrt{9} \times \sqrt{81}$
           $= 3 \times \square$
           $= \square$

  c $1764 = 36 \times 49$

    Use this fact to work out $\sqrt{1764}$.

  d $2025 = 25 \times 81$

    Use this fact to work out $\sqrt{2025}$.

Q5c hint

$\sqrt{1764} = \sqrt{36} \times \sqrt{49} = \square \times \square = \square$

6 a Complete these cube roots.

    $\sqrt[3]{8} = 2$ $\sqrt[3]{64} = \square$ $\sqrt[3]{125} = \square$ $\sqrt[3]{1000} = \square$

  b Complete the workings to calculate $\sqrt[3]{64\,000}$.
Use the fact that $64000 = 64 \times 1000$.

    $64\,000 = 64 \times 1000$
    $\sqrt[3]{64\,000} = \sqrt[3]{64} \times \sqrt[3]{1000}$
           $= 4 \times \square$
           $= \square$

  c $8000 = 8 \times 1000$

    Use this fact to work out $\sqrt[3]{8000}$.

  d $1728 = 27 \times 64$

    Use this fact to work out $\sqrt[3]{1728}$.

Q6c hint

$\sqrt[3]{8000} = \sqrt[3]{8} \times \sqrt[3]{1000} = \square \times \square = \square$

Working with brackets

1 Work out these. The first one has been started for you.

a $(6 \times 3 - 10)^2$

$6 \times 3 - 10 = \square$

$\square^2 = \square$

b $(18 - 3 \times 5)^3$

c $8(10 - 4)$

d $(12 - 3)^2 - 11$

e $5 \times (\sqrt{9} + 7)$

f $7 \times (8 - \sqrt{25})^2$

Q1c hint

$8(10 - 4) = 8 \times (10 - 4)$

$= 8 \times \square$

Q1e hint

Work out the brackets first, then multiply by 5.

2 Work out these. The first one has been started for you.

a $\sqrt{23 + 26}$

$\sqrt{23 + 26} = \sqrt{49} = \square$

b $\sqrt{5^2 - 9}$

Q2b hint

Work out the calculation under the square root first.

3 Work out these.

a $\dfrac{32 - 2}{4 + 1} = \dfrac{\square}{\square}$

b $\dfrac{32 - 4^2}{4}$

c $\dfrac{6 + 39}{3^2}$

d $\dfrac{5^2 - 15}{\sqrt{4}}$

e $\dfrac{\sqrt[3]{64} + 46}{5^2}$

f $\dfrac{1 + \sqrt{81}}{\sqrt[3]{1000}}$

Q3a hint

Calculate the top and bottom of the fraction first.

4 Write down the number that you square for each calculation.

a 2×3^2

b $2^2 \times 3$

c $(2 \times 3)^2$

d $4^2 \times (5 - 2)$

e $4 \times (5 - 2)^2$

f $4 \times (5 - 2^2)$

Q4c hint

The whole bracket is squared, so $2 \times 3 = \square$

5 Match each calculation to the correct answer.

i	$7^2 \times 2$	**A**	45
ii	7×2^2	**B**	75
iii	$(7 + 2)^2$	**C**	98
iv	$3^2 \times (1 + 4)$	**D**	15
v	$3 \times (1^2 + 4)$	**E**	28
vi	$3 \times (1 + 4)^2$	**F**	81

Enrichment

1 Here are some number cards.

−3   9   −4   6   −2   11

a Find two numbers that sum to 7.

b Find two other numbers that sum to 7.

c The product of two numbers is −18. Which two numbers could they be?

d Write a calculation using three of the number cards, using addition and subtraction to make the largest possible answer.

Q1 hint

Adding numbers gives the sum. Multiplying numbers gives the product.

2 Reflect Write down five different ways you used your multiplication and division skills in these strengthen lessons.

Your first two might be:

- When dividing a negative number by a negative number, I divided the numbers and then wrote an answer which was positive.
- When squaring a number, I multiplied it by itself.

Master
P29

Check
P44

Strengthen
P46

EXTEND

Test
P54

2 Extend

You will:

- Extend your understanding with problem-solving.

1 Problem-solving / Finance Carlos buys a new sofa that costs £984.
He pays a **deposit** of £300.
He then pays the remaining amount in 12 equal monthly **instalments**.
How much does Carlos pay each month?

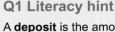

> **Q1 Literacy hint**
>
> A **deposit** is the amount you pay on the day you buy an item.
> An **instalment** is the amount you pay on a regular basis, e.g. monthly.

2 Work out
    a 3587 ÷ 17   **b** 7856 ÷ 15   **c** 9017 ÷ 17   **d** 1108 ÷ 12

3 Problem-solving Andrea has 988 followers on Twitter.
Andrea has 26 times as many followers as Nicola.
How many fewer people follow Nicola than follow Andrea?

988
×26

4 Problem-solving At the end of each month a restaurant owner shares
the tips equally between the members of staff. Any remainder is put
towards the tips for next month.
One month the tips are £856. There are 18 members of staff.

(1·2)

    a How much does each member of staff receive?

    b How much is put towards next month's tips?

5 Write these numbers in ascending order.

 2^3 3^3 4^2 4^3 5^2

6 Reasoning Which of these numbers do you think is bigger: 15^2 or 2^{15}?
Use your calculator to see if you are correct.

7 a Write down all the factors of
    i 16   **ii** 40   **iii** 56

1·6 (?) early

    b Write down the HCF of 16, 40 and 56.

8 a Write down the first 10 multiples of
    i 3   **ii** 4   **iii** 6

    b Write down the LCM of 3, 4 and 6.

9 Problem-solving Sophie and Will start swimming at the same time
from the same end of a swimming pool.
It takes Sophie 40 seconds to swim one length of the pool.
It takes Will 30 seconds to swim one length of the pool.
After how many seconds will they meet for the first time at the same
end of the pool?

> **Q9 Strategy hint**
>
> Draw a diagram to help. Make sure they are meeting at the same end of the pool.

10 Problem-solving / Reasoning The answer to a calculation is −12.
Write four different calculations that each give an answer of −12.
Use each sign +, −, ×, ÷ at least once.

(1·3)

11 Problem-solving Here are some number cards.

$$\boxed{-6} \quad \boxed{7} \quad \boxed{-2} \quad \boxed{8} \quad \boxed{-5}$$

   a i Which two cards could you use to make this calculation correct?

$$\boxed{} + \boxed{} = 2$$

   ii Which other two cards could you use to make the calculation correct?

   b i Which two cards could you use to make this calculation correct?

$$\boxed{} - \boxed{} = -1$$

   ii Which other two cards could you use to make the calculation correct?

   c Which cards could you use in this calculation to give you

     i the greatest possible answer

     ii the smallest possible answer?

$$\boxed{} - \boxed{} \times \boxed{} =$$

12 Problem-solving / Reasoning The area of a square is 28 cm².
Lamar says, 'I think the side length of the square is about 4.8 cm.'
Without working out the side length, explain how you know there is a better
estimate.

[handwritten: 14]

[handwritten square labelled x by x]

13 Problem-solving The area of a square is 70 cm².
Estimate the perimeter of the square.

[handwritten: 1·4]

[handwritten: $x^2 = 70$, $x = \sqrt{70}$, $P = 4x = 4\sqrt{70}$]

Q13 hint
The perimeter is the distance around the edge of the square.

14 Problem-solving Square A has a side length of 6.5 cm.
Square B has a perimeter of 25.6 cm.
Square C has an area of 47 cm².

[handwritten: 1·4]

   a Which square has the smallest perimeter?

   b Which square has the greatest area?

[handwritten: 6.5 cm, A, B, C, P = 25.6, A = 47]

15 STEM Jenson works out the time it takes a car to cover different
distances. He uses the rule $\text{time} = \sqrt{\dfrac{2 \times \text{distance}}{\text{acceleration}}}$

[handwritten: 1·5]

Time is measured in seconds. Distance is measured in metres.
Acceleration is measured in metres per second per second.

   a Work out the time taken when

     i distance = 50 and acceleration = 4

     ii distance = 400 and acceleration = 8

     iii distance = 90 and acceleration = 5

   b Estimate the time taken when

     i distance = 120, acceleration = 6

     ii distance = 300, acceleration = 10

Q15a hint
$\text{time} = \sqrt{(2 \times 50) \div 4}$

16 Give both possible answers to each calculation.
~~The first one is done for you.~~

   a $\sqrt{31 - 2 \times 3}$

     $= \sqrt{31 - 6}$

     $= \sqrt{25}$

     $= 5 \text{ or } -5$

   b $\sqrt{21 + 28}$

   c $\sqrt{6 \times 5 - 14}$

   d $\sqrt{7 \times 6 - 3 \times 11}$

Topic links: Area and perimeter, Range, Mean   **Subject links:** Science (Q15, Q27)

17 Work out

a $(-4)^2$ **b** $(3-5)^2$ **c** $(4-2\times5)^2$

d $(2\times11-4\times8)^2$ **e** $(-3)^2+3\times7$ **f** $40-(-5)^2$

g $12+(12-19)^2$ **h** $(-9)^2-(2\times-4)^2$

Q17 hint

$(-4)^2 = -4 \times -4 = \square$

18 a i Copy and complete.

$(-1)^3 = -1 \times -1 \times -1 = -1$

$(-2)^3 = -2 \times -2 \times -2 = \square$

$(-3)^3 = \square \times \square \times \square = \square$

$(-4)^3 = \square \times \square \times \square = \square$

$(-5)^3 = \square \times \square \times \square = \square$

     ii Is the cube of a negative number always positive or negative?

b i Copy and complete

$(-1)^4 = -1 \times -1 \times -1 \times -1 = \square$

$(-2)^4 = -2 \times -2 \times -2 \times -2 = \square$

$(-3)^4 = \square \times \square \times \square \times \square = \square$

$(-4)^4 = \square \times \square \times \square \times \square = \square$

$(-5)^4 = \square \times \square \times \square \times \square = \square$

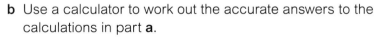

     ii Explain why a negative number raised to the power of 4 will always give a positive answer.

c Will the answer be positive or negative when a negative number is raised to the power of

     i 5   **ii** 6   **iii** 7   **iv** 8?

Discussion How can you tell by looking at the power and the base number whether the answer will be positive or negative?

Q18c hint

Is $(-1)^5$ positive or negative?

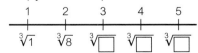

Q18 Literacy hint

The base number is the number that is being raised to a power. In 2^3, 2 is the base, 3 is the index or power.

19 Reasoning Is the answer to each question positive or negative? Explain how you know. You don't need to write the final answers.

a $15 \times (-8)^2$ **b** $24 \times (-6)^3$ **c** $-4 \times (-15)^2$

d $(-12)^5 \div 3$ **e** $(-9)^4 \div 6$ **f** $(-7)^3 \div -2$

20 a Estimate the answer to each calculation.

     i 12×2.8^2 **ii** $4.1^2 + 5.2 \times 9.8$ **iii** $8.2^2 - 5.1^2$

     iv $\sqrt{18} \times 22$ **v** $6.7 \times 7.9 - \sqrt{50}$ **vi** $\dfrac{\sqrt{83}}{\sqrt{8}}$

b Use a calculator to work out the accurate answers to the calculations in part **a**.

Were your estimates close to the accurate answers?

Q20a iv hint

Round 18 to the nearest square number, so it is easy to find the square root.

21 a Copy and complete this number line.

$$\overset{1}{\underset{\sqrt[3]{1}}{|}} \quad \overset{2}{\underset{\sqrt[3]{8}}{|}} \quad \overset{3}{\underset{\sqrt[3]{\square}}{|}} \quad \overset{4}{\underset{\sqrt[3]{\square}}{|}} \quad \overset{5}{\underset{\sqrt[3]{\square}}{|}}$$

b Use the number line to estimate a value for these cube roots.

     i $\sqrt[3]{20}$ **ii** $\sqrt[3]{30}$ **iii** $\sqrt[3]{90}$

c Use a calculator to work out the accurate cube roots of the numbers in part **b**.

How close were your estimates to the accurate answers?

Q21b hint

Draw the number line on squared paper.

22 Work out

   a $(-2)^3 + 10$ **b** $30 + (-3)^3$ **c** $-2 \times (-5)^3$

   d $(-4)^3 \div -8$ **e** $2^3 + (-2)^3$ **f** $3^3 - (-3)^3$

23 a Write down the missing numbers.

   i $\sqrt[3]{\square} = -2$ **ii** $\sqrt[3]{\square} = -3$ **iii** $\sqrt[3]{\square} = -4$

Q23a i hint

Which number has a cube root of 2?
What about −2?

   b Work out

   i $12 + \sqrt[3]{-8}$ **ii** $-5 \times \sqrt[3]{-27}$ **iii** $26 - \sqrt[3]{-64}$ **iv** $\sqrt[3]{-125} \div -5$

24 Here are four number cards.

   | $\sqrt{7^2 + 15}$ | $20 - (4 + \sqrt[3]{64})$ | $6 \times (\sqrt[3]{27} + 2^2)$ | $\sqrt[3]{6^2 - 44}$ |

   1.5

   a Work out the mean of the value of the number cards.

   b Work out the range of the values of the number cards.

25 **Problem-solving** The sum of these two values is 8.

   1.5

   | $\dfrac{32 + \square}{5^2}$ | $\dfrac{45 - \sqrt{81}}{2 \times 3}$ |

   Work out the missing number. $10 - 9 = 1$ $10 - 9 = 1$

Q25 hint

Work out the number on the right first.

26 **Reasoning** Kai and Bo work out $10 - (-3)^2$ and $10 - 3^2$.
   Kai says 'I get the same answer for both.'
   Bo says 'I get different answers.'
   Who is correct? Copy and complete this sentence to explain.
   _____ is correct because _____

27 **STEM / Reasoning** The energy of an object is related to its mass
   and velocity (speed).
   Jenny is working out the energy of different roller coaster cars.

   1.5

   She uses the rule   energy $= \dfrac{\text{mass} \times \text{velocity}^2}{2}$

   a Work out the energy for each car.

Q27a hint

energy $= \dfrac{450 \times 20^2}{2} = \square$

Roller coaster car	A	B	C
Mass (kg)	450	625	450
Velocity (m/s)	20	38	40
Energy (Joules)			

   b Car C has the same mass as Car A. Its velocity is twice as fast.
   Does it have twice as much energy?

28 **Reflect** In these extend lessons you used brackets for different
   calculations.
   Which questions wouldn't have made sense without brackets?
   Write a calculation that needs brackets for it to make sense.
   Now write a calculation that *doesn't* need brackets.
   Use a calculator and swap with a partner to make sure.

Reflect

Master
P29

Check
P44

Strengthen
P46

Extend
P50

TEST

2 Unit test

Log how you did on your
Student Progression Chart.

1 Look at this list of numbers.
   1   2   3   5   8   13
   Which of the numbers are
   a cube numbers
   b prime numbers?

2 What is the highest common factor of 12 and 16?

3 What is the lowest common multiple of 12 and 15?

4 A lottery win of £992 is shared equally between 16 people.
   How much does each person win?

5 Work out
   a $890 \div 16$ **b** $6911 \div 22$ **c** $7 \div 8$

6 Match each calculation with the correct answer.

6^2	125
4^3	36
5^2	81
5^3	64
9^2	25

7 Work out
   a $9 + -5$ **b** $8 - -12$ **c** $9 + -12$ **d** $-9 + 2$
   e $-22 + -8$ **f** $-8 - 9$ **g** $-1 - -1$

8 Work out an estimate for $\sqrt{8}$.

9 Work out
   a $6(3 + 4)$ **b** $(12 - 8)^2$
   c $\sqrt{90 - 26}$ **d** $3^2 \times (\sqrt{25} + 1)$
   e $6^2 + (10 - 5)^2$

10 Write down both answers to $\sqrt{100}$.

11 Work out
   a 4×3^3 **b** $2 \times 2^2 \times 2^3$ **c** $\dfrac{10^3}{4}$ **d** $\dfrac{500}{5^3}$

12 Here are four calculation cards.

   A $2 \times 7^2 - 11$ **B** $\dfrac{100}{\sqrt[3]{64}} + 3 \times 21$ **C** $12 \times \sqrt[3]{27} + 50$ **D** $3 \times 7 + 4^3$

   Work out the value of the calculation on each card.

13 Work out the missing numbers in each calculation.

    a $5 \times -2 = \square$ **b** $-8 \times 6 = \square$

    c $-3 \times \square = 12$ **d** $\square \times 9 = -27$

14 Estimate the answer to each calculation.

    a $21 \times 39 + 19 \times 13$ **b** $89 - 7.8 \times 3.2$ **c** $48.6 + \dfrac{13}{4.3}$

15 Work out

    a $2 \times (-12)^2$ **b** $(-5)^3 \times -4$ **c** $(-2)^4 \div 8$

16 Work out $\sqrt[3]{-8}$

17 $576 = 4 \times 9 \times 16$

    Use this fact to work out $\sqrt{576}$.

18 $-216 = -8 \times 27$

    Use this fact to work out $\sqrt[3]{-216}$.

19 Work out

    a $\dfrac{4 + 6^2}{5}$ **b** $\dfrac{3^3 - 3}{2^2}$ **c** $\dfrac{\sqrt{64}}{3^2 - 1}$ **d** $\dfrac{\sqrt[3]{1000} + 40}{5^2}$

20 Work out

    a $3^2 \times 4$ **b** 3×4^2 **c** $(3 \times 4)^2$ **d** $3^2 \times 4^2$

Challenge

21 Copy this secret code box.

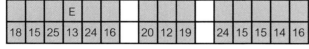

		E											
18	15	25	13	24	16		20	12	19		24	15	15	14	16

    Work out the answer to each calculation below.

    Then use your answers to fill in the letters in the code box and find the secret message.

    The first one is done for you.

    $5 - -5 + 3 = 5 + 5 + 3 = 13$, so **E** = 13

E $5 - -5 + 3$	**D** $6 \times \sqrt{81} - 35$	**T** $5 \times \sqrt[3]{8} + 4$
A $6 \times -3 + 38$	**S** $5^2 - 3^2$	**P** $-3 \times -7 - 3$
W $\dfrac{2 \times 5^3}{\sqrt{100}}$	**O** $\dfrac{\sqrt[3]{27} \times 10}{2}$	**N** $2 \times (9 - 3)$
R $(3^2 - 3)^2 - 3 \times 4$		

    What is the secret message?

22 Write your own secret code questions and code box.

23 **Reflect** In this unit you have mostly done calculations involving:

    • negative numbers

    • powers

    • roots

    • factors

    • estimation.

    Which type of calculation did you find easiest? What made it easy?

    Which type of calculation did you find hardest? What made it hard?

    Write a hint, in your own words, for the type of calculation you found hardest.

Q23 hint

Look back through the unit to remind yourself of each type of calculation.

Reflect

3.1 Simplifying algebraic expressions

You will learn to:
- Simplify expressions by collecting like terms

Why learn this?
Algebra is a language that people in every country in the world can understand. It doesn't need to be translated into Japanese, Spanish or any other language.

Fluency
Write these additions as multiplications:
- 5 + 5 + 5
- 9 + 9 + 9 + 9 + 9
- 10 + 10
- 18 + 18 + 18 + 18 + 18

Explore
Why do we 'simplify' in algebra?

Exercise 3.1

1 Write using index notation.
  a $3 \times 3 \times 3 \times 3$
  b $2 \times 2 \times 2$
  c $5 \times 5 \times 5 \times 5 \times 5 \times 5$

> **Key point**
> An **algebraic expression** e.g. $3x + 2y$, contains numbers and letters.
> Each part of an algebraic expression is called a **term**.

Worked example

Simplify $x + x + x$

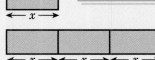

Think of a rod that is x cm long.

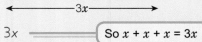

When you put three rods together the total length is $3x$ cm.

$3x$ So $x + x + x = 3x$

2 Simplify
  a $n + n$
  b $y + y + y + y + y$
  c $2a + 3a$
  d $5b + 6b$
  e $5a - 3a$
  f $8b - 3b$
  g $7y + 2y - 3y$
  Discussion Why is $x + x + x + x$ the same as $4x$?

> **Key point**
> **Like terms** contain the same letter (or do not contain a letter).
> You simplify an expression by collecting like terms.

3 Simplify by collecting **like terms**.
  a $2x + 4x + 2 = 6x + \square$
  b $2b + 6c - 3c$
  c $6y - 2y + 8 - 3b$
  d $4y - 2 + 3y$
  e $9x + 3 - 3y - 7x$
  f $9a - 7b + 2a + 5$
  Discussion Are the two expressions $3x + 2y$ and $2y + 3x$ equivalent?

> **Q3e hint**
> $9x - 7x = \square$

Topic links: Order of operations, Indices

4 Copy and complete these addition pyramids. Each brick is the sum of the two bricks below.

a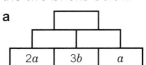

| 2a | 3b | a |

b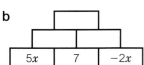

| 5x | 7 | −2x |

c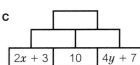

| 2x + 3 | 10 | 4y + 7 |

5 Simplify

  a $b \times b$

  b $t \times t \times t$

  c $m \times m \times m \times m$

6 Simplify

  a $2x^2 + 3x^2 = \square x^2$

  c $2b^2 + 3b + b^2$

  e $8x^4 − x^4$

  b $4a + 2b^2 + 3b^2$

  d $5x + 2x^2 + 7x$

  f $12x^2 + 3x^3 − 2x^3$

7 Simplify

  a $a \times b$

  c $p \times p \times p \times y \times y$

  e $x \times 5$

  b $t \times t \times b$

  d $m \times 2$

  f $q \times 7 \times p$

Worked example

Simplify

a $3b \times 2b$

$3b \times 2b = 3 \times b \times 2 \times b$

$\qquad = 3 \times 2 \times b \times b$ ——— The order of multiplication does not matter.

$\qquad = 6b^2$

b $\dfrac{8b}{4}$

$\dfrac{8b}{4} = 2b$ ——— $\dfrac{8b}{4}$ means $8b \div 4$. Work out $8 \div 4$

8 Simplify

  a $2b \times 5b$

  d $\dfrac{12b}{4}$

  b $9a \times 3a$

  e $\dfrac{9a}{2}$

  c $3a \times 2a \times 3a$

  f $\dfrac{36b}{12}$

9 Match the equivalent expressions.

| $2x$ | $4x − 3x$ | $x \times x$ | x | $3x + 4x$ |

| $x + x$ | $4x^2$ | $3x$ | $2x \times 2x$ | x^2 |

| $x \times 2x$ | $7x$ | $\dfrac{9x}{3}$ | $2x^2$ |

10 Copy and complete these multiplication pyramids.
Each brick is the product of the two bricks below.

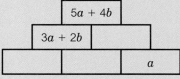

a

| 2 | 3 | a |

b

| 5 | a | 4 |

c

| a | a | a |

Key point

The identity symbol ($\equiv$) shows that two expressions are always equivalent.
For example, $a + 2b \equiv 2b + a$

11 In between which pairs of expressions can you write $\equiv$?
  a $a + b \;\square\; b + a$
  b $a - b \;\square\; b - a$
  c $ab \;\square\; ba$
  d $a \div b \;\square\; b \div a$

Q11 hint

Test with some numerical values for a and b.

Investigation

1 This is an addition pyramid. Work out the missing values.

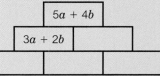

	$5a + 4b$	
$3a + 2b$		
		a

2 How many different possibilities can you find for this addition pyramid?

	$5a + 4b$	
$3a + 2b$		

DI
3.2
Inv

3 This is a multiplication pyramid. How many different possibilities can you find?

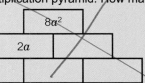

	$8a^2$	
$2a$		

12 Explore Why do we 'simplify' in algebra?
Is it easier to explore this question now you have completed the lesson?
What further information do you need to be able to answer this?

13 Reflect In algebra, letters are used to represent values we do not know. This lesson may be the first time you have done algebra.
Choose **A**, **B** or **C** to complete each statement.
In this lesson, I did...   **A** well   **B** ok   **C** not very well
So far, I think algebra is...   **A** easy   **B** ok   **C** difficult
When I think about the next lesson,
   I feel...   **A** confident   **B** ok   **C** unsure
If you answered mostly **A**s and **B**s, did your experience surprise you? Why?
If you answered mostly **C**s, then look back at the questions you found most tricky. Ask a friend or your teacher to explain them to you. Then answer the statements above again.

Explore

Reflect

3.2 Writing algebraic expressions

You will learn to:
- Construct expressions using four operations.

Why learn this?
Computers are programmed using a computer algebra system (CAS).

Fluency
Work out:
- 3^2
- 5^3
- 1^4

Explore
Think of a number. Double it. Add 10. Halve it. Take away your original number. Try this with different numbers. What answer do you get? Why?

CONFIDENCE

Exercise 3.2

Warm up

1 Simplify

  a $2x + 3x - 5x$ **b** $3x^2 - 4x + 2x^2$ **c** $3x + 5 - 2x + 4$

2 Simplify

  a $y \times y$ **b** $b \times b \times b$ **c** $4 \times 2n$

  d $4b \times 2b$ **e** $\dfrac{16c}{4}$

3 John collects coins. He has b coins. Write an expression for how many he has when there are

  a 2 more   **b** 4 fewer   **c** 17 more

  d 5 times as many   **e** half as many.

Q3a hint

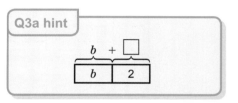

Q3d hint

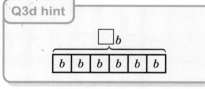

Q3e hint

Finding half is the same as dividing by 2.

4 a On Monday a shop sells x newspapers and y magazines. Write an expression for the total number of newspapers and magazines it sells.

  b Write an expression for the total number of newspapers and magazines sold

    i on Tuesday when they sell 3 fewer newspapers but the same number of magazines

    ii on Wednesday when they sell 4 more newspapers and 7 fewer magazines than on Monday.

5 Edward is m years old. Write expressions for the ages of each of these people.

  a Laila is 4 times as old as Edward.

  b Maggie is 5 years older than Edward.

  c Ami is 6 years younger than Edward.

  d Iman is half the age of Edward.

  e Rashid is 5 years older than twice Edward's age.

  f Ruth is 3 years less than 5 times Edward's age.

6 Write an algebraic expression for

  a y more than x **b** x multiplied by y
  c y less than x **d** x more than 2 times y
  e 3 times y add 4 times x **f** y multiplied by itself
  g 4 times x multiplied by itself   **h** 7 less than y multiplied by itself
  i x divided by y **j** 2 more than 20 divided by x

Q6a hint

Try it with numbers. How would you write 5 more than 3?

7 t represents a number. Write and simplify an expression for

  a 2 more than triple the number   **b** 5 less than double the number
  c 4 more than double the number   **d** the number added to itself
  e the number subtract 5   **f** the number multiplied by itself
  g the number divided by 3   **h** 3 divided by the number.

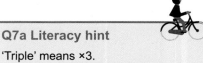

Q7a Literacy hint

'Triple' means ×3.

Worked example

Write an expression for each function machine.

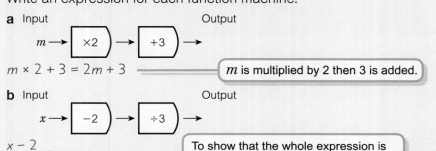

a Input   Output

$m \rightarrow \boxed{\times 2} \rightarrow \boxed{+3} \rightarrow$

$m \times 2 + 3 = 2m + 3$ ——— m is multiplied by 2 then 3 is added.

b Input   Output

$x \rightarrow \boxed{-2} \rightarrow \boxed{\div 3} \rightarrow$

$\dfrac{x - 2}{3}$ ——— To show that the whole expression is divided by 3 draw a long division line.

8 Write an expression for the output of each function machine.

  a $\rightarrow \boxed{\times 3} \rightarrow \boxed{-17} \rightarrow$

  b $\rightarrow \boxed{\div 4} \rightarrow \boxed{+3} \rightarrow$

  c $\rightarrow \boxed{\times 5} \rightarrow \boxed{\times 5} \rightarrow$

  d $\rightarrow \boxed{+2} \rightarrow \boxed{\div 5} \rightarrow$

9 A rectangle has height b. The width is 5 more than the height.

DI
3.4
  a Write an expression for the width.
  b Write and simplify an expression for the perimeter.
  c Calculate the perimeter of the rectangle when $b = 10$ cm.

10 Explore Think of a number. Double it. Add 10. Halve it. Take away your original number. Try this with different numbers. What answer do you get? Why?
Is it easier to explore this question now you have completed the lesson?
What further information do you need to be able to answer this?

11 Reflect This lesson suggested bar modelling and function machines to help you with writing expressions. Did they help you? How?
Did you use any other methods? Explain the method(s) you used.

3.3 STEM: Using formulae

You will learn to:
- Substitute into formulae.

Why learn this?
You can substitute into formulae to work out all sorts of things – from the volume of the Earth to the cooking time of a meal.

Fluency
Work out:
- $2 + 3 \times 4$
- $\dfrac{4 + 5}{2}$
- $\dfrac{4 \times (5 + 2)}{2}$

Explore
How can you predict your adult height?

Exercise 3.3

1 A recipe gives this formula to work out how long it takes to cook a chicken:
(50 × weight (in kg) + 40) minutes
How long does it take to cook a 2 kg chicken?

2 **STEM** To calculate the maximum pulse rate when exercising, use
maximum heart rate = 220 − age.
Work out the maximum heart rate for these ages:
   a 18 **b** 45 **c** 79

3 Work out the value of each expression when $a = 3$.
   a $2a$ **b** $a + 3$ **c** $a - 5$ **d** a^2 **e** $10 - a$

> **Q3a hint**
> $2a = 2 \times a = 2 \times \square$

4 Given $x = 3$, $y = 5$, $z = 8$ work out the value of
   a xy **b** $xz + 5$ **c** $2(x + 1)$ **d** $\dfrac{z}{2}$ **e** $\dfrac{x + y}{2}$

> **Q4a hint**
> $\square \times \square$

Worked example

The **formula** used to calculate speed is: speed = $\dfrac{\text{distance}}{\text{time}}$

Work out the speed of a cyclist who travels 1000 metres in 20 seconds.

$Speed = \dfrac{1000}{20}$

$= 50$ m/s

> Substitute the values into the formula.
> Write the units.
> m/s means metres per second.

> **Key point**
> A **formula** is a general rule for a relationship between quantities. You use a formula to work out an unknown quantity by substituting.

5 **STEM** Use the formula speed = $\dfrac{\text{distance}}{\text{time}}$ to work out the speed of each of these cyclists in metres per second.
   a distance = 3000 m   time = 360 seconds
   b distance = 600 m   time = 50 seconds
   c distance = 10 000 m   time = 640 seconds

Topic links: Order of operations, Negative numbers

Subject links: Science (Q5–12)

6 **STEM** In physics the formula $F = ma$ is used to calculate force, F, where m = mass and a = acceleration.
Work out the value of the force (F) when:
a $m = 2$, $a = 27$ b $m = 5$, $a = 32$ c $m = 25$, $a = 7$
Discussion When $F = 20$ and $a = 5$ could you work out the value of m?

7 **STEM** Weight (W) in newtons (N) is calculated using the formula
$W = mg$ where m = mass in kg and g = acceleration due to gravity in m/s².
a On Earth $g = 10$ m/s². Work out the weight, in newtons, of
  i a 5kg dog
  ii a 70kg man
  iii a 30kg monkey.
b On the Moon $g = 1.6$ m/s²
Work out the weight of the dog, the man and the monkey on the Moon.

8 **STEM** The formula to calculate pressure (P) in N/m² is $P = \dfrac{F}{A}$ where
F = force in N and A = area in m². Work out the pressure when
a $F = 20$, $A = 2$
b $F = 100$, $A = 25$

9 **STEM** An engineer uses the formula $V = IR$ to work out the voltage in a circuit where I is the current (in amps) and R is the resistance (in ohms).
Work out the voltage, V, of a circuit with
a current 4 amps and resistance 10 ohms
b current 3.1 amps and resistance 15 ohms
c current 7.2 amps and resistance 20 ohms.

10 The formula for the perimeter of a rectangle is $P = 2l + 2w$.
Work out the perimeter when
a $l = 12$cm and $w = 2$cm
b $l = 4$m and $w = 5$m
c $w = 10.5$cm and $l = 6$cm.

11 **STEM** To convert from °C (C) to Kelvin (K) scientists use the formula $K = C + 273$.
Convert these temperatures to Kelvin.
a 100°C   b –20°C   c 0°C   d –100°C

12 **STEM** The formula for converting from temperature in Fahrenheit (F) to Celsius (C) is $C = \dfrac{5(F - 32)}{9}$.
Convert these temperatures into °C.
a 41°F   b 59°F   c 77°F   d 23°F

13 **Explore** How can you predict your adult height?
Is it easier to explore this question now you have completed the lesson?
What further information do you need to be able to answer this?

14 **Reflect** Look back at the formula in Q6.
a Would it matter if this formula used the letters x and y instead of m and a?
b Do the letters help you to understand a formula?

Q14 hint
If you used different letters would your answers be different?

Explore

Reflect

3.4 Writing formulae

You will learn to:

- Derive formulae from a description.

CONFIDENCE

E3		fx	=B3+C3+D3		
	A	B	C	D	E
1	The Cupcake Shop - First Quarter Sales				
2		January	February	March	Total
3	Red velvet	£1,292	£1,156	£1,208	£3,656
4	Lemon drizzle	£2,047	£1,987	£1,999	£6,033
5	Vanilla	£1,795	£1,896	£1,689	£5,380
6	Fudge	£1,250	£1,346	£1,287	£3,883
7	Total revenues	£6,384	£6,385	£6,183	£18,952

Why learn this?
You can write formulae into a spreadsheet so that it automatically does all the calculations for you.

Fluency
Work out the mean of 6, 12, 12

Explore
What is the formula to convert weeks into minutes?

Exercise 3.4

Warm up

1 Write algebraic expressions for
  a 2 more than x
  b 5 less than y
  c the cost of x apples at 20p each.

2 There are r red marbles and b blue marbles.
  Write an expression for the total number of marbles.

3 When $x = 2$ and $y = 7$ work out the value of
  a xy **b** $2x + 4$ **c** $9x - 2y$ **d** $3y + 2x$

4 An online company charges £5 to rent a film and £10 to download a film. It uses the formula $C = 5r + 10d$.
  a What do you think r stands for?
  b What do you think d stands for?
  c How much would 3 rentals and 2 downloads cost?

5 Alice earns £9 per hour.
  a How much does she earn in 5 hours?
  b How much does she earn in 12 hours?
  c Write an expression for how much she earns in x hours.
  d Write a formula for her earnings, E, in x hours.
  Discussion What is the difference between an expression and a formula?

Q5d hint
E = your expression from part **c**.

Worked example

Storing furniture in a warehouse costs £12 per week.
Write a formula for the cost, C, of storing furniture for y weeks.

$12y$ Write down the cost each week.
         Multiply the cost by the number of weeks.

$C = 12y$ Write C = your expression.

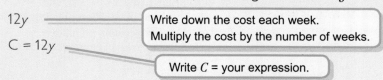

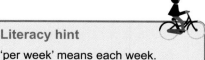

Literacy hint
'per week' means each week.

Topic links: Order of operations, Negative numbers   **Subject links:** PE (Q8), ICT(Q12), Food technology (Q14)

6 Renting a go-cart costs £15 per hour.
   a Write an expression for the cost for x hours.
   b Write a formula, $C = \square$

Q6a Strategy hint

Start by trying different numbers of hours to see the pattern.

7 The amount of bread a restaurant orders depends on the number of bookings each day. They order 10 more loaves that they have bookings. Write a formula that connects the number of bookings, b, to the number of loaves of bread, L.

8 Ranjit and Meadow are running a relay race. Ranjit runs x metres and Meadow runs y metres.
Write a formula that connects the total distance they run, R, to x and y.

9 A library buys bookcases. Each bookcase has 6 shelves.
Write a formula that connects the total number of shelves in the library, L, to the number of bookcases, B.

10 Modelling
   a Write an algebraic expression for finding the mean of three numbers x, y and z.
   b Write a formula for the mean of three numbers.
   c Use your formula to work out the mean when $x = 5$, $y = 22$ and $z = 12$.

DI
3.6

Q10 hint

Write $m = \square$.

11 STEM / Real The mean pulse rate is worked out for three different readings. The readings are a, b and c.
Write a formula to work out mean pulse rate, P.

12 Real A broadband provider charges £12.50 per month and £4 per gigabyte (GB) of data.
   a Work out the cost when
      i 10 GB are used
      ii no data is used.
   b Write a formula for the monthly cost, C, when n gigabytes of data are used.

13 A function machine multiplies each input by 5 and then adds 3.
   What is the output if the input is
   a i 5   **ii** –2   **iii** –7   **iv** x?
   b Write a formula which connects the output, y, with the input, x.

DI
3.6

Q13 hint

Draw the function machine.

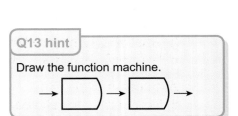

14 The cooking time for a joint of meat is 45 minutes per kg plus an extra 20 minutes.
   a Work out the cooking time for a 3 kg joint.
   b Write a formula that connects the cooking time (in minutes), C, to the mass in kg, k.

15 Explore What is the formula to convert weeks into minutes?
Is it easier to explore this question now you have completed the lesson?
What further information do you need to be able to answer this?

16 Reflect In this lesson you wrote your own formulae. In lesson 3.3 you were given formulae to work with. Which did you find more difficult?
What made it more difficult?
Are there particular kinds of questions you need more practice on? If so, what kinds?

Explore

Reflect

3.5 Brackets and powers

You will learn to:
- Expand expressions involving brackets
- Substitute into expressions involving powers.

Why learn this?
Science formulae often contain powers and brackets.

Fluency
Work out
- $5(2 + 3)$
- $2(10 - 4)$
- $4(3 - 6)$

Explore
How do you convert temperatures in degrees Celsius to degrees Fahrenheit?

Exercise 3.5

1 Simplify

  a $3 \times y$ **b** $a \times 6$ **c** $p \times -3$ **d** $7 \times 2s$ **e** $9z \times 5$

2 Simplify

  a $b \times b$ **b** $m \times 2m$ **c** $a \times a \times a$ **d** $3b \times 2b$ **e** $6n \times 3n$

3 a Work out

    i $3(2 + 5)$ **ii** $3 \times 2 + 3 \times 5$

    What do you notice?

  b Work out

    i $4(6 - 1)$ **ii** $4 \times 6 + 4 \times -1$

    What do you notice?

Worked example

Expand

a $2(x + 3)$

$2(x + 3) = 2 \times x + 2 \times 3$

$\quad\quad\quad = 2x + 6$

b $5(y - 2)$

$5(y - 2) = 5 \times y + 5 \times -2$

$\quad\quad\quad = 5y - 10$

Key point

Expand a bracket means multiply every number inside the bracket by the number or letter outside the bracket.

4 Expand

  a $3(x + 4)$ **b** $2(n + 12)$ **c** $3(p - 7)$ **d** $4(y - 5)$

  e $2(2 + r)$ **f** $5(8 - b)$ **g** $8(2 - q)$ **h** $10(10 - a)$

  Discussion How could you check that your answers are correct?

5 Anne earns x pounds per hour. Jamil earns £3 more per hour than Anne. On Sunday he gets paid double.

  Write an algebraic expression in terms of x for the amount Jamil earns per hour on Sunday.

Q5 hint

$2(\square + \square)$

Topic links: Order of operations

6 A company making mobile phones works out their profit, P, by subtracting £50 from the cost of the phone, T, and multiplying the answer by the number of phones sold, x.
Write a formula for calculating P.

7 The length of a rectangle is x cm.
Its height is 5 cm less than its length.
  a Write an expression for the height of the rectangle.
  b Write and simplify an expression for the area of the rectangle.
  c Copy and complete the formula for calculating the area, $A = \square$
  d Use the formula to work out the area of the rectangle when
     i $x = 10$ 　 **ii** $x = 12$

x

8 Expand
  a $b(b + 4)$ 　**b** $y(y - 2)$ 　**c** $t(10 + t)$ 　**d** $r(2 - r)$
  e $w(3w + 2)$ **f** $p(10 + 4p)$ **g** $q(15 - 2q)$ **h** $2r(3r + 1)$
  i $8m(2m - 3)$ **j** $2b(20 - 4b)$

Q8a hint

$b \times b + b \times 4 = b^2 + \square$

9 Work out the value of the expressions when $a = 2$ and $b = 5$.
  a $a^2 + 5$ 　**b** $3a^2$ 　**c** $a^2 + 2b$ 　**d** $a^2 + b^2$
  e $\dfrac{b^2}{5}$ 　**f** $(2a)^2$ 　**g** $(a + b)^2$ 　**h** $2b^2 + 5a$
  i $2b^2 - 3a^2$ **j** $\left(\dfrac{a}{2}\right)^2$

Q9 hint

Remember to follow the priority of operations.

10 BMI can be calculated using the expression $\dfrac{m}{h^2}$ where m is your mass in kg and h is your height in metres.
Work out the BMI (to the nearest whole number) when
  a $m = 65, h = 1.6$ 　**b** $m = 90, h = 1.85$ 　**c** $m = 100, h = 1.5$

Q10 Literacy hint

BMI means body mass index.
A healthy BMI is roughly between 18.5 and 25.

11 Ray is x years old. Anne's age is the square of Ray's.
Bryony is 5 years older than Anne.
  a Write an expression for Anne's age.
  b Write an expression for Bryony's age.
  c Write and simplify an expression for the sum of their ages.
  d Ray is 5 years old. What is the sum of their ages?
  Discussion How did you answer part **d**? Is there more than one way?
  Which is the quickest way?

12 Work out the value of the expressions when $t = 2$ and $r = 3$.
  a $t^3 + 5$ 　**b** $r^3 - 27$ 　**c** $\dfrac{t^3}{2}$ 　**d** $\dfrac{t^5}{4}$
  e $t^3 + r^3$ **f** $5r^3$ 　**g** $(2t)^3$ 　**h** $(t - 1)^4$
  i $(3t - 5)^3$ **j** $3t^3 + \dfrac{r^3}{9}$

Q12 hint

$t^3 + 5 = t \times t \times t + 5$

13 **Explore** How do you convert temperatures in degrees Celsius to degrees Fahrenheit?
Is it easier to explore this question now you have completed the lesson?
What further information do you need to be able to answer this?

14 **Reflect** Write a definition, in your own words, for
  • expand
  • simplify.
Compare your definitions with those written by others in your class.
Can you improve your definitions?

Q14 hint

Look back at questions where you were asked to 'expand' or 'simplify'. What did you do?

Explore

Reflect

3.6 Factorising expressions

You will learn to:
- Factorise an algebraic expression.

CONFIDENCE

Why learn this
Factorising is useful when solving many different types of equations.

Fluency
What are the common factors of
- 9 and 12
- 25 and 15?

Explore
Is $4x + 7y$ divisible by 2?

Exercise 3.6

Warm up

1 Expand
- **a** $2(x + 3)$
- **b** $4(3x + 2)$
- **c** $9(2 - x)$
- **d** $5(4 - 7x)$

2 Work out the highest common factor (HCF) of
- **a** 18 and 27
- **b** 20 and 12
- **c** 21 and 35

3 Write the common factors of
- **a** 6 and $2a$
- **b** $12b$ and 3
- **c** $10x$ and 15
- **d** 8 and $12y$

> **Q3a hint**
> $2a = \boxed{2} \times a$
> $6 = \boxed{2} \times 3$

4 Write the HCF of
- **a** $16b$ and 8
- **b** 36 and $24x$

Worked example

Factorise $3x + 9$.

$3x + 9$

$= 3(x + 3)$

> 3 is a common factor of both $3x$ and 9.
> Write 3 in front of the bracket.
> Divide both terms by 3 to find the values in the bracket.

> **Key point**
> Expanding removes brackets from an expression. **Factorising** inserts brackets into an expression.
>
> expand
> $6(a + 3) = 6a + 18$
> factorise
>
> To factorise $6a + 18$, write the common factor of its terms, 6, outside the brackets. This is called 'taking out the common factor'.

5 Copy and complete:
- **a** $4x + 8 = 4(\Box + 2)$
- **b** $12x + 3 = 3(\Box + \Box)$
- **c** $9x - 15 = 3(\Box - \Box)$
- **d** $14x - 21 = 7(\Box - \Box)$
- **e** $12x + 6 = \Box(2x + \Box)$
- **f** $9x - 3 = \Box(3x - \Box)$
- **g** $11x + 33 = \Box(\Box + 3)$
- **h** $10 - 5x = \Box(2 - \Box)$
- **i** $12 + 3x = \Box(\Box + x)$

6 **Factorise** each expression.
- **a** $3x + 12$
- **b** $5p - 15$
- **c** $22z - 11$
- **d** $2y - 20$
- **e** $10 + 5m$
- **f** $26 - 13n$
- **g** $14 + 7s$
- **h** $7 - 28t$

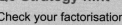

> **Q6 Strategy hint**
> Check your factorisation by expanding the brackets.

Topic links: HCF

DI 3.3 Inv.

7 Problem-solving Match the equivalent expressions.

a $2x + 4$

b $5x + 30$

c $2x - 6$

d $6x + 36$

e $5x - 20$

f $6x + 12$

i $6(x + 2)$

ii $2(n - 3)$

iii $5(x - 4)$

iv $2(x + 2)$

v $6(x + 6)$

vi $5(x + 6)$

8 How many different ways can the expression $12x + 24b$ be factorised?

9 Factorise completely.

a $4x + 8$
b $8y + 12$
c $14m + 28$
d $12n - 6$
e $20 - 10s$
f $8 + 20t$
g $90y + 45$
h $66 + 33z$

Key point

To factorise completely, write the highest common factor outside the brackets.

10 Factorise

a $4m + 2n + 16$

b $15+ 10b + 55c$

c $pq + 2p + 12p$

Q10a hint

$2(□ + □ + □)$

$m(70 + 10)$

11 Jim pays £70 deposit for a bike. Then he pays £10 a month.
Write a formula for the amount paid after m months.

Q11 hint

Use brackets in your formula.

12 Kaz pays £120 deposit for a laptop, then pays £25 a month.
Write a formula for the amount paid after n months.

13 Explore Is $4x + 7y$ divisible by 2?
Is it easier to explore this question now you have completed the lesson?
What further information do you need to be able to answer this?

14 Reflect Write down a definition of 'factor'.
Use your definition to write a definition, in your own words, of 'highest common factor (HCF)'.
Use your definition of HCF to help you write a definition, in your own words, of 'factorising'. Be as accurate as possible.
How did your definitions of 'factor' and 'HCF' help you to define factorising?

3 Check up

Log how you did on your Student Progression Chart.

Simplifying expressions

1 Expand
  a $3(x + 4)$ **b** $2(a - w)$ **c** $5(11 - x)$

2 Simplify
  a $x + x$ **b** $4x + 7x$ **c** $10c - 5c$
  d $4t - t$ **e** $7x + 2b - 5x$

3 Simplify
  a $y \times y \times y$ **b** $x \times x$ **c** $3 \times t \times t$
  d $2 \times r \times r \times r \times 5$ **e** $5r \times r$ **f** $7t \times 2t$

  g $y \div 7$ **h** $\dfrac{12y}{6}$

4 Simplify
  a $x^2 + 3x^2$ **b** $x + x^2 + x$ **c** $2 + x^2 + 2x^2 - 5$

5 Expand
  a $x(x + 3)$ **b** $b(b - 2)$ **c** $a(10 - a)$
  d $2x(3x + 1)$ **e** $4t(10 - 2t)$

6 Factorise
  a $4x + 20$ **b** $6x - 9$ **c** $14a - 21b$

Substitution

1 Area of rectangle = length × width
   Work out the area of a rectangle with width = 12 cm and length = 7 cm.

2 $T = 5B$ What is the value of T when $B = 12$?

3 Density $= \dfrac{\text{mass}}{\text{volume}}$
   Work out the density of a block with mass 20 kg and volume 4 m³.

4 The approximate perimeter, P, of a semicircle can be
   calculated using the formula $P = a + \dfrac{3a}{2}$
   Work out the approximate perimeter when $a = 4$ cm.

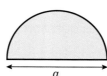

5 Use the formula $b = 10t - c$ to work out the value of b when
   a $t = 3$, $c = 5$ **b** $t = -1$, $c = 7$
   c $t = 4$, $c = -2$ **d** $t = -3$, $c = -4$

6 Work out the value of the expression $ab + 2c$ when $a = 2$, $b = 5$, $c = 9$.

7 What is the value of x^2 when $x = 7$?

8 Work out the value of each expression when $x = 3$, $y = 5$.
   a $3(x + 2)$ **b** $(x + y)^2$ **c** x^3
   d $5x^2$ **e** $10 + x^2$

Writing expressions and formulae

1 Marion has x stamps. Write expressions for the number of stamps each person has.
  a Christian has 7 fewer than Marion.
  b Nick has 12 times as many as Marion.
  c Michael has half as many as Marion.
  d Olivia has m times as many as Marion.

2 Jack is paid £5 for each hour he babysits.
  Write a formula that connects the total amount he is paid, T, and the number of hours he babysits, x.

3 Write an algebraic expression for
  a a more than b
  b 3 more than a, multiplied by b
  c a multiplied by itself
  d b divided by 5.

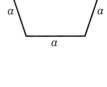

4 A regular pentagon has 5 sides of equal length.
  Write a formula that connects the perimeter, P, to the length of one of the sides, a.

5 A class has 30 students. A teacher buys sweets to share between them.
  Write a formula that connects the number of sweets each student receives, S, and the number of sweets the teacher buys, p.

6 A square has sides a cm long.
  Write a formula for finding the area of the square, A, using the length of the side, a.

7 A cup of tea costs £2 and a cup of coffee costs £3.
  Write a formula that connects the total cost, C, to the number of teas, t, and coffees, c.

8 **How sure are you of your answers? Were you mostly**
  ☹ **Just guessing**   😐 **Feeling doubtful**   ☺ **Confident**
  What next? Use your results to decide whether to strengthen or extend your learning.

Challenge

9 A pattern is made of squares and rectangles.

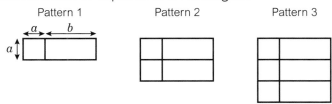

Pattern 1   Pattern 2   Pattern 3

Write and simplify an algebraic expression for the area of
  a Pattern 1   b Pattern 2   c Pattern 3
  d Pattern 10   e Pattern n.

10 Find a value of x so that
  a x^2 is equal to $2x$ b x^2 is equal to x^3.

11 $a + b = -2$ and $ab = -15$.
  a and b are whole numbers. What are the values of a and b?

> **Q11 hint**
> Try different values for a and b.

3 Strengthen

You will:
* Strengthen your understanding with practice.

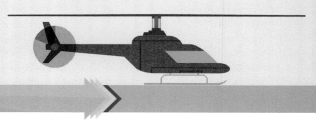

Simplifying expressions

1 Copy and complete.

a $p + p + p = \square\, p$

b $m + m + m + m = \square m$

c $d + d$

d $t + t + t + t + t$

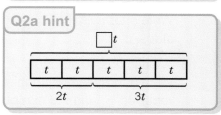

Q1 hint

Draw bars to help.

| p | p | p |

2 Simplify

a $2t + 3t$

b $5g + 7g$

c $10y - 3y$

d $5p - p$

e $10y + 2b + 3y$

f $6m + n + 5m$

g $4a + 3b - a$

h $3q + 2b - 3b$

i $4t + 7 - 2t$

j $4y + 8 - 2 + 3y$

Q2a hint

| $\square t$ |

| t | t | t | t | t |

$\underbrace{\quad}_{2t} \underbrace{\quad}_{3t}$

Q2e hint

Add the y terms first.

| $10y$ | $3y$ |

| $\square y$ |

Q2i hint

Numbers, e.g. 7, can only be added to other numbers.

3 Expand $3(2 + 4)$

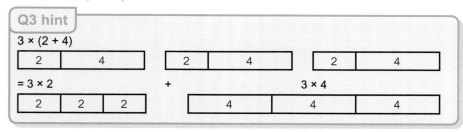

Q3 hint

$3 \times (2 + 4)$

| 2 | 4 | | 2 | 4 | | 2 | 4 |

$= 3 \times 2$ + 3×4

| 2 | 2 | 2 | | 4 | 4 | 4 |

4 Copy and complete.

a $2(x + 3) = \square x + \square$

b $3(x + 4) = (x + 4) + (x + 4) + (x + 4) = \square + \square$

c $4(b + 2)$

d $5(t + 3) = \square \times t + \square \times 3 = \square t + \square$

e $3(6 + a)$

f $2(r - 3) = \square \times r + \square \times -3$

g $6(10 - b)$

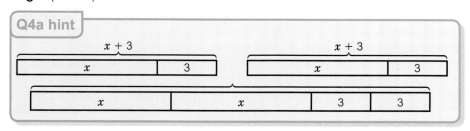

Q4a hint

| $x + 3$ | | $x + 3$ | |
| x | 3 | x | 3 |

| x | x | 3 | 3 |

5 Fill in the missing numbers.

  a $6 \times 6 \times 6 = 6^{\square}$

  b $5 \times 5 \times 5 \times 5 = 5^{\square}$

  c $11 \times 11 = 11^{\square}$

6 Match each expression on a blue card to one on a yellow card.

a $a \times a \times a$	**i** a^4
b $a \times a$	**ii** a^6
c $a \times a \times a \times a \times a$	**iii** a^2
d $a \times a \times a \times a$	**iv** a^3
e $a \times a \times a \times a \times a \times a$	**v** a^5

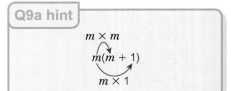

> **Q6 hint**
>
> How many times is a multiplied by itself?

7 Copy and complete.

  a $2w \times 3w =$ **b** $4a \times 2a =$

  c $3b \times 5b =$ **d** $8m \times 3m =$

  e $9n \times 11n =$

8 Simplify these. Which is the 'odd one out'?

  a $n \times n$ **b** $n + n$

  c $2 \times n$ **d** $n \times 2$

9 Copy and complete.

  a $m(m + 1) =$ **b** $b(b + 2) =$

  c $d(3 + d) =$ **d** $r(r - 1) =$

  e $m(m - 3) =$ **f** $t(10 - t) =$

> **Q9a hint**
>
> $m \times m$
> $m(m + 1)$
> $m \times 1$

> **Q9d hint**
>
> Draw the arrows.

10 a Complete the pattern.

    $t + t = 2t$

    $t^2 + t^2 = 2t^2$

    $t^3 + t^3 = 2t^3$

    $t^4 + t^4 = \square$

  b Simplify by collecting like terms.

    i $p^2 + p^2$

    ii $x^3 + x^3$

    iii $m^2 + m^2 + m^2$

    iv $2x^2 + 3x^2$

11 Simplify by collecting like terms.

  a $t^2 + t^2 + 3t = \square t^2 + \square$

  b $p^3 + p + p$

  c $3x + x^2 + 2x$

> **Q11 hint**
>
> You can only add terms with the same letters and powers.

12 a What is the highest common factor (HCF) of 3 and 9?

  b Copy and complete.

    $3x + 9 = \square(\square + \square)$

> **Q12 hint**
>
> The HCF is outside the bracket.

13 Copy and complete.

  a $4x + 8 = 4(\square + \square)$ **b** $2x + 6 = 2(\square + \square)$

  c $15x + 5 = \square(3x + 1)$ **d** $18x - 12 = \square(3x - 2)$

  e $3x + 15 = 3(\square + \square)$ **f** $7x - 14 = 7(\square + \square)$

Substitution

1 Molly earns £9 per hour. She uses this formula to work out her pay.
Pay = 9 × number of hours
Work out how much she is paid for 8 hours.

2 The formula to work out the distance a car travels is
distance = speed × time
A car travels at a speed of 50 km per hour for 2 hours.
How far does it travel?

3 Work out the value of each expression when $m = 2$ and $n = 6$.
  a $m + 3$ **b** $n - 5$ **c** $m + n$

  d $4m$ **e** $3n$ **f** $\dfrac{n}{2}$

  g mn **h** $mn + 2$ **i** $\dfrac{n}{m}$

4 The formula for the area of a rectangle is $l \times w$ where l = length and w = width.
Work out the area of a rectangle when
  a $l = 3$, $w = 5$
  b $l = 9$, $w = 7$
  c $l = 4$, $w = 4$
  d $l = 20$, $w = 1$

5 $P = 10(a + b)$
Work out the value of P when
  a $a = 9$, $b = 3$
  b $a = 2$, $b = 5$
  c $a = 3$, $b = 12$

6 Use the formula $P = 10 + m$ to work out the value of P when
  a $m = -2$ **b** $m = -5$ **c** $m = -10$

7 Work out the value of n^2 when
  a $n = 5$ **b** $n = 1$ **c** $n = 7$

8 Copy and complete the calculations when $m = 2$.
  a $m^4 = \square \times \square \times \square \times \square = \square$ **b** $m^2 + 1 = \square \times \square + 1 = \square$
  c $m^2 - 2 = \square \times \square - 2 = \square$ **d** $3m^2 = 3 \times \square \times \square = \square$

Writing expressions and formulae

1 Match each algebraic expression to its description.

a $x + 3$	**i** 3 less than x
b $x - 3$	**ii** x less than 3
c $3x$	**iii** 3 more than x
d $\dfrac{x}{3}$	**iv** one third of x
e $3 - x$	**v** 3 times x

Q1 hint

Pay = 9 × $\underset{8}{\underline{\text{number of hours}}}$

  = 9 × 8 = $\square$

Q3a hint

$\underset{\smile}{m} + 3$
2 + 3 = $\square$

Q3g hint

$mn = m \times n = \square \times \square.$

Q4a hint

Area = $\underset{\smile}{l} \times \underset{\smile}{w}$
    = 3 × 5
    = $\square$

Q5a hint

$P = 10(a + b)$
  = 10(9 + 3)
  = 10 × 12

Q6a hint

$P = 10 + -2$
  = 10 − 2

Q7a hint

$5^2 = \square$

Q8b hint

Remember to calculate powers first.

2 To estimate the number of bulbs that will sprout, S. Eddie divides the number planted, p, by 3.
Copy and complete the formula $S = \dfrac{\square}{\square}$

3 Write an expression for each function machine. The first one has been done for you.

a
$a \rightarrow \boxed{+3} \rightarrow a + 3$

b
$m \rightarrow \boxed{\div 2} \rightarrow \square$

c
$n \rightarrow \boxed{\times 5} \rightarrow \square$

4 To convert a decimal, m, to a percentage, p, multiply by 100.
Choose the correct formula connecting m and p.

$p = m + 100$ $\qquad$ $p = 100m$ $\qquad$ $p = \dfrac{m}{100}$ $\qquad$ $p = 100 - m$

> **Q4 hint**
>
> Draw a function machine.

5 Write a formula to convert mm, x, into cm, y.

6 Write a description for each expression.

a $x + y$ $\qquad$ **b** xy $\qquad$ **c** $x - y$ $\qquad$ **d** $\dfrac{x}{y}$

e $y + x$ $\qquad$ **f** $y - x$ $\qquad$ **g** $\dfrac{y}{x}$ $\qquad$ **h** yx

> **Q6a hint**
>
> Use these phrases: *more than, less than, multiplied by, divided by.*
> E.g. y more than ….

7 William works out the money he has, M. He adds the money in his bank account, b, to the money in his savings account, s.
Which formula shows the correct relationship between M, b and s?

$M = b - s$ $\qquad$ $M = b + s$ $\qquad$ $M = \dfrac{b}{s}$ $\qquad$ $M = bs$

8 To convert from km, K, to miles, M, divide by 8 then multiply by 5.
Write the formula.

9 To find the mean, M, of two values, a and b, add them together and divide by 2.
a Write an expression for a add b divided by 2.
b Write a formula for finding the mean of a and b. $M = $ _____

10 I think of a number, add 3, and then divide by 8.
a What would the result be if the original number was 21?
b Copy and complete the function machine.

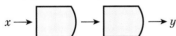

c Which of the formulae below connect x with y?

$y = \dfrac{x + 3}{8}$ $\qquad$ $y = 8(x + 3)$ $\qquad$ $y = \dfrac{x}{3} + 8$ $\qquad$ $y = 3x + 8$

Enrichment

1 a When $x = 1$ work out the value of
i x^2 $\qquad$ **ii** x^3 $\qquad$ **iii** x^4 $\qquad$ **iv** x^5
b Predict the value of x^{119}.

2 Victoria says, '$x + 2 < x + 3$ for any value of x'.
Is she correct? Explain your answer.

3 Reflect Look back at the questions you answered in this section.
Which hints were most useful to you? What made them more useful?
Which hints were least useful to you? What made them less useful?
What do your answers tell you about how you learn maths best?

Reflect

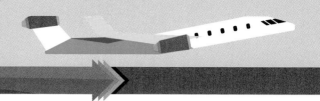

3 Extend

You will:
- Extend your understanding with problem-solving.

1 A square has sides of length x. Write and simplify an expression for its
  a perimeter   **b** area.

2 A cube has edges of length 10 cm.
  a Work out the area of one of the square faces.
  b The cube is painted. Work out the total area that is painted.
  Another cube has edges of length x.
  c Write an algebraic expression for the area of one of the faces.
  d Write an algebraic expression for the total area of all the faces.

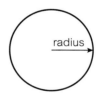

3 You can estimate the area of a circle, A, using the formula $A = 3r^2$ where
  r = radius, the distance from the centre of a circle to the edge.
  a Work out an estimate for the area of the circle when
    i $r = 10$
    ii $r = 12$
  b The area of a circle is approximately 27 cm². Estimate its radius.

4 **Finance** Company 1 uses the formula $C = 0.05M + 0.02T$ for calculating
  the cost of a mobile phone bill, where M = number of minutes of calls
  and T = number of texts.
  a Work out the cost of bills for each of these customers.
    Customer A: 10 minutes of calls, 1000 texts
    Customer B: 300 minutes of calls, 20 texts
    Customer C: 1000 minutes of calls
  b Company 2 uses the formula $C = 0.1M + 0.01T$
    Work out the bill for each of the customers if they used this company.
  c Which company should each customer use?

5 **Problem-solving** Jamie is working out coordinates using a rule.
  She takes the x-coordinate and puts it into the function machine to
  get a y-coordinate:

> **Q5 hint**
> Start with $x = 0$

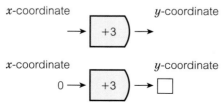

Work out several pairs of coordinates and plot them on a coordinate
grid. Join them with a line. What do you notice? Design your own
function machine and generate coordinates. Plot them and join them
with a line. What do you notice?

6 A triangle has side length n cm.
The second side is 5 less than double this length.
The third side is twice the length of the second side.
Write an expression for the perimeter of the triangle. Simplify your expression as much as possible.

Q6 hint

Sketch and label the triangle.

7 In the pyramid, each brick is the sum of the two bricks below.
Work out the missing expressions.

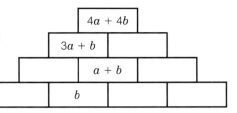

DI
3.4

8 A magician uses this number trick: *Think of a number. Add 3. Multiply it by 2. Subtract double the number you first thought of. The number you have is 6.*
Explain the trick.

Q8 hint

Call the unknown number 'x' and construct an algebraic expression.

9 In a magic square the diagonals, rows and columns all sum to the same total.

DI
3.2
$Q9$

a Write the numbers 1–9 in the magic square (using each number only once) so that all the diagonals, rows and columns sum to 15. Three numbers have been written for you.

	1	
	5	
4		

b Write the algebraic expressions in the magic square so that all the rows, columns and diagonals sum to $3c$.

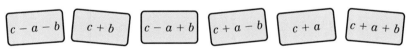

$c - a - b$ $c + b$ $c - a + b$ $c + a - b$ $c + a$ $c + a + b$

	c	
$c - b$		$c - a$

10 When $a = -2$ all but one of these expressions have the same value. Which is the 'odd one out'?

$a^2 + 2$ $3a + 12$ $-3a$ $-\dfrac{12}{a}$ $-4a + 2$ $2a + 10$

11 This is part of a spreadsheet a shop uses to calculate wages.

a What value will be calculated in cell D2?

b What expressions should be written in cells D3 and D4 to calculate the wages of Mr Grantwich and Mrs Angelica?

c The value in cell B4 is changed to £19. What value will show in cell D4?

d The expression in C5 calculates the mean number of hours worked.
What is this value?

e What does the expression in cell B5 calculate?

	A	B	C	D
1		Pay per hour	Number of hours	Pay
2	Mrs Burns	8	25	= B2 * C2
3	Mr Grantwich	7	17	
4	Mrs Angelica	15	15	
5		= (B2+B3+B4)/3	= (C2+C3+C4)/3	
6				

Key point

In spreadsheets * is used instead of ×.

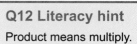

12 The product of two terms is $6x^3$. What could the two terms be?

13 The sum of two terms is $8x$. Their product is $15x^2$. What are they?

14 The length of a rectangle is three times the width. Write and simplify an expression for
  a the area
  b the perimeter.

Q12 Literacy hint
Product means multiply.

Q12 hint
$\square \times \square = 6x^3$

Investigation   Problem-solving

This blue square has width a.
1 Write an expression for the area of the blue square.

 a

This yellow square has sides twice as long.
$2a$
2 Write and simplify an expression for the area of the yellow square.
3 How many blue squares will fit inside the yellow square?

Discussion When you double the length of the sides of a square what happens to the area?

---

15 A secret message, is written using this code:

1	2	3	4	5	6	7	8	9	10	11	12	13
A	B	C	D	E	F	G	H	I	J	K	L	M

14	15	16	17	18	19	20	21	22	23	24	25	26
N	O	P	Q	R	S	T	U	V	W	X	Y	Z

To decode the message substitute $x = 2$ and $y = 3$ into each expression and then identify the letter. Each new line is a new word.

$10x + y \qquad 4x \qquad (x + y)^2$

$10x + y = 20 + 3 = 23 \qquad 23 = W$
$4x = 8 \qquad\qquad\qquad 8 = H$
$(x + y)^2 = 25 \qquad\qquad 25 = Y$

$y^2 \qquad 5y + 2x$

$y(x + 1) \qquad 10x$

$3x - y \qquad \dfrac{y}{3} \qquad yx^2 \qquad 2xy \qquad x + y \qquad \dfrac{4(x + y)}{5}$

$2y \quad y - x \quad 3x - y \quad 7y - 1 \quad 3x + 3y \quad 6y \quad 2(x + y) - 1 \quad 10x - 1 \quad 5x - 1 \quad y^2 + x + \quad 2x + y?$

Worked example

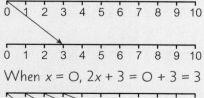

Draw a pair of number lines from 1 to 10.
Show the mapping: $x \to 2x + 3$

0 1 2 3 4 5 6 7 8 9 10

0 1 2 3 4 5 6 7 8 9 10
When $x = 0$, $2x + 3 = 0 + 3 = 3$

> Substitute each number on the top number line into the function $2x + 3$.

0 1 2 3 4 5 6 7 8 9 10

0 1 2 3 4 5 6 7 8 9 10

When $x = 1$, $2x + 3 = 2 + 3 = 5$
When $x = 2$, $2x + 3 = 4 + 3 = 7$
When $x = 3$, $2x + 3 = 6 + 3 = 9$

Topic links: Calculate the mean, Calculations involving negative numbers.

Subject links: ICT (Q11).

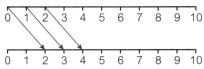

16 The function $x \rightarrow x + 2$ is shown on a **mapping diagram**.
Copy and complete the mapping diagram.

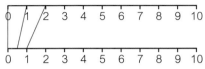

17 Show each mapping on a pair of number lines from 0 to 10.

a $x \rightarrow x - 5$ b $x \rightarrow 3x - 3$ c $x \rightarrow \dfrac{(2x + 4)}{2}$

Key point

A mapping diagram is a visual representation of a function.

18 Show each mapping on a pair of number lines from –5 to 5.

a $x \rightarrow x + 2$ b $x \rightarrow 2x + 4$ c $x \rightarrow 2 - x$

19 a Copy and complete the mapping diagram for $x \rightarrow \frac{1}{2}x$

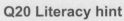

b What value maps to 10?

20 The first of three **consecutive** whole numbers is x.
  a Write expressions for the next two numbers: x, $x + \square$, $x + \square$.
  b Write and simplify an expression for the sum of the three numbers.
  c Factorise the expression.
  d Write an expression for the mean of the three numbers.
  What do you notice?

Q20 Literacy hint

Consecutive numbers follow each other. 4, 5, 6 are consecutive.

21 a When $x = -1$ work out the value of
  i x^2 **ii** x^3 **iii** x^4 **iv** x^5
  b Predict the value of x^{119}.

22 What value(s) of x would make these statements true?
  a $2x < x$ **b** $x^2 = 2x$ **c** $x^2 > 2x$ **d** $x^2 < 2x$

23 Look at these advertisements.

2U Taxis	**A 2 B Taxis**
Fare: £1 per mile	Fare: £2 per passenger + 50p per mile

  a Work out the cost of a 10-mile journey with 3 passengers with each company.
  b For each company write a formula for calculating the cost of a journey, T, with distance d and number of passengers p.
  c Which company is cheaper for 2 passengers to travel 15 miles?
  d A journey with 2U costs £20. What distance was the journey?
  e A journey for 2 passengers with A2B costs £20. What distance was the journey?

Q23 hint

Remember 50p = £0.50

24 Reflect Look back at Q12, 13 and 14. How did you use algebra to solve the problems? Did you use expressions, equations or formulae? Or all three?

3 Unit test

Log how you did on your Student Progression Chart.

1 To convert between hours and minutes use the formula
Minutes = number of hours × 60
Work out the number of minutes in 7 hours.

2 The formula for calculating the perimeter of a shape, P, is $P = 2a + 3b$.
Work out the value of P when $a = 5$ and $b = 7$.

3 Use the formula $m = \dfrac{c}{100}$ for converting centimetres, c, to metres, m.
Work out the value of m when $c = 325$.

4 Use the formula $D = \dfrac{n(n-3)}{2}$ to work out the value of D when $n = 4$.

5 Expand
   a $3(x + 4)$
   b $5(x - 7)$
   c $7(10 - x)$

6 Write an expression for
   a 2 less than y
   b 5 times m
   c y divided by 10
   d x more than y.

7 Angela is paid £10 more than Imogen.
Write a formula connecting the amount Angela is paid, A, and the amount Imogen is paid, I.

8 Write an expression for
   a b multiplied by itself
   b double b
   c a divided by b.

9 Henry runs or cycles every day. When he runs he covers 2 miles.
When he cycles he covers 5 miles.
Write a formula connecting the total distance he travels, T, with the number of days he runs, r, and the number of days he cycles, c.

10 Work out the value of these expressions when $p = 3$, $q = 6$.
   a $2(p + 3)$
   b $5(2p + q)$

11 Simplify by collecting like terms.
   a $x + 2x$
   b $6x + 2y - 3x$
   c $10 + 12y + 7 - 14y$

12 When $a = 5$, $b = 11$ and $c = 9$ work out the value of

  a $4a + 2c$

  b $20 - 3a$

  c $10c - 2b + a$

13 Use the formula $z = 2m - a$ to work out the value of z when

  a $m = -1$, $a = 5$

  b $m = -3$, $a = -2$

14 Simplify

  a $r \times r \times r \times r \times r$

  b $2 \times y \times 7 \times y \times y$

  c $3y \times y$

  d $3m \times 5m$

  e $18x \div 3$

15 Simplify by collecting like terms.

  a $3r^3 + 10r^3$

  b $12x + 3x^2 - 5x$

16 Expand

  a $x(x + 7)$

  b $r(r - 5)$

  c $2b(b + 5)$

  d $3b(2b - 4)$

17 Find the value of each expression when $b = 2$ and $m = 9$.

  a b^3

  b $b^2 - m$

  c $\dfrac{b + 2m}{2}$

  d $m^2 - b^2$

  e $3(m - b)$

  f $(m - b)^2$

18 Factorise

  a $2x + 12$

  b $12x - 15$

  c $50 - 20x$

Challenge

19 Are there any values of x that make these pairs of expressions equal?

  a $2x^2$ and $2x$

  b $4x - 5$ and $5x - 4$

  c $\dfrac{3x}{2}$ and $\dfrac{2x}{3}$

  d $2(3x + 5)$ and $2(3x - 5)$

20 Reflect Look back at the work you have done in this unit. Find a question that you could not answer straightaway, but that you really tried at, and then answered correctly.

How do you feel when you struggle to answer a maths question?

Write down the strategies you use to overcome your difficulty.

How do you feel when you eventually understand and get the correct answer?

4.1 Working with fractions

You will learn to:
- Compare and simplify fractions
- Write one number as a fraction of another
- Work out simple fractions of amounts.

Why learn this?
You can compare fractions to find the best deals.

Fluency
What fraction of this rectangle is
- shaded
- unshaded?

οο1

Explore
What fraction of the stages in the Tour de France are mountain stages?

Confidence

Exercise 4.1

Warm up

1 Work out the highest common factor (HCF) of
  a 8 and 12   **b** 6 and 15
  c 7 and 35   **d** 24 and 40

2 Which fraction is larger in each pair?
  a $\frac{1}{2}$ or $\frac{1}{4}$ **b** $\frac{1}{5}$ or $\frac{1}{3}$
  c $\frac{1}{8}$ or $\frac{3}{8}$ **d** $\frac{5}{9}$ or $\frac{4}{9}$

3 Sort these fractions into pairs of **equivalent fractions**.
  $\frac{1}{4}$ $\frac{4}{5}$ $\frac{1}{2}$ $\frac{15}{20}$ $\frac{2}{8}$ $\frac{3}{4}$ $\frac{3}{6}$ $\frac{8}{10}$

4 Use the fraction wall to work out which is larger.
  Write < or > between each pair of fractions.   оо3
  a $\frac{2}{7}$ ☐ $\frac{3}{8}$
  b $\frac{5}{6}$ ☐ $\frac{3}{4}$
  c $\frac{1}{3}$ ☐ $\frac{3}{7}$
  d $\frac{3}{5}$ ☐ $\frac{1}{2}$

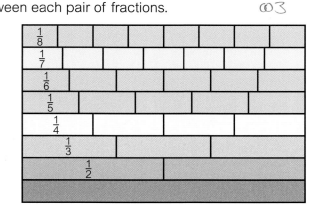

> **Key point**
> **Equivalent fractions** have the same value.

> **Q3 hint**
>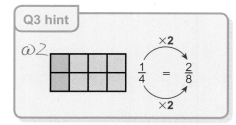
> ω2
> $\frac{1}{4} = \frac{2}{8}$
> ×2

> **Q4 hint**
> > means 'is greater than' and < means 'is less than.'

Topic links: Pie charts, Area, Using formulae   **Subject links:** Science (Q11)

5 Write these fractions in order of size. Start with the smallest.

$\frac{5}{8}$ $\frac{1}{2}$ $\frac{2}{5}$ $\frac{4}{7}$

6 Problem-solving Which is larger, $\frac{3}{4}$ or $\frac{7}{10}$?

7 Problem-solving Which is larger, $\frac{3}{4}$ or $\frac{4}{5}$?

8 Simplify

  a $\frac{12}{20}$

  b $\frac{9}{12}$

  c $\frac{10}{15}$

  d $\frac{5}{10}$

  e $\frac{3}{9}$

  f $\frac{14}{35}$

> **Key point**
>
> You can write a fraction in its **simplest form** by dividing the numerator and denominator by their highest common factor (HCF) to give an equivalent fraction.

Discussion Is there more than one way to simplify $\frac{12}{20}$?

Q6 Strategy hint

Make two copies of this grid and shade in parts to compare. Use equivalent fractions to help you.

$\frac{3}{4} = \frac{\square}{20}$

$\frac{7}{10} = \frac{\square}{20}$

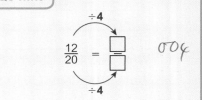

Q8 hint

$\frac{12}{20} = \frac{\square}{\square}$ $\div 4$ $\div 4$ ᴏᴏ4

Q8 Literacy hint

$5 \rightarrow$ numerator
$6 \rightarrow$ denominator

Investigation   **Problem-solving**

a Copy and complete these equivalent fractions, and write each fraction as a coordinate pair. $\frac{1}{2}, \frac{2}{4}, \frac{3}{\square}, \frac{\square}{8}, \frac{5}{\square}$

  (1, 2), (2, 4), (3, $\square$), ($\square$, 8), (5, $\square$)

b Copy the grid.
  Plot all the coordinate pairs on the grid.
  The first one has been done for you.

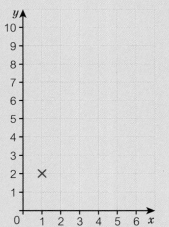

c Join together all the points you have plotted.
  Discussion Why do you think all the points lie on a straight line?

d Go through parts **a** to **c** again, but this time with three fractions that are equivalent to $\frac{1}{3}$.

e Discussion Do think you will always have a straight line, whatever equivalent fractions you use?

ᴏᴏ5

8·1 /ᴍ

9 A shop sells 18 rugby shirts. 9 of them are Harlequins shirts.
  What fraction are Harlequins shirts?
  Write your answer in its simplest form.

10 Out of the top 15 football clubs in Europe with the highest match attendance figures, 5 are British clubs.
  What fraction of the top 15 clubs are British?
  Write your answer in its simplest form.

Q9 hint

$\frac{\text{Harlequins shirts sold}}{\text{Total shirts sold}}$

Simplify your fraction.

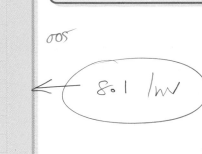

11 **STEM** The pie chart shows the composition of pink gold. Write the fraction of pink gold that is
a gold
b copper
c silver.

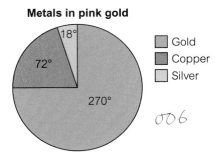

Metals in pink gold

- Gold
- Copper
- Silver

18°
72°
270°

006

Q11 hint

How many degrees are there altogether in a pie chart? Simplify your answer.

12 **Real life / Problem-solving** The table shows the number of games won by each player in each set of a match in a Wimbledon tournament.

	Set 1	Set 2	Set 3
Player A	4	3	2
Player B	6	6	6

What fraction of all the games in the match did Player B win?
Write your answer in its simplest form.

13 Work out
a $\frac{1}{2}$ of £40
b $\frac{1}{4}$ of 20 kg
c $\frac{1}{3}$ of 300 ml
d $\frac{1}{5}$ of 75 cm

Q13a hint

£40 ÷ 2 = ...

14 Work out
a $\frac{3}{4}$ of £80
b $\frac{3}{5}$ of 35 m
c $\frac{2}{3}$ of 150 mm
d $\frac{4}{9}$ of 27 kg

Q14a hint

To work out $\frac{3}{4}$ of a number, first work out $\frac{1}{4}$, then multiply by 3.

15 Which is larger, $\frac{2}{3}$ of 18 m or $\frac{5}{6}$ of 24 m?

16 **Problem-solving** A rectangle is 12 cm long and 5 cm wide.
Ibrahim shades $\frac{7}{10}$ of the rectangle.
What area of the rectangle does Ibrahim shade?

17 **Explore** What fraction of the stages in the Tour de France are mountain stages?
Is it easier to explore this question now you have completed the lesson?
What further information do you need to be able to answer this?

18 **Reflect** After this lesson John says, 'Fractions are not really like whole numbers.'
Farooq says, 'Yes! Fractions can be written in many different ways.'
Look back at your work on fractions.
What do you think John means?
What do you think Farooq means?

Q18 hint

List all the ways you think fractions are not like whole numbers.
List all the different ways you can write fractions.

Explore

Reflect

Active Learn Delta 1, Section 4.1

4.2 Adding and subtracting fractions

You will learn to:
- Write an improper fraction as a mixed number
- Add and subtract fractions.

Why learn this?
Engineers add and subtract fractions when they calculate the size of bolts needed to join different pieces of metal.

Fluency
Sort these fractions into their equivalent pairs.

$\frac{5}{10}$ $\frac{2}{3}$ $\frac{16}{24}$ $\frac{1}{2}$

Explore
Can you add different unit fractions to get 1 whole?

Exercise 4.2

1 Write each fraction in its simplest form.
  a $\frac{4}{8}$
  b $\frac{6}{9}$
  c $\frac{6}{10}$
  d $\frac{12}{14}$

2 Work out the lowest common multiple (LCM) of
  a 2 and 3
  b 5 and 10
  c 6 and 8

3 Work out these divisions. Write each answer as a whole number and a remainder.
  a $8 \div 3$
  b $12 \div 5$
  c $18 \div 4$
  d $31 \div 2$

> **Q3a hint**
> $10 \div 3 = 3$ remainder $\square$

4 How many
  a quarters are in 1
  b fifths are in 1
  c thirds are in 1
  d tenths are in 1?

5 Which is larger $1\frac{4}{5}$ or $\frac{11}{5}$?

6 Write these improper fractions as mixed numbers.
  a $\frac{7}{4}$
  b $\frac{12}{5}$
  c $\frac{31}{7}$
  d $\frac{23}{3}$

> **Key point**
> A **mixed number** has a whole number part and a fraction part.
> In an **improper fraction** the numerator is greater than the denominator.
> A fraction greater than 1 can be written as a mixed number or an improper fraction.

> **Q6a hint**
> $7 \div 4 = 1$ remainder 3, so $\frac{7}{4} = 1\frac{\square}{4}$

Warm up

7 Work out

   a $\frac{1}{3} + \frac{1}{3}$

   b $\frac{3}{7} + \frac{3}{7}$

   c $\frac{8}{11} - \frac{3}{11}$

   d $1 - \frac{3}{5}$

8 Work out these. Give each answer in its simplest form.

   a $\frac{2}{9} + \frac{1}{9}$

   b $\frac{7}{12} - \frac{5}{12}$

9 Problem-solving Karl adds together two different fractions with the same denominator. He simplifies his answer and gets $\frac{2}{5}$.
Write down two fractions that Karl may have added.

   Discussion What method did you use to solve this problem?

10 Work out these. Give each answer in its simplest form.

   a $\frac{3}{10} + \frac{2}{5}$

   b $\frac{11}{12} - \frac{3}{4}$

   c $\frac{4}{9} + \frac{1}{3}$

   d $\frac{7}{10} - \frac{1}{6}$

$8.2?$

11 Real life An engineer bolts together a piece of metal that has a thickness of $\frac{3}{8}$ inch and a piece of wood that has a thickness of $\frac{5}{16}$ of an inch. What is the total thickness of the metal and wood when they are bolted together?

12 Work out these. Give each answer in its simplest form.

   a $\frac{1}{2} + \frac{1}{3}$

   b $\frac{9}{10} - \frac{3}{8}$

   Discussion Can you use a common denominator that isn't the LCM?

13 Work out these. Give your answers as mixed numbers.

   a $\frac{5}{6} + \frac{2}{3}$

   b $\frac{1}{9} + \frac{9}{10}$

   c $\frac{3}{4} + \frac{3}{5}$

   d $\frac{1}{2} + \frac{8}{9}$

Key point

When two fractions have the same denominator, add or subtract by adding or subtracting the numerators.

Q7a hint

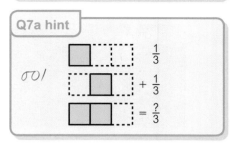

Key point

When you add or subtract fractions with different denominators, first write them as equivalent fractions with the same denominator (**common denominator**).

Q10a hint

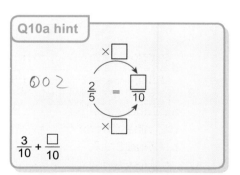

Q12a hint

Work out the LCM of 2 and 3.

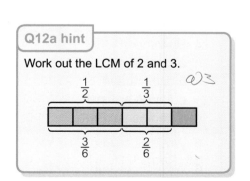

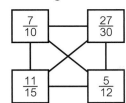

14 Problem solving The diagram shows four fractions linked by lines.

$\frac{7}{10}$ ——— $\frac{27}{30}$

$\frac{11}{15}$ ——— $\frac{5}{12}$

004

    a Work out the total of any two linked fractions.
    b Which two fractions give the greatest total?
       Work out this total and write it as a mixed number in its simplest form.
    c Work out the difference between any two linked fractions.
    d Which two fractions give you the greatest difference?
       Work out this difference and write it in its simplest form.
    Discussion How did you work out your answers to parts **b** and **d**?

15 Work out these. Give each answer in its simplest form, and as a mixed number where necessary.

    a $\frac{1}{2} + \frac{2}{3} + \frac{3}{4}$

    b $\frac{4}{5} + \frac{1}{4} + \frac{1}{2}$

    c $\frac{5}{8} + \frac{7}{12} - \frac{11}{24}$

    d $\frac{24}{25} - \frac{2}{5} - \frac{13}{50}$

overlaps with Core

> **Q15a hint**
>
> $\frac{1}{2} + \frac{2}{3} + \frac{3}{4} + \frac{\square}{12} + \frac{\square}{12} + \frac{\square}{12}$

16 Problem-solving The table shows the fraction of class 7T that support three different rugby teams.

Rugby team	Scarlets	Blues	Dragons
Fraction of class	$\frac{2}{15}$	$\frac{3}{10}$	$\frac{1}{6}$

    a What fraction of the class do not support the Scarlets, Blues or Dragons?
    b How many students do you think are in class 7T? Explain your answer.

> **Q16a hint**
>
> Start by working out the total fraction of the class that support the Scarlets, Blues and Dragons.

Investigation   **Problem-solving**

Two fractions add to $\frac{1}{4}$.
What could the fractions be?
Find at least four different pairs.

---

17 Explore Can you add different unit fractions to get 1 whole? Is it easier to explore this question now you have completed the lesson? What further information do you need to be able to answer this?

18 **Reflect** Look back at Q11.
What steps did you take to work out these calculations?
You might begin with 'Step 1: I looked at the denominators and…'.
Do your steps also work for subtracting fractions?

Explore

Reflect

4.3 Fractions, decimals and percentages

You will learn to:
- Work with equivalent fractions, decimals and percentages
- Use division to write a fraction as a decimal.

Why learn this?
Proportions can be given as fractions, decimals or percentages.

Fluency
Which of these are equivalent?

$\frac{1}{2}$ $\frac{1}{4}$ $\frac{3}{4}$ $\frac{1}{10}$

0.1   0.25   0.5   0.75

75%   10%   50%   25%

Explore
Which vegetables contain the greatest percentage of water?

CONFIDENCE

Exercise 4.3

Warm up

1 Copy and complete

a $\frac{1}{5} = \frac{\square}{10}$ **b** $\frac{2}{5} = \frac{\square}{10}$ **c** $\frac{3}{5} = \frac{\square}{10}$

2 Work out these.
   a $8\overline{)7}$ **b** $20\overline{)9}$

3 What fraction of an hour is 25 minutes?

4 Copy and complete this table.

Fraction		$\frac{1}{5}$		$\frac{3}{10}$			$\frac{3}{5}$			$\frac{4}{5}$	
Decimal			0.25			0.5		0.7			0.9
Percentage	10%			40%					75%		

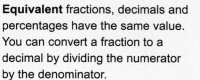

Q4 hint

$10\% = \frac{1}{10}$

$\times 2 \Big(\qquad \Big) \times 2$

$20\% = \frac{\square}{10}$

5 Copy and complete this table.

Mixed number	$1\frac{3}{4}$					$1\frac{2}{5}$
Decimal		1.5			1.7	
Percentage			130%	120%		

Discussion What does it mean when people say 'house prices have increased by 200%'?

6 Finance A newspaper article states

> A business increased its profits by 250%.

   a Write 250% as a decimal.
   b The business originally made a profit of £182 000.
      How much profit do they make now?

7 Write these fractions as decimals.
   a $\frac{4}{5}$ **b** $\frac{3}{20}$ **c** $\frac{12}{16}$ **d** $\frac{15}{8}$ **e** $\frac{24}{60}$

Key point

Equivalent fractions, decimals and percentages have the same value. You can convert a fraction to a decimal by dividing the numerator by the denominator.

Key point

When a positive mixed number is greater than 1, its decimal equivalent is greater than 1, and its percentage equivalent is greater than 100%.
For example, $1\frac{1}{4}$ = 1.25 = 125%

Topic links: Bar charts

8 In a rugby match the Cardiff Blues won 13 out of the 20 line-outs.

  a What fraction of the line-outs did they win?

  b Write your answer to part **a** as a decimal.

  c What percentage of the line-outs did they win?

9 Modelling / STEM A new medicine was trialled on 5 groups of people. The table shows the number of people in each group and the number of people successfully treated.

Group	A	B	C	D	E
Number in group	150	200	80	350	420
Number successfully treated	132	182	68	320	382

  a What fraction of each group was successfully treated?

  b Shaya says, 'There is about a 0.9 success rate for each group'. Do you agree with Shaya? Explain your answer.

10 Problem-solving The bar chart shows the number of slices of cake sold one day in a café. Steve thinks that approximately 45% of the slices of cake sold were carrot cake. Is Steve correct? Explain your answer.

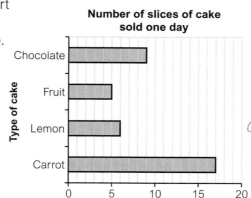

Number of slices of cake sold one day

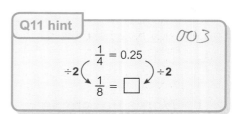

Q10 Strategy hint

Work out the fraction of cake sold that was carrot cake. Then convert the fraction to a decimal, then a percentage.

002

11 Use the fact that $\frac{1}{4} = 0.25$ to work out these fractions as decimals.

  a $\frac{1}{8}$

  b $\frac{1}{16}$

  c $\frac{1}{32}$

Q11 hint

003

$$\frac{1}{4} = 0.25$$
$$\div 2 \left(\right) \div 2$$
$$\frac{1}{8} = \square$$

12 Use the fact that $\frac{1}{100} = 0.01$ to write these fractions as decimals.

  a $\frac{1}{200}$

  b $\frac{1}{400}$

  c $\frac{1}{50}$

  d $\frac{1}{25}$

Q12 hint

004

$$\frac{1}{100} = 0.01$$
$$\times 2 \left(\right) \times 2$$
$$\frac{1}{50} = \square$$

13 Explore Which vegetables contain the greatest percentage of water? Is it easier to explore this question now you have completed the lesson? What further information do you need to be able to answer this?

14 Reflect After this lesson Hillary says, 'Decimals are just another way to write fractions.' Do you agree with Hillary? Explain.

Explore

Reflect

MASTER

Check
P95

Strengthen
P97

Extend
P101

Test
P105

4.4 Multiplying and dividing fractions

You will learn to:
- Work out fractions of amounts
- Divide an integer and a fraction by a fraction
- Multiply a fraction by a fraction.

CONFIDENCE

Why learn this?
Some medicine doses for children are fractions of adult doses. Doctors need to calculate with fractions to make sure they prescribe the right amount.

Fluency
$4 \times 5 = 5 \times \square$
$3 \times 8 = \square \times 3$

Explore
How many episodes of a TV series can you watch in 24 hours?

Exercise 4.4

Warm up

1 Work out
  a $\frac{1}{4}$ of £120
  b $\frac{1}{5}$ of 45 m
  c $\frac{2}{3}$ of 18 cm
  d $\frac{5}{9}$ of 36 kg

2 Write each fraction in its simplest form.
  $\frac{4}{6}, \frac{12}{15}, \frac{16}{28}, \frac{35}{50}$

3 Work out
  a $\frac{1}{7} \times 56$
  b $\frac{3}{4} \times 24$
  c $60 \times \frac{1}{3}$
  d $27 \times \frac{2}{9}$
  e $\frac{2}{5} \times 25$
  f $\frac{3}{4} \times 12$
  g $18 \times \frac{2}{9}$
  h $64 \times \frac{5}{8}$

> **Q3a hint**
> $\frac{1}{7} \times 56$ is the same as $\frac{1}{7}$ of 56.

Worked example

Work out $\frac{3}{8}$ of 12 kg.

> 12 ÷ 8 isn't a whole number, so work out 3 × 12 first.

$\frac{3}{8} \times 12 = \frac{3 \times 12}{8} = \frac{36}{8}$

$36 \div 8 = 4$ remainder 4

> Divide 36 by 8 and write as a whole number and a remainder.

$\frac{3}{8}$ of 12 kg $= 4\frac{4}{8}$ kg $= 4\frac{1}{2}$ kg

> Write your answer as a mixed number in its simplest form.

4 Work out these fractions of amounts. Write each answer as a mixed number in its simplest form.
  a $\frac{2}{5}$ of 18 kg
  b $\frac{3}{4}$ of 13 m
  c $\frac{5}{6}$ of 20 mm
  d $\frac{2}{9}$ of 21 km

5 **Real life** The formula to convert a distance in kilometres to a distance in miles is
  distance in miles $= \frac{5}{8}$ of distance in kilometres
  Carlos sees this sign.
  How many miles is Carlos from Barcelona?

  Barcelona 42 km

Topic links: Using formulae, Imperial units, Area

6 Copy and complete these divisions.

a $1 \div \frac{1}{2} = 1 \times 2 = \square$

b $1 \div \frac{1}{3} = 1 \times 3 = \square$

c $1 \div \frac{1}{4} = 1 \times \square = \square$

d $1 \div \frac{1}{5} = 1 \times \square = \square$

Discussion How many ways can you complete this sentence?
Dividing by $\square$ is the same as multiplying by $\square$.

Q6a hint

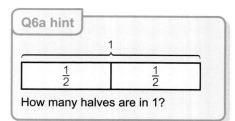

How many halves are in 1?

7 Copy and complete these divisions.

a $4 \div \frac{1}{2} = 4 \times \frac{2}{1} = 4 \times \square = \square$

b $8 \div \frac{2}{3} = 8 \times \frac{3}{2} = \frac{8 \times \square}{\square} = \frac{\square}{\square} = \square$

c $6 \div \frac{3}{5} = 6 \times \frac{\square}{\square} = \square$

d $15 \div \frac{5}{8} = 15 \times \frac{\square}{\square} = \square$

Discussion When you divide a positive number by a fraction that is
smaller than 1, is your answer bigger or smaller than the number?

Key point

To divide by a fraction, you can
turn the fraction upside down and
multiply instead.

Q8a hint

How many halves are in 4?

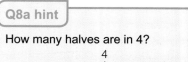

8 **Real life / Problem-solving** Approximately $\frac{1}{4}$ of cars in the UK are silver
and $\frac{1}{5}$ are blue.
Rasheed and Kamal did a survey on car colours.

a Rasheed found 120 people had silver cars.
How many people could he have asked?

b Kamal found 120 people had blue cars.
How many people could he have asked?

Worked example

Work out $\frac{3}{4} \times \frac{1}{2}$

$\frac{3}{4}$ of $\frac{1}{2}$

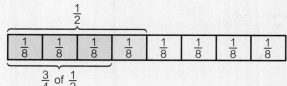

$\frac{3}{4} \times \frac{1}{2} = \frac{3 \times 1}{4 \times 2} = \frac{3}{8}$

Key point

To multiply two fractions, multiply
their numerators and multiply their
denominators.

9 Work out these multiplications. Write each answer in its simplest form.

a $\frac{1}{2} \times \frac{1}{3}$ **b** $\frac{1}{4} \times \frac{2}{3}$

c $\frac{2}{5} \times \frac{1}{2}$ **d** $\frac{2}{3} \times \frac{2}{3}$

Key point

You can cancel common factors
before multiplying fractions.

10 $\frac{1}{6}$ of the members of a school committee are students.

$\frac{3}{4}$ of these students are girls.

What fraction of the committee are girls?

11 Shelley uses this method to multiply fractions.

$$\frac{3}{4} \times \frac{8}{9} = \frac{3 \times 8}{4 \times 9} = \frac{\overset{1}{\cancel{3}} \times \overset{2}{\cancel{8}}}{\underset{1}{\cancel{4}} \times \underset{3}{\cancel{9}}} = \frac{2}{3}$$

Key point

You can cancel common factors before multiplying fractions.

Use Shelley's method to work out these multiplications.

a $\frac{1}{2} \times \frac{6}{7}$ **b** $\frac{3}{5} \times \frac{10}{21}$

c $\frac{9}{16} \times \frac{2}{3}$ **d** $\frac{5}{6} \times \frac{9}{10}$

Discussion $\frac{5 \times 9}{6 \times 10} = \frac{45}{60}$. Simplify the answer.

Which is the easiest way to work out $\frac{5}{6} \times \frac{9}{10}$?

12 Work out the area of each rectangle.

a
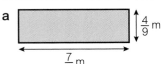
$\frac{4}{9}$ m

$\frac{7}{8}$ m

b
$\frac{8}{15}$ m

$\frac{5}{12}$ m

13 Copy and complete these divisions. The first two have been started for you.

Write each answer in its simplest form.

a $\frac{2}{5} \div \frac{7}{10} = \frac{2}{5} \times \frac{10}{7} = \frac{\square}{\square}$

b $\frac{4}{5} \div \frac{12}{13} = \frac{4}{5} \times \frac{13}{12} = \frac{\square}{\square}$

c $\frac{8}{15} \div \frac{4}{5}$

d $\frac{3}{8} \div \frac{9}{16}$

Q13c hint

Turn the fraction you are dividing by upside down and multiply.

Investigation Problem-solving

These are the tickets on a jacket that is reduced in price in a sale.

Sale Price!
$\frac{1}{3}$ off normal price

Further reduction!
$\frac{1}{4}$ off sale price

Strategy hint

Choose any price for the jacket. Work out the sale price then the price after the further reduction.

1 What is the total fraction off the normal price?

2 What is the final price as a fraction of the normal price?

3 Investigate other calculations involving normal and sale prices, such as $\frac{1}{2}$ off normal price then $\frac{3}{4}$ off sale price. How can you work out the total fraction off for any pair of fractions?

14 Explore How many episodes of a TV series can you watch in 24 hours?

Is it easier to explore this question now you have completed the lesson?

What further information do you need to be able to answer this?

15 Reflect Write down two new things you have learned in this lesson.

Write down the questions that used these new things.

When you answered these questions, did you make any mistakes?

If so, check that you understand where you went wrong.

4.5 Working with mixed numbers

You will learn to:
- Add and subtract mixed numbers
- Enter time as a mixed number into a calculator
- Multiply and divide a mixed number by a fraction.

Why learn this?
Writing time as a mixed number is useful when calculating the average speed of a car.

Fluency
What is each of these as a fraction of an hour in its simplest form?
- 30 minutes
- 15 minutes
- 45 minutes
- 20 minutes
- 10 minutes

Explore
What is the average speed of an intercity train?

Exercise 4.5

1 Work out

  a $\frac{1}{3} + \frac{2}{5}$

  b $\frac{7}{8} - \frac{5}{6}$

2 Work out

  a $\frac{2}{3} \times \frac{3}{5}$

  b $\frac{2}{5} \div \frac{8}{15}$

3 Write each improper fraction as a mixed number.

  a $\frac{5}{3}$

  b $\frac{7}{2}$

  c $\frac{9}{5}$

  d $\frac{16}{7}$

4 Write each time as a mixed number.
The first one is done for you.

  a 2 hours 15 minutes $= 2\frac{1}{4}$ hours

  b 5 hours 20 minutes

  c 4 hours 12 minutes

  d 7 hours 10 minutes

5 Write these improper fractions as decimals.

  a $\frac{13}{4} = 3.\square\square$

  b $\frac{11}{5}$

  c $\frac{36}{10}$

Q5 hint

Write as a mixed number first. Then write the fraction part as a decimal.

Warm up

6 Work out these additions. Write your answer in its simplest form.

   a $2\frac{3}{4} + 1\frac{1}{8} = 3 + \frac{3}{4} + \frac{1}{8} = 3 + \frac{\square}{8} + \frac{1}{8}$

   b $11\frac{3}{5} + 9\frac{2}{15}$

   c $3\frac{7}{10} + 2\frac{3}{5} = 5 + \frac{7}{10} + \frac{3}{5} = \square$

   d $1\frac{2}{3} + 3\frac{5}{6}$

   e $3\frac{1}{2} + 2\frac{2}{3}$

   f $4\frac{3}{4} + 7\frac{7}{10}$

Key point

When you add mixed numbers, add the whole numbers first, then add the fraction parts.

Q6c hint

$\frac{7}{10} + \frac{6}{10} = \frac{\square}{10}$

Worked example

Work out $5\frac{1}{4} - 2\frac{3}{5}$

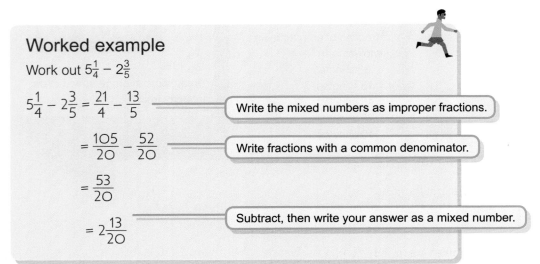

$5\frac{1}{4} - 2\frac{3}{5} = \frac{21}{4} - \frac{13}{5}$ ——— Write the mixed numbers as improper fractions.

$= \frac{105}{20} - \frac{52}{20}$ ——— Write fractions with a common denominator.

$= \frac{53}{20}$

$= 2\frac{13}{20}$ ——— Subtract, then write your answer as a mixed number.

Discussion Why didn't the worked example subtract the whole numbers first, then the fraction parts?

7 Work out these subtractions. Write each answer in its simplest form.

   a $4\frac{2}{3} - 2\frac{1}{6}$

   b $5\frac{3}{5} - 3\frac{1}{2}$

   c $7\frac{5}{8} - 4\frac{5}{12}$

   d $3\frac{1}{3} - 1\frac{1}{2}$

   e $5\frac{1}{4} - 3\frac{5}{8}$

   f $10\frac{2}{5} - 7\frac{2}{3}$

   g $9\frac{2}{7} - 6\frac{3}{4}$

8 Helena travels to stay with her sister. She has a 45-minute walk to the train station. She waits for 20 minutes for a train and then travels for $1\frac{1}{2}$ hours on the train. She has a $\frac{1}{4}$ hour wait for the next train and then another journey of 2 hours 40 minutes.
Finally she has a 50-minute walk to her sister's house.

   a Work out the total time it takes Helena to get to her sister's house.

   b Helena sets off at 9.45 am.
   At what time does she arrive at her sister's house?

Q8 hint

Use the fraction button on your calculator.

9 Here are some mixed number cards.

$6\frac{5}{7}$ $8\frac{7}{9}$ $4\frac{9}{13}$ $3\frac{5}{6}$ $8\frac{1}{2}$

Work out the range.

10 Work out these. The first one has been started for you.
Write each answer in its simplest form.

a $3\frac{1}{2} \times 5 = \frac{7}{2} \times 5 = \frac{7 \times 5}{2} = \square\frac{\square}{2}$

b $8 \times 3\frac{5}{12}$

c $2\frac{1}{4} \times \frac{2}{3}$

d $\frac{4}{7} \times 2\frac{4}{5}$

e $5\frac{3}{7} \times 1\frac{1}{6}$

> **Key point**
>
> When you multiply or divide a mixed number by a fraction, start by writing the mixed number as an improper fraction.

11 **Problem solving** Work out the area of the brown section of this rectangle.

$5\frac{2}{3}$ m

$\frac{3}{4}$ m

$1\frac{8}{9}$ m

12 Work out these. The first one has been started for you.
Write each answer in its simplest form.

a $4\frac{1}{8} \div 3 = \frac{33}{8} \div \frac{3}{1} = \frac{33}{8} \times \frac{1}{3} = \frac{\square}{8} = \square\frac{\square}{8}$

b $5\frac{2}{3} \div 2$

c $2\frac{5}{8} \div \frac{1}{2}$

d $3\frac{1}{4} \div \frac{3}{8}$

e $2\frac{3}{5} \div \frac{7}{10}$

13 **Problem-solving** Jayne cuts pieces of ribbon $\frac{5}{8}$ m in length from a roll of ribbon $13\frac{4}{5}$ m long.

a How many pieces of ribbon can Jayne cut from this roll?

b How many centimetres of ribbon does Jayne have left?

14 **Explore** What is the average speed of an intercity train?
Is it easier to explore this question now you have completed the lesson?
What further information do you need to be able to answer this?

15 **Reflect** What is the same when you calculate with fractions or with mixed numbers?
What is different?

4 Check up

Log how you did on your Student Progression Chart.

Equivalence

1 Which is larger, $\frac{5}{8}$ or $\frac{7}{10}$?

2 Write each fraction in its simplest form.

a $\frac{6}{12}$

b $\frac{16}{24}$

3 A shop sells 30 pairs of flip-flops in one day.
10 pairs are men's flip-flops.
What fraction of the flip-flops sold are men's?
Write your answer in its simplest form.

4 Work out these. Give each answer in its simplest form.

a $\frac{1}{6} + \frac{2}{3}$

b $\frac{1}{2} + \frac{2}{9}$

c $\frac{4}{5} - \frac{3}{4}$

d $\frac{11}{15} - \frac{2}{3}$

5 Copy and complete this table.

Fraction		$\frac{2}{5}$		$\frac{7}{10}$			$3\frac{1}{5}$
Decimal			0.5			2.75	
Percentage	25%				150%		

6 The table shows some students' favourite sport.

Favourite sport	Football	Tennis	Athletics	Rugby	Hockey
Number of students	32	12	5	14	17

What fraction of the students chose football as their favourite sport?
Write your answer in its simplest form.

7 Write these fractions as decimals.

a $\frac{7}{8}$

b $\frac{22}{5}$

Multiplying and dividing with fractions

8 Work out

a $\frac{1}{4}$ of £20

b $\frac{2}{5}$ of 25 kg

9 Work out $21 \times \frac{5}{7}$

10 Mr Jones orders $\frac{5}{8}$ of a lorry load of gravel.
The lorry holds 20 tonnes of gravel when full.
How much does Mr Jones order?
Write your answer as a mixed number in its simplest form.

11 Work out

    a $12 \div \frac{1}{2}$ **b** $35 \div \frac{5}{6}$

12 $\frac{1}{5}$ of the students in a class are left handed.

    $\frac{1}{2}$ of the left-handed students are boys.
What fraction of the class are left-handed boys?

13 Work out $\frac{2}{3} \times \frac{9}{10}$

14 Work out these divisions.

    a $\frac{3}{4} \div \frac{1}{8}$ **b** $\frac{5}{9} \div \frac{2}{3}$

Working with mixed numbers

15 Work out

    a $3\frac{2}{3} + 6\frac{3}{4}$ **b** $4\frac{5}{6} - 3\frac{1}{5}$

16 Write each of these times as a mixed number in its simplest form.
    a 4 hours 45 minutes
    b 3 hours 10 minutes

17 Work out $9 \times 3\frac{1}{4}$

18 Work out $4\frac{5}{8} \div 2$

19 **How sure are you of your answers? Were you mostly**
    😞 **Just guessing**   😐 **Feeling doubtful**   🙂 **Confident**
    What next? Use your results to decide whether to strengthen or
    extend your learning.

8.2 as ⊝n or as Inv?

Challenge

20 Here are some fraction cards and money cards.

$\boxed{\frac{3}{4}}$ $\boxed{\frac{1}{3}}$ $\boxed{\frac{7}{10}}$ $\boxed{\frac{2}{5}}$ $\boxed{£15}$ $\boxed{£60}$ $\boxed{£30}$ $\boxed{£40}$

Sharon arranges the cards like this:

$\boxed{\frac{?}{?}}$ of $\boxed{£\ \ }$ + $\boxed{\frac{?}{?}}$ of $\boxed{£\ \ }$ =

Which cards does she use to get
    a the largest possible answer
    b the smallest possible answer?

21 In this spider diagram, the four
calculations give the answer in
the middle.
each of
Write three calculations for the
missing ones.

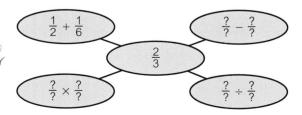

$\frac{1}{2} + \frac{1}{6}$ $\frac{?}{?} - \frac{?}{?}$ $\frac{2}{3}$ $\frac{?}{?} \times \frac{?}{?}$ $\frac{?}{?} \div \frac{?}{?}$

U8 Ext ? or 8·4 Inv.

Master
P81

Check
P95

STRENGTHEN

Extend
P101

Test
P105

4 Strengthen

You will:
- Strengthen your understanding with practice.

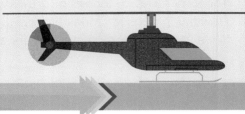

Equivalence

1 Write each fraction in its simplest form.
The first one has been started for you.

a $\frac{2}{4} = \frac{\square}{\square}$

b $\frac{12}{16}$

c $\frac{25}{30} = \frac{?}{?}$

d $\frac{15}{40}$

e $\frac{24}{33}$

> **Q1b hint**
>
> Start by dividing both numbers by 2, then check to see if you can divide again.

2 Out of a group of 32 students, 12 are girls.
Complete the workings to show the fraction of the students who are girls.

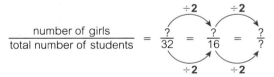

$$\frac{\text{number of girls}}{\text{total number of students}} = \frac{?}{32} = \frac{?}{16} = \frac{?}{?}$$

3 There are 15 dogs in a dog training class. 5 of them are collies.
What fraction of the dogs are

a collies

b not collies?

Give each answer in its simplest form.

> **Q3a hint**
>
> $$\frac{\text{number of collies}}{\text{total number of dogs}}$$

4 The table shows favourite ice cream flavours.

Favourite flavour	Vanilla	Chocolate	Caramel	Strawberry	Other
Number of students	24	8	12	16	4

a Work out the total number of students.

b What fraction of the students chose these flavours as their favourite?
Write each answer in its simplest form.

   i Chocolate

   ii Vanilla

5 Copy and complete these equivalent fractions, decimals and percentages.

a $\frac{1}{4} = 0.25 = 25\%$
×3 ⟶ $\frac{3}{4} = \square = \square\%$ ×3

b $\frac{1}{5} = 0.2 = 20\%$
×2 ⟶ $\frac{2}{5} = 0.4 = \square\%$ ×2

$\frac{3}{5} = 0.6 = \square\%$

$\frac{4}{5} = \square = \square\%$

c $\frac{1}{10} = 0.1 = 10\%$ $\frac{2}{10} = 0.2 = \square\%$ $\frac{3}{10} = 0.3 = \square\%$ $\frac{4}{10} = \square = \square\%$ $\frac{5}{10} = \square = \square\%$

$\frac{6}{10} = \square = \square\%$ $\frac{7}{10} = \square = \square\%$ $\frac{8}{10} = \square = \square\%$ $\frac{9}{10} = \square = \square\%$

6 Use your answers to Q5 to complete this table.

Fraction	$1\frac{1}{4}$	$1\frac{2}{5}$			
Decimal			2.5	2.6	
Percentage					310%

Q6 hint

$1\frac{1}{4} = 1.\square\ \square$

7 Write these fractions as decimals. The first one has been started for you.

a $\frac{1}{8} = 1 \div 8$

$1 \div 8 = 8\overline{)\ 1\ .^1 0\ ^2 0\ \ 0}$ quotient $0\ .\ 1\ \square\ \square$

b $\frac{11}{8}$

c $\frac{9}{4}$

d $\frac{7}{20}$

Multiplying and dividing with fractions

1 Work out

a $\frac{2}{3}$ of £18   **b** $\frac{3}{5}$ of 35 kg   **c** $\frac{5}{7}$ of 21 km

Q1a hint

£18

$\frac{1}{3} = £6$ $\frac{1}{3} = £6$ $\frac{1}{3} = £6$

$\frac{2}{3}$

2 Work out

a $\frac{2}{3} \times 39$ **b** $28 \times \frac{3}{7}$ **c** $32 \times \frac{5}{8}$

Q2a hint

$\frac{2}{3} \times 39 = \frac{2}{3}$ of 39

3 Work out these. The first two have been started for you.

a $\frac{2}{3}$ of 13 kg $\frac{2 \times 13}{3} = \frac{26}{3}$ $26 \div 3 = 8$ r $\square$ Answer: $8\frac{\square}{3}$

b $\frac{4}{5}$ of 17 km $\frac{4 \times 17}{\square} = \frac{\square}{\square}$ $\square \div 5 = \square$ r $\square$ Answer: $\square\frac{\square}{5}$

c $\frac{2}{7}$ of 19 m

d $\frac{5}{6}$ of 21 km

Q3a hint

$\frac{1}{3}$ of 13 isn't a whole number. Multiply, then simplify.

4 Work out

a $3 \div \frac{3}{4}$ **b** $3 \times \frac{4}{3}$

What do you notice?

Q4a hint

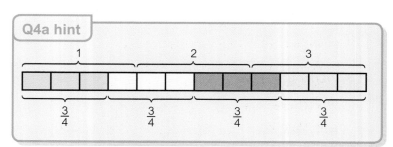

1   2   3

$\frac{3}{4}$ $\frac{3}{4}$ $\frac{3}{4}$ $\frac{3}{4}$

5 Work out

a $6 \div \frac{2}{3}$ **b** $6 \times \frac{3}{2}$

What do you notice?.

6 Work out $8 \div \frac{4}{5}$

7 Use the bar models to help work out these multiplications.

a $\frac{1}{2} \times \frac{2}{3}$ **b** $\frac{1}{2} \times \frac{1}{4}$

c $\frac{1}{3} \times \frac{2}{5}$ **d** $\frac{3}{5} \times \frac{1}{4}$

8 Work out

a $\frac{1}{7} \times \frac{1}{2} = \frac{1 \times 1}{7 \times 2} = \frac{\square}{\square}$

b $\frac{3}{5} \times \frac{2}{7} = \frac{\square \times \square}{\square \times \square} = \frac{\square}{\square}$

c $\frac{3}{4} \times \frac{2}{5}$

d $\frac{4}{5} \times \frac{5}{12}$

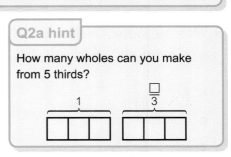

Q8 hint

Simplify your answers.

9 Work out

a $\frac{1}{3} \div \frac{2}{5} = \frac{1}{3} \times \frac{5}{2} = \frac{1 \times 5}{3 \times 2} = \frac{\square}{\square}$

b $\frac{1}{4} \div \frac{5}{8} = \frac{1}{4} \times \frac{8}{5} = \frac{\square \times \square}{\square \times \square} = \frac{\square}{\square}$

c $\frac{5}{12} \div \frac{10}{21}$

Working with mixed numbers

1 Write these mixed numbers as improper fractions.

a $2\frac{1}{4}$ **b** $3\frac{1}{2}$

c $5\frac{2}{3}$ **d** $2\frac{3}{10}$

e $2\frac{5}{6}$ **f** $10\frac{3}{5}$

2 Write these improper fractions as whole numbers or mixed numbers.

a $\frac{15}{3}$ **b** $\frac{12}{4}$

c $\frac{13}{4}$ **d** $\frac{20}{6}$

e $\frac{10}{3}$ **f** $\frac{16}{7}$

3 Work out

a $3\frac{1}{3} + 5\frac{5}{6} = \frac{\square}{3} + \frac{\square}{6} = \frac{\square}{6} + \frac{\square}{6} =$

b $1\frac{3}{4} + 7\frac{4}{5}$ **c** $6\frac{1}{6} + 3\frac{13}{18}$ **d** $1\frac{3}{8} + 2\frac{5}{24}$

Q1a hint

How many quarters are there?

Q2a hint

How many wholes can you make from 5 thirds?

Q3c hint

Convert to improper fractions first. Simplify your answer.

4 Work out

  a $4\frac{2}{3} - 1\frac{2}{9} = \frac{\square}{3} - \frac{\square}{9}$ **b** $9\frac{3}{5} - 9\frac{1}{3}$

  c $3\frac{3}{10} - 2\frac{4}{5}$ **d** $3\frac{3}{4} - 2\frac{1}{12}$

5 **a** Copy and complete these fractions of an hour.
  Write each answer in its simplest form.

     i 10 minutes $= \frac{10}{60}$ hour $= \frac{\square}{6}$ hour

     ii 12 minutes $= \frac{12}{60}$ hour $= \frac{\square}{5}$ hour

     iii 15 minutes $= \frac{15}{60}$ hour $= \frac{\square}{4}$ hour

     iv 25 minutes $= \frac{\square}{60}$ hour $= \frac{\square}{\square}$ hour

     v 45 minutes

     vi 40 minutes

  b Write each of these times as a mixed number in its simplest form.
     i 1 hour 15 minutes
     ii 4 hours 55 minutes

 6 Work out
  a 1 hour 15 minutes + 3 hours 20 minutes
  b 6 hours 15 minutes − 2 hours 45 minutes
  c 3 hours 25 minutes − 1 hour 40 minutes

7 Work out
  a $8\frac{2}{5} - 3\frac{3}{4}$ **b** $7\frac{3}{7} - 2\frac{4}{5}$

8 Work out
  a $8 \times 2\frac{1}{5}$ **b** $6\frac{2}{3} \times 4$ **c** $2\frac{1}{4} \div 1\frac{1}{8} = \frac{\square}{4} \div \frac{\square}{4}$

Enrichment

1 Here are five fraction cards.

   $\frac{3}{4}$ $\frac{2}{3}$ $\frac{9}{10}$ $\frac{3}{5}$ $\frac{5}{8}$

  a Which two fractions sum to $1\frac{1}{2}$?
  b Which two fractions have a product of $\frac{1}{2}$?
  c Which two fractions will give the greatest total? What is that total?
  d Which two fractions will give the greatest difference? What is that difference?

2 **Reflect** Look back at the questions you got wrong in the Check up.
  Were there mostly questions about
  • equivalence
  • multiplying and dividing fractions
  • working with mixed numbers?
  Now look back at the Strengthen questions you answered.
  Write down one thing you now understand better.
  Is there anything you still need help with?
  Ask a friend or your teacher to help you with it.

Q4a hint
Convert to improper fractions first.

Q4c hint
Simplify your answer.

Q5 hint
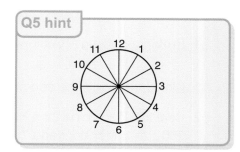

Q6 hint
Convert to fractions of an hour.
On your calculator, enter $1\frac{1}{4} + 3\frac{1}{3}$

Q8a hint
Use the grid method.

Q8c hint
Convert to improper fractions first.

Q1 hint
Adding gives the sum. Multiplying gives the product. Subtracting gives the difference.

Reflect

4 Extend

You will:
- Extend your understanding with problem-solving.

1 **Problem-solving / Reasoning** Here are six fractions.

$\frac{15}{20}$ $\frac{30}{36}$ $\frac{19}{38}$ $\frac{28}{49}$ $\frac{34}{51}$ $\frac{36}{45}$

$3/4$ $5/6$ $1/2$ $\boxed{4/7}$ $2/3$ $4/9$

Which fraction is the odd one out? Explain your answer.

Q1 Strategy hint

Start by writing each fraction in its simplest form.

2 **Real life** The recipe for a loaf of bread uses 150 g of rye flour, 150 g of barley flour and 100 g of rice flour.
   a What is the total mass of flour in the loaf?
   b What fraction of the flour used in the loaf is rice flour? Give your answer in its simplest form.

3 **Problem-solving / Real life** The bar chart shows the composition of a piece of Cheddar cheese. The total mass of the piece of cheese is 120 g.

DI
5.2

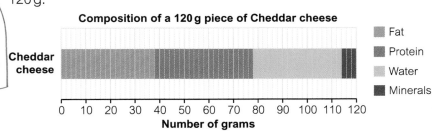

Composition of a 120 g piece of Cheddar cheese

Cheddar cheese

| Fat | Protein | Water | Minerals |

0 10 20 30 40 50 60 70 80 90 100 110 120
Number of grams

What fraction of the piece of cheese is protein?
Give your answer in its simplest form.

4 Copy and complete these fraction pyramids.
Each brick is the sum of the two bricks below it.

8.2

w/o
scaff

 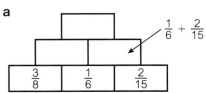

a

$\frac{1}{6} + \frac{2}{15}$

$\frac{3}{8}$ $\frac{1}{6}$ $\frac{2}{15}$

b

$\frac{20}{27}$

$\frac{1}{2}$

$\frac{1}{18}$

5 Here is a set of dominoes.

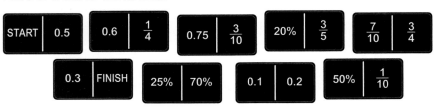

| START | 0.5 | 0.6 | $\frac{1}{4}$ | 0.75 | $\frac{3}{10}$ | 20% | $\frac{3}{5}$ | $\frac{7}{10}$ | $\frac{3}{4}$ |

| 0.3 | FINISH | 25% | 70% | 0.1 | 0.2 | 50% | $\frac{1}{10}$ |

Work out how to link the dominoes together. One domino can only touch another domino when they have an equivalent fraction, decimal or percentage.

Q5 hint
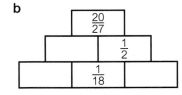

| START | 0.5 | | 50% | $\frac{1}{10}$ |

6 STEM / Problem-solving The pie chart shows the composition of a fertiliser.

Composition of fertiliser

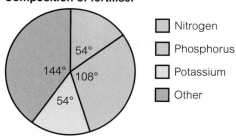

- Nitrogen
- Phosphorus
- Potassium
- Other

Work out the amount of nitrogen and phosphorus in 12 tonnes of fertiliser.

Give each answer as a mixed number.

Q6 Strategy hint

Work out the fractions of fertiliser that are nitrogen and phosphorus first.

7 The rectangle contains four fractions and the oval contains four numbers.

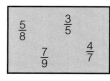

$$\frac{5}{8} \qquad \frac{3}{5}$$
$$\frac{7}{9} \qquad \frac{4}{7}$$

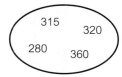

315   320
280   360

a Choose a fraction from the rectangle and multiply it by a number from the circle.

b Which fraction and number, when you multiply them together, will give you

   i the largest answer possible   **ii** the smallest answer possible?

8 Reasoning

a Sally says, 'When you add two positive fractions, the answer is always bigger than the individual fractions'.
Is Sally correct? Explain why.

b Lauren says, 'When you subtract two positive fractions, the answer is always smaller than the individual fractions'.
Is Lauren correct? Explain why.

9 Reasoning Eleri writes the fraction $\frac{15}{16}$ as a decimal.
This is what she writes.

$$15\overline{)16 \ . \ {}^{1}0 \ {}^{10}0 \ {}^{10}0 \ {}^{10}0} \quad \text{so } \frac{15}{16} = 1.0666...$$
$$\quad 1 \ . \ 0 \ 6 \ 6 \ 6 \ ...$$

a Explain the mistake that Eleri has made.

b Work out the correct decimal equivalent of $\frac{15}{16}$.

10 Work out

  a $1\frac{1}{2} + 2\frac{2}{3} + 3\frac{5}{6}$

  b $4\frac{4}{5} + 1\frac{7}{10} + 2\frac{7}{20}$

  c $7\frac{3}{4} + 5\frac{2}{9} - 4\frac{11}{12}$

Q10 hint

Simplify your answers.

11 Work out the perimeter of each shape.

a

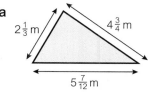

$2\frac{1}{3}$ m $4\frac{3}{4}$ m

$5\frac{7}{12}$ m

b

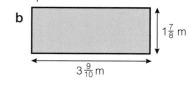

$1\frac{7}{8}$ m

$3\frac{9}{10}$ m

12 STEM The Millennium Stadium in Cardiff is made from 4000 tonnes of concrete, 12000 tonnes of structural steel and 40000 tonnes of steel reinforcement.
What fraction of the stadium is made from
  a concrete
  b steel reinforcement?
Give each fraction in its simplest form.

13 STEM By volume, dry air contains approximately 78% nitrogen, 21% oxygen and the remainder is other gases and water vapour.
What fraction of dry air is
  a nitrogen   **b** oxygen
  c other gases and water vapour?
Give each fraction in its simplest form.

> **Q13a hint**
> $78\% = \dfrac{\square}{100}$

14 Problem-solving Sort these cards into five groups of correct calculations. There must be one triangular, one rectangular and one circular card in each group.

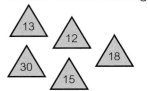
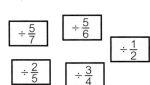
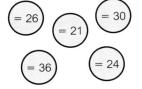

> **Q14 Strategy hint**
> Start by rewriting each yellow card
> as $\times \dfrac{\square}{\square}$ instead of $\div \dfrac{\square}{\square}$

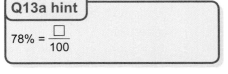

15 Work out these divisions.
Write each answer as a mixed number in its simplest form.
  a $9 \div \frac{2}{3}$ **b** $7 \div \frac{4}{5}$ **c** $4 \div \frac{6}{7}$ **d** $6 \div \frac{8}{9}$

16 You can work out the distance, in miles, a car travels using the formula
    distance = average speed × time
Work out the distance a car travels when
  a average speed = 60 miles per hour and time = 1 hour 30 minutes
  b average speed = 50 miles per hour and time = 2 hours 45 minutes
  c average speed = 48 miles per hour and time = 4 hours 10 minutes
  d average speed = 62 miles per hour and time = 3 hours 24 minutes

> **Q16 hint**
> Enter the time as a mixed number on your calculator.

17 Reasoning
  a Work out

    i $\frac{1}{2}$ of £30 and then $\frac{1}{3}$ of the answer
    ii $\frac{1}{3}$ of £30 and then $\frac{1}{2}$ of the answer.
    iii What do you notice about your answers to parts **i** and **ii**?
      What is the overall fraction of £30 that you have found?
      How can you combine $\frac{1}{2}$ and $\frac{1}{3}$ to give you this overall fraction?
  b Work out
    i $\frac{3}{4}$ of £80 and then $\frac{2}{5}$ of the answer
    ii $\frac{2}{5}$ of £80 and then $\frac{3}{4}$ of the answer.
    iii What is the overall fraction of £80 that you have found?
      How can you combine $\frac{2}{5}$ and $\frac{3}{4}$ to give you this overall fraction?
  c Will your method for **a iii** and **b iii** work for any fraction of an amount followed by a fraction of an amount?

> **Q17a hint**
> $\frac{1}{2}$ of £30 = £$\square$, $\frac{1}{3}$ of £$\square$ = £$\square$

Topic links: Bar charts, Pie charts, Rounding, Perimeter, Mean   **Subject links:** Science (Q6, Q13, Q16)

18 Sort these cards into groups that give the same answer.

$9\frac{13}{30} - 6\frac{9}{10}$ $4\frac{2}{5} - 2\frac{1}{4}$ $5\frac{17}{20} - 3\frac{7}{10}$

$5\frac{19}{36} - 3\frac{7}{9}$ $8\frac{2}{3} - 6\frac{2}{15}$ $7\frac{2}{3} - 5\frac{11}{12}$

19 Problem-solving Copy and complete this calculation.

$$\square\frac{\square}{\square} - \square\frac{\square}{\square} = 4\frac{1}{5}$$

20 Reasoning Hassan says, 'When you multiply a positive number by a fraction less than 1, your answer will always be smaller than the number you started with'.
Is Hassan correct? Explain why.

21 Finance / Problem-solving Martha spends $\frac{1}{4}$ of her pocket money on food.
She spends $\frac{3}{5}$ of what is left on clothes. She saves the rest.
What fraction of her money does she save?

22 Ethan says, '$\frac{3}{8} \div 4$ equals 3 over 2, which is the same as one and a half'.
Is Ethan correct?

23 Which of these three fractions, $\frac{3}{10}$, $\frac{2}{3}$ or $\frac{9}{6}$, is the missing fraction in this calculation?

$$\frac{5}{9} \div \frac{\square}{\square} = \frac{5}{6}$$

24 These are the ages of the five members of a family.

$42\frac{1}{2}$ $38\frac{2}{3}$ $14\frac{5}{6}$ $12\frac{5}{12}$ $8\frac{3}{4}$

8.5

Work out the mean age.

Investigation   **Reasoning**

1 Work out $1 + \frac{1}{2}$

2 Work out $1 + \frac{1}{2} + \frac{1}{3}$

3 Work out $1 + \frac{1}{2} + \frac{1}{3} + \frac{1}{4}$

4 Look at this sum of fractions.

$$\frac{1}{1} + \frac{1}{2} + \frac{1}{3} + \frac{1}{4} + \frac{1}{5} + \frac{1}{6} + \frac{1}{7} + \frac{1}{8} + \dots + \frac{1}{x}$$

a Explain what happens to the sum of the series as x gets bigger and bigger.

b How many fractions must be added to get a sum greater than 3?

c Will the sum ever be greater than 4? Explain your answer.

---

25 Reflect The word fraction is used in lots of ways. For example,
 • In everyday English, a fraction means 'a small amount'. For example, when hanging a picture 'move it up a fraction' or you might ask someone to 'budge up a fraction' so you can sit beside them.
 • In chemistry, the fractionating process separates a mixture into its components.
Write a definition, in your own words, of 'fraction' in mathematics.
What do you think 'fractional ownership' means? When might it be a good idea?

4 Unit test

Log how you did on your Student Progression Chart.

1 Write each fraction in its simplest form.

$\frac{6}{9}$ $\frac{7}{14}$ $\frac{9}{12}$ $\frac{25}{30}$ $\frac{24}{40}$

2 There are 40 chocolates in a box. 15 of the chocolates contain nuts.
   What fraction of the chocolates contain nuts?
   Write your answer in its simplest form.

3 Write these amounts in order of size, starting with the smallest.

$\frac{1}{5}$ of 100 kg $\frac{2}{3}$ of 36 kg $\frac{6}{7}$ of 21 kg

4 A chef uses $\frac{3}{5}$ of a 4 litre container of cooking oil.
   How much cooking oil does the chef use?
   Write your answer as a mixed number in its simplest form.

5 Work out these. Give each answer in its simplest form.

   a $\frac{1}{8} + \frac{3}{4}$

   b $\frac{2}{9} + \frac{5}{12}$

   c $\frac{21}{25} - \frac{1}{5}$

   d $\frac{9}{10} - \frac{5}{6}$

6 Write $\frac{27}{4}$ as a mixed number.

7 Write $6\frac{7}{10}$ as an improper fraction.

8 Work out

   a $\frac{4}{9} \times 27$

   b $32 \times \frac{5}{8}$

9 Copy and complete this table.

Fraction		$\frac{4}{5}$		$\frac{3}{10}$			$6\frac{2}{5}$
Decimal			0.75			4.7	
Percentage	50%				125%		

10 Write $\frac{17}{5}$ as a decimal.

11 Work out these. Write each answer in its simplest form.

   a $5\frac{3}{4} + 2\frac{5}{8}$

   b $1\frac{2}{5} + 1\frac{2}{3}$

   c $8\frac{8}{9} - 4\frac{1}{3}$

   d $3\frac{9}{11} - 3\frac{1}{2}$

12 The table shows the amounts of money raised for charity by a scout group.

Event	Cake sale	Concert	Sponsored swim	Quiz night
Amount	£75	£165	£250	£160

What fraction of the money was raised at the sponsored swim?
Write your answer in its simplest form.

13 Work out

a $16 \div \frac{1}{4}$

b $42 \div \frac{7}{8}$

14 Write each length of time as a mixed number of hours.
   a 3 hours 30 minutes   **b** 3 hours 12 minutes

15 Josh used his calculator to solve a problem involving time.
He got the answer $5\frac{7}{10}$ hours.
Write this time in hours and minutes.

16 $\frac{2}{3}$ of the students in a class have a mobile phone.
$\frac{2}{5}$ of the students who have a mobile phone have a smartphone.
What fraction of the class have a smartphone?

17 Work out $5\frac{2}{15} + 6\frac{1}{6} - 3\frac{2}{3}$. Write your answer in its simplest form.

18 Work out these multiplications.
   a $\frac{5}{8} \times \frac{4}{7}$ **b** $\frac{7}{18} \times \frac{9}{28}$

19 Work out $5 \times 2\frac{2}{3}$

20 Work out $9\frac{1}{3} \div \frac{5}{9}$

Challenge

21 This rectangle has a perimeter of $10\frac{5}{6}$ cm.
Work out the area of the rectangle.
Give your answer as a fraction in its simplest form.

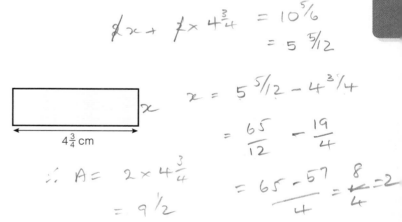

$4\frac{3}{4}$ cm

$$\not{2}x + \not{2}x \, 4\frac{3}{4} = 10\frac{5}{6}$$
$$= 5\frac{5}{12}$$
$$x = 5\frac{5}{12} - 4\frac{3}{4}$$
$$= \frac{65}{12} - \frac{19}{4}$$
$$= \frac{65 - 57}{4} = \frac{8}{4} = 2$$

$$\therefore A = 2 \times 4\frac{3}{4}$$
$$= 9\frac{1}{2}$$

22 Work out the missing values in each of these.

   a $1\frac{3}{10} + \square\frac{\square}{4} = 6\frac{1}{20}$

   b $\frac{5}{9} \times \frac{\square}{15} = \frac{7}{27}$

   c $\square\frac{2}{\square} \div \frac{8}{9} = 4\frac{1}{8}$

23 **Reflect** In this Unit, did you work
   • slowly
   • average speed
   • quickly?
   Did you find the work easy, OK or hard?
   How did that affect how fast you worked?
   Is it always good to work quickly? Explain
   Is it always bad to work slowly? Explain

5.1 Angles and parallel lines

You will learn to:
- Work out unknown angles when two or more lines meet or cross at a point
- Work out unknown angles involving parallel lines.

CONFIDENCE

Why learn this?
The angles of a keyboard stand keep the keyboard horizontal.

Fluency
- What do the angles on a straight line add up to?
- What do the angles round a point add up to?
- What is 90 − 35, 180 − 110, 360 − 250?

Explore
What different shapes can you make when you intersect pairs of parallel lines?

Exercise 5.1

Warm up

1 For each angle

 A   B    C

a state whether it is acute, obtuse or reflex
b estimate its size
c measure it accurately.

2 This shape is made from two squares and their diagonals.
  a Write a line that is
    i parallel to CF   **ii** perpendicular to DF.
  b Are the lines BD and CE parallel?
    Explain your answer.
  c Copy the diagram.
    Mark the parallel sides using arrows.

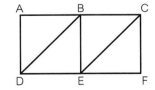

3 a Draw two lines crossing like the ones shown here.
  b Measure one acute angle and the angle opposite.
    What do you notice?
  c Measure the other two **vertically opposite** angles.
    What do you notice?
  d Repeat for another two sets of crossing lines.
  e Copy and complete this rule.
    Vertically opposite angles are _____
  Discussion Do everybody's angles fit the rule?
  Is this enough evidence to show that the rule is true?

> **Key point**
>
> **Vertically opposite** angles are equal. The green angles are equal. The blue angles are equal.
>
>

Worked example

Work out the angles marked with letters. Give a reason for each answer.

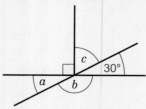

a $a = 30°$ (vertically opposite angles are equal)
b $b = 180° - 30° = 150°$ (angles on a straight line add up to 180°)
c $c = 360° - 90° - 30° - 150° - 30° = 60°$
   (angles at a point add up to 360°)

> You need to write a reason.

4 Reasoning Work out the angles marked with letters. Give your reasons.

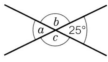

5 Reasoning Work out the angles marked with letters. Give reasons for your answers.

a

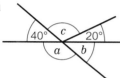

b

c

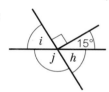

Key point

The blue angles are **alternate angles**. They are on different (alternate) sides of the diagonal.
The red angles are **corresponding angles**. They are on the same (corresponding) sides of the diagonal.

6 a Copy the diagram.
Mark each pair of **alternate angles**.
Use a different colour for each pair.

  b Copy the diagram again.
Mark each pair of **corresponding angles**. Use a different colour for each pair.

> **Q6 hint**
> There are four pairs of alternate angles and four pairs of corresponding angles.

Investigation   Reasoning

Copy this diagram on to squared paper.
1 Measure the acute alternate angles. What do you notice?
2 Find two alternate angles that are obtuse and measure them.
  What do you notice?
3 Copy and complete this rule. Alternate angles are _____
4 Draw another line that crosses the parallel lines at a different angle.
  Check your rule works for the alternate angles.
5 Draw two more parallel lines.
6 Measure a pair of corresponding angles. What do you notice?
7 Copy and complete this rule. Corresponding angles are _____
8 Check your rule works by measuring other pairs of corresponding angles.

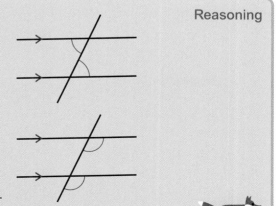

7 Reasoning Work out the angles marked with letters.
Give reasons for your answers.

a
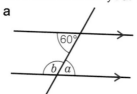

b
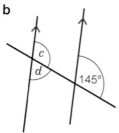

c
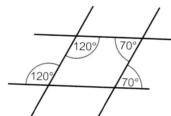

d
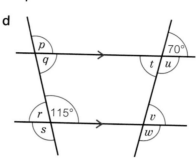

Q7 hint

You don't have to work out the angles in the order of the letters but it may help.

8 a Reasoning Sketch this diagram. Do not use a protractor.

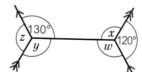

b Work out all the unmarked angles and write them on your diagram.
c Mark the parallel lines.

Q8c hint

Use arrows to show parallel lines.

9 Reasoning Work out the angles marked with letters.
Give a reason for each answer.

a
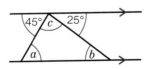

b
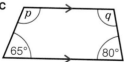

c

d
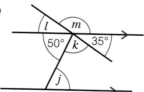

Q9c hint

Copy the diagram. Extend each of the lines.

10 Explore What different shapes can you make when you intersect pairs of parallel lines?
Is it easier to explore this question now you have completed the lesson?
What further information do you need to be able to answer this?

11 Reflect In this lesson you learned about opposite angles, corresponding angles and alternate angles.
How can you help yourself remember the difference between them?
What do all the pairs of angles have in common?

*Active*Learn   Delta 1, Section 5.1

5.2 Triangles

You will learn to:

- Describe the line and rotational symmetry of triangles
- Understand how to prove that a result is true
- Use properties of a triangle to work out unknown angles
- Use the properties of isosceles and equilateral triangles to solve problems.

Why learn this?
The isosceles shape of a step ladder makes it strong and stable.

Fluency
Work out 180° − 40° − 40°
180° − 35° − 110°
55° + ☐ = 180°
What is the missing angle?

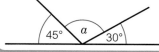

Explore
What is the angle at the top of a folding ladder?

Exercise 5.2

1 **a** For each triangle say whether it is equilateral, isosceles or scalene?
  b Which angles are equal?

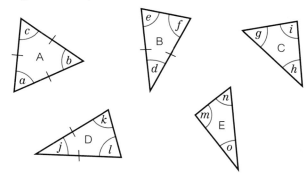

Key point

A **line of symmetry** divides a shape into two halves that fit exactly on top of each other.
The **order of rotational symmetry** of a shape is the number of times it exactly fits on top of itself when rotated a full turn.

2 lines of symmetry

rotational symmetry order 2

2 Copy and complete this table showing the number of lines of symmetry and order of rotational symmetry of triangles.

Q2 hint

If a shape has no line or rotational symmetry, write 'None'.

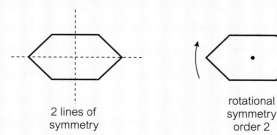

Triangle	Equilateral	Isosceles	Scalene
number of lines of symmetry			
order of rotational symmetry			

3 Reasoning **Prove** that the angles of a triangle add up to 180°.

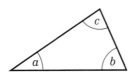 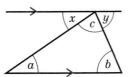

  a Copy the triangle and draw a line parallel to the base as shown.

  b Copy and complete this proof.

    Angle x = angle ☐ (alternate angles)

    Angle y = angle ☐ (_____ angles)

    $x + c + y = ☐°$ (angles on a _____ _____)

    $x + c + y = a + c + b$ (because $x = a$, $y = b$), so $c = ☐°$

    This proves that the angles in a triangle add up to ☐°.

4 Reasoning Work out the unknown angle in each triangle.
Give a reason for each answer.

  a    **b** 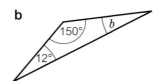   **c**

5 Reasoning Work out the angles marked with letters.
Give a reason for each step.

  a   **b**

  c 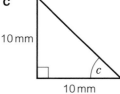   **d**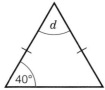

6 Problem-solving One angle of an isosceles triangle is 100°.
What are the other two?

7 Work out the angles marked by letters.
Give a reason for each answer.

  a 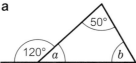   **b** 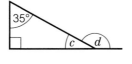   **c**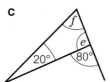

8 a Copy and complete the table for triangles **a**, **b** and **c** in Q7.

	a	b	c
exterior angle	120°		
sum of opposite interior angles	50° + ☐ = ☐		

  b What do you notice about the **exterior angle** and opposite **interior angles**?

Key point

Showing that a rule works for a few values is not enough. You need to **prove** it works for *all* values. A **proof** uses logical reasoning to show a rule is true.

Q3 Strategy hint

You must always give a reason for each statement you make.

Q4a hint

$a = ☐$

Angles in a triangle add up to ☐°

Q5 Strategy hint

Explain how you know each triangle is isosceles.
Next, identify the two equal base angles.

Key point

An **interior angle** is inside a shape.
An **exterior angle** is outside the shape on a straight line with the interior angle.

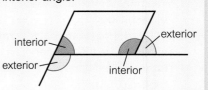

Q8a hint

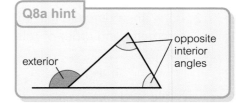

9 Reasoning Prove that an exterior angle of a triangle is equal to the sum of the opposite interior angles.

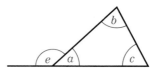

The exterior angle e is opposite the two interior angles b and c.
You must prove that $e = b + c$.
Copy and complete this proof.
$e + a = \square°$ because they lie on a _____
$b + c + a = \square°$ because the angles in a triangle sum to $\square°$.
This proves that $e = b + c$.
Discussion Why does the last statement follow from the other two statements?

10 Reasoning **a** What are the interior angles of an equilateral triangle? Give a reason for your answer.
 b What is the exterior angle of an equilateral triangle? Give a reason for your answer.

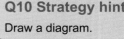

Q10 Strategy hint
Draw a diagram.

11 Reasoning Work out the angles marked with letters. Give a reason for each step.

a

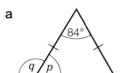

b

c

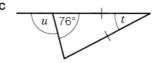

12 Reasoning / Problem-solving The diagram shows the front of a tent.

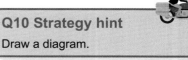

Q12 Strategy hint
Sketch a diagram. Write on the diagram each angle you work out.

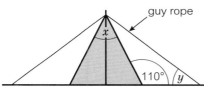

guy rope

Two equal guy ropes hold up the central pole.
 a Work out angle x.
 b The angle between the two guy ropes is 100°. Work out angle y.
 c Work out the angle the guy rope makes with the side of the tent.

13 Explore What is the angle at the top of a folding ladder? Is it easier to explore this question now you have completed the lesson? What further information do you need to answer this?

14 Reflect After this lesson Safia says, 'I measured all the angles in 3 different triangles and they all add up 180°.'
Do you think Safia's statement proves that the angles in all triangles add up to 180°?
Look back at Q3. In what way is the proof different to Safia's statement?

5.3 Quadrilaterals

You will learn to:
* Describe the line and rotational symmetry of quadrilaterals
* Describe the properties of quadrilaterals
* Solve problems involving quadrilaterals.

CONFIDENCE

Why learn this?
Quadrilaterals help you draw 3D solids.

Fluency
What is the sum of the angles of a triangle?
How many sides does a quadrilateral have?
What are these angles called?

Explore
What is the quickest way to draw a kite? a rhombus?

Warm up

Exercise 5.3

1 a Write the coordinates of each point.
For example, A(3, 6).
b What quadrilateral do the points make?

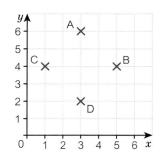

2 Copy and complete this table showing the number of lines of symmetry and order of rotational symmetry of these quadrilaterals.

Quadrilateral	Square	Rectangle	Parallelogram	Rhombus	Kite	Arrowhead	Trapezium	Isosceles trapezium
number of lines of symmetry								
order of rotational symmetry								

3 Sketch each shape in Q2.
* Mark equal sides with dashes. Use double dashes for a second pair of equal sides.
* Mark equal angles with arcs. Use double arcs for a second pair of equal angles.
* Mark right angles.
* Mark parallel sides with arrows. Use double arrows for a second pair of parallel sides.

The arrowhead has been done for you.

Arrowhead

line of symmetry means sides and angles are equal.

Q3 hint

Use line and rotational symmetry to find equal sides and angles.

Discussion What can you say about opposite angles in a parallelogram? Is this the same for a rhombus?

4 Work out the angles and sides marked with letters.

a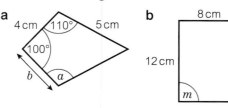
4 cm 110° 5 cm
100°
b *a*
kite

b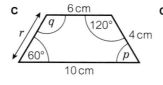
8 cm
12 cm *n*
m
rectangle

c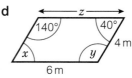
6 cm
r *q* 120°
4 cm
60° *p*
10 cm
isosceles
trapezium

d
z
140° 40°
x *y* 4 m
6 m
parallelogram

Investigation　　　　　　　　　　　　　　　　　　　　　　　　**Reasoning**

Sketch these quadrilaterals: square, rectangle, parallelogram, rhombus and kite.
1 Draw the **diagonals**.
2 Use line and rotational symmetry to find equal lengths and angles. Mark them on your diagram.
3 Do any of the diagonals **bisect** each other?
4 Copy and complete this table to show the properties of the quadrilaterals.

Quadrilateral	Diagonals bisect each other	Diagonals bisect the interior angles	Diagonals cross at right angles
rectangle			

---

5 Work out the angles and sides marked with letters.

a
f
e
square

b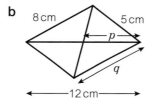
8 cm 5 cm
p
q
12 cm
parallelogram

c
x
y
80°
rhombus

Literacy hint

A **diagonal** is a straight line joining two opposite corners (**vertices**) of a shape.
Bisect means to cut in half.

Q5 hint

Use the table in the investigation.

Q6 hint

Do any of these shapes have the same properties as a rectangle?

6 A rectangle has opposite sides equal and all angles 90°.
Which of these shapes is a rectangle?
parallelogram　　　　　square　　　　　kite

7 Reasoning　A square is a special type of rectangle.
a Copy and complete this sentence.
A rectangle is a special type of _____
b Write two more sentences like this about different shapes.

8 Problem-solving　**a** What shape am I?
　i I have two pairs of equal angles and two pairs of parallel sides.
　ii My diagonals cross at right angles and I have two pairs of equal sides.
　iii My opposite sides are parallel and my diagonals divide me into four identical triangles.
　iv I have two pairs of equal sides and one line of symmetry.
b Write your own description of a shape for your classmates to work out.

9 Problem-solving　**a** Draw a coordinate grid on squared paper with both axes going from 0 to 10. Plot the points A(2, 5), B(0, 3) and C(2, 1).
b Work out possible coordinates of a fourth point
　i D so that ABCD is a square
　ii E so that ABCE is a kite
　iii F so that ABCF is an arrowhead
　iv G so that ABCG is a trapezium.

Key point

You can describe a shape using the letters at its **vertices** (the plural of **vertex**).

10 Reasoning Prove that the angles of a quadrilateral add up to 360°.

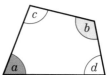 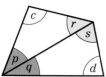

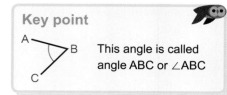
Prove that $a + b + c + d = 360°$.

Copy and complete this proof. Give a reason for each statement.

$p + r + c = \square°$ because the angles in a triangle sum to $\square°$.

$q + s + d = \square°$ because the angles in a triangle sum to $\square°$.

$p + q + r + s + c + d = \square° + \square° = \square°$

$a + b + c + d = 360°$ (beause $a = p + q$ and $b = r + s$

This proves that the angles in a quadrilateral sum to $\square°$.

11 a Work out ∠BCD.   **b** Work out ∠JML.

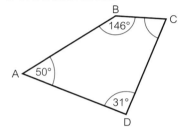 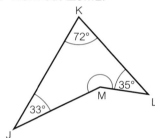

Worked example

a Name the shape

b Work out the angles marked with letters.

Give a reason for each answer.

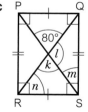

a PQRS is a kite (two pairs of equal sides next to each other)

b $a = 100°$ (PR is a line of symmetry)

$b = 360° - 100° - 100° - 90° = 70°$

(angle sum of a quadrilateral is 360°)

12 Reasoning

For each shape

i name the shape

ii work out the angles marked with letters. Give a reason for each answer.

a 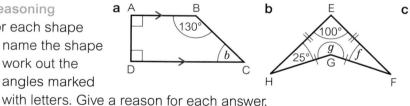   **b**   **c**   **d**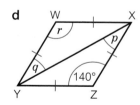

13 Explore What is the quickest way to draw a kite? a rhombus?

Is it easier to explore this question now you have completed the lesson?

What further information do you need to be able to answer this?

14 Reflect Frankie says that to identify a shape, he begins by asking himself:

• Are its sides straight?

• Are any sides equal lengths?

• Are the equal sides next to each other, or opposite?

Write down all the questions you ask yourself to identify a shape.

Test your questions on some quadrilaterals. Can you improve your questions?

Compare your questions with other people's. Can you improve your questions any more?

5.4 Polygons

You will learn to:

• Work out the interior and exterior angles of a polygon.

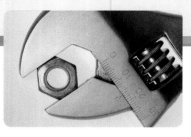

Why learn this?
Spanners are designed to fit hexagonal nuts and bolts.

Fluency
What is 180 − 45?
What is 360 ÷ 6?
What is an interior angle of a shape?

Explore
After turning, a bolt appears to be in the same position. What angle could it have turned through?

Exercise 5.4

1 Work out the angles marked with letters.

a

b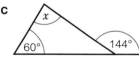

c

2 a i How many lines of symmetry does a regular pentagon have?

ii What is the order of rotational symmetry for a regular pentagon?

b Find the number of lines of symmetry and order of rotational symmetry for three different regular polygons.

c What do you notice?

Discussion Is a rectangle a polygon?
Is a square a regular polygon?

> **Key point**
>
> A **polygon** is a closed shape with straight sides.
> In a **regular polygon**, the sides and angles are all equal.
>
> **regular polygons**
>
>
>
> pentagon   hexagon   heptagon
>
> **irregular polygons**
>
> hexagon   pentagon

Warm up

Investigation   Reasoning

 1 Draw a pentagon and divide it into triangles using diagonals.
The diagonals must all start from the same vertex (corner) of the pentagon.

2 Fill in the 'pentagon' row in this table.

Shape	Number of sides	Number of triangles	Sum of interior angles
triangle	3	1	180°
quadrilateral	4	2	360°
pentagon	5	3	
hexagon	6		

3 Use the triangle method above to work out the sum of the interior angles in a hexagon.
4 Copy and complete the table.
5 Write down how to work out the number of triangles from the number of sides.
6 Write down how to work out the sum of the interior angles from the number of sides.
7 Add decagon to your table.

3 Work out the unknown angle.

a

b
135° 150°
b
30°
135° 150°

Q3 hint

What kind of polygon is it? What is the sum of its interior angles?

4 Problem-solving The sum of the interior angles of a polygon is 2340°.
Work out how many sides it has.

Q4 Strategy hint

First work out how many triangles it divides into. ☐ × 180° = 2340°

Worked example

Work out the interior angle of a regular octagon.

$S = 180° \times (n - 2)$ ⟵ Write down the formula. Substitute $n = 8$.

$n = 8$

$S = 180° \times (8 - 2)$

$180° \times 6 = 1080°$

Each interior angle $= 1080° \div 8 = 135°$ ⟵ A regular octagon has 8 equal angles. Divide 1080° by 8.

Key point

Sum of interior angles of an n-sided polygon
$S = (n - 2) \times 180°$

---

5 Work out the interior angle of a regular
  a hexagon   **b** nonagon.

6 a Work out the interior angle of a regular pentagon.
  b Work out the exterior angle of a regular pentagon.
  c How many exterior angles are there in a regular pentagon?
  d Work out the sum of the exterior angles.

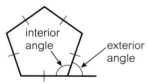

interior angle   exterior angle

Q6c hint

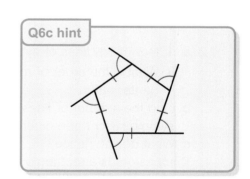

7 Repeat Q6 for a regular hexagon.
What do you notice?

8 a Draw an irregular pentagon.

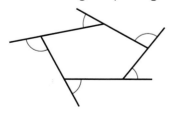

  b Measure the exterior angles.
  c Work out their sum. What do you notice?
  d Copy and complete this rule.
     The exterior angles of any polygon add up to ☐°
  e Write a rule in words to work out the exterior angle of a regular polygon.
  f Modelling Use algebra to write an expression for the exterior angle of a regular polygon with n sides.

9 Reasoning a What is the sum of the exterior angles of a regular nonagon?

b Work out the size of one of its exterior angles.

c Work out the size of one of its interior angles.

10 Problem-solving The exterior angle of a regular polygon is 15°.

a Work out the interior angle.

b How many sides does the polygon have?

Q10b hint

□ × 15° = □°

11 A regular polygon has 30 sides. Work out the size of its

a exterior angle

b interior angle.

Discussion Is it easier to work out the exterior or interior angle of a regular polygon first?

12 Real / Problem-solving The diagram shows parts of some floor tiling using regular polygons.

Work out the angles marked with letters. Give reasons.

Q12 hint

Work out the interior angle of each polygon.

a

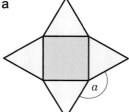

b

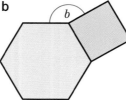

c

d

13 Problem-solving The diagram shows the face of a gem stone.

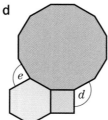

The face has two lines of symmetry. Work out the angle marked x. Give reasons for your working.

14 Explore After turning, a bolt appears to be in the same position. What angle could it have turned through?

Is it easier to explore this question now you have completed the lesson? What further information do you need to be able to answer this?

15 Reflect Look back at the investigation. You used lots of different maths topics to work on it. Write a list of all the different maths you used in the investigation.

Compare your list with a friend.

Explore

Reflect

5 Check up

Log how you did on your Student Progression Chart.

Angles and parallel lines

1 Work out the angles marked with letters. Give reasons for your working.

a

b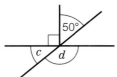

c

2 Work out angle x. Give reasons for your working.

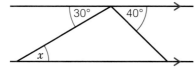

3 Work out angles w and x. Give a reason for your answer.

a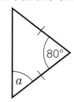

b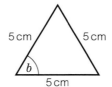

Triangles and quadrilaterals

4 Work out the unknown angles. Give a reason for each answer.

a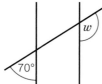

b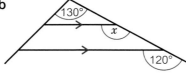

5 Work out the angles marked with letters. Give a reason for each answer.

a

b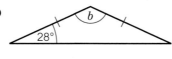

6 The diagram shows a flag on a pole. Work out angle x. Give a reason for your answer.

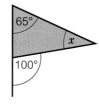

7 The diagram shows an isosceles trapezium.
   a Copy the diagram.
      Draw on the lines of symmetry.
   b Mark the equal sides, equal angles and parallel lines.
   c What is the order of rotational symmetry of an isosceles trapezium?

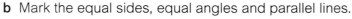

8 The diagram shows three vertices of the parallelogram ABCD.
Write down the coordinates of point C.

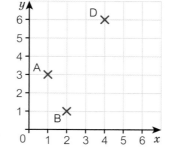

9 Name two quadrilaterals whose diagonals bisect each other at right angles.

10 Work out the angles marked with letters. Give reasons for your working.

a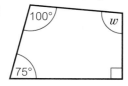

b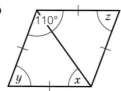

Interior and exterior angles

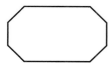 **11** Work out the sum of the interior angles of this polygon.

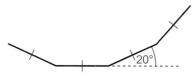

12 a Work out the exterior angle of a regular decagon (10-sided polygon). Show your working.
b Work out the interior angle of a regular decagon.

13 The diagram shows the exterior angle of a regular polygon. Work out how many sides the polygon has.

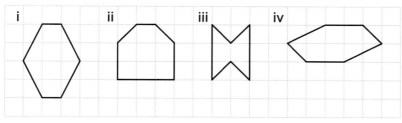

14 How sure are you of your answers? Were you mostly
☹ Just guessing   😐 Feeling doubtful   🙂 Confident.

Challenge

15 The diagram shows hexagons drawn on squared paper.

| i | ii | iii | iv |

a Describe the line symmetry of each hexagon.
b Describe the rotational symmetry of each hexagon.
c Draw a different hexagon with no symmetry.
d Draw three pentagons with different line and rotational symmetry.
e Draw four octagons with different line and rotational symmetry.

> **Q15a and b hint**
> ☐ lines of symmetry
> rotational symmetry order ☐

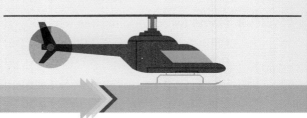

5 Strengthen

You will learn to:
- Strengthen your understanding with practice.

Angles and parallel lines

1 Work out the angles marked with letters.

a
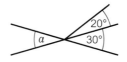

b

2 Work out the angles marked with letters.
Choose one of these reasons for each answer:
  i angles on a straight line add up to 180°
  ii angles at a point add up to 360°
  iii vertically opposite angles are equal.

a

b
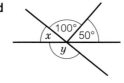

c

d
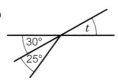

3 Copy the diagrams. Look for the Z-shape.
Write the size of the marked **alternate angle**.
Give a reason for your answer.

a
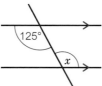

b

c
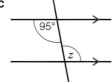

4 Copy the diagrams. Look for the F-shape.
Write the size of the marked **corresponding angle**.
Give a reason for your answer.

a
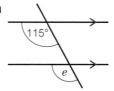

b

c
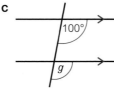

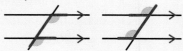

5 Work out the angles marked with letters.
Copy and complete the sentences.

a
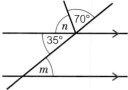

b
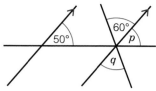

$m =$ ____ (alternate angles)

$n =$ ____ (angles on a straight line)

$p =$ ____ (corresponding angles)

$q =$ ____ (vertically opposite angles)

Q5 hint

Look for ⋏Z⊰ and ⋏Ⴑ.

Triangles and quadrilaterals

1 Work out the angles marked with letters.
Give a reason for each answer.

a
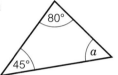

b
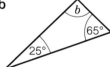

c

Q1a hint

The angles in a triangle add up to 180°. Start with 180° and subtract the other angles.
$x = 180 - 80 - \square = \square°$ (angle sum of a triangle)

2 Work out angle x for each quadrilateral.

a
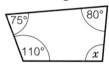

b
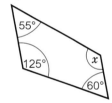

c
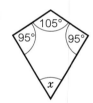

Q2a hint

Start with
$x = 360 - 110 - \square - \square = \square°$
(angle sum of a quadrilateral)

3 All of these triangles are isosceles. Work out the angles marked with letters. Give a reason for each answer.

a

b

c

d
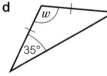

e

Q3 hint

The two angles at the base of the equal sides of an isosceles triangle are equal.

4 a Which is the exterior angle, x or y?
b Work out angle x.
Give reasons for your working.
c Work out angle y.
Give reasons for your working.

5 Work out the angles marked with letters.

a
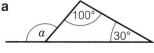

b

c
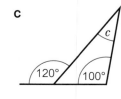

Q5 hint

Follow the method in Q4.

6 Copy these quadrilaterals.
Draw the lines of symmetry using dashed lines.

| A | B | C | D | E | F | G | H |

square   rectangle   parallelogram   rhombus   kite   trapezium   isosceles   arrowhead
trapezium

Which quadrilaterals have
a rotational symmetry of order 2
b no rotational symmetry?

Q6 hint

Use a mirror to check for line symmetry.
Use tracing paper to check for rotational symmetry.

7 The dashed lines are lines of symmetry. Use the symmetry of each shape to find equal angles. Work out the angles marked with letters.

a 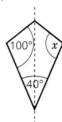   **b**    **c**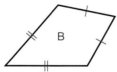

Q7 hint

Look at Q6 to work out what shapes they are first.

8 a Work out the angles marked with letters.
b Copy and complete this sentence.
Opposite angles of a parallelogram are _____

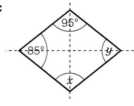

Q8 hint

Does the parallelogram have rotational symmetry?
Which angles must be equal?

9 Look at each quadrilateral.

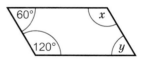

a What type of quadrilateral is it?
b Sketch each quadrilateral and mark equal angles using arcs.
Use double arcs for a second pair of equal angles.

Q9b hint

Draw lines of symmetry to find the equal angles.

10 Work out the angles marked with letters.

$a = \square°$ (opposite angles of a parallelogram)
$b = \square°$ (alternate angles)
$c = \square°$ (angle sum of a triangle)

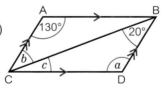

Interior and exterior angles

1 a Name these polygons.
b Write down the number of sides of each polygon.
c Write down the number of interior and exterior angles of each polygon.
d What do you notice about your answers to parts **b** and **c**?

A   B   C

2 Follow these steps to find the angle sum of a polygon.
1 Sketch the polygon.
2 Hold your pencil on one vertex.
3 Draw lines to the other vertices.
4 Write 180° in each triangle.
5 Work out the total, e.g. 3 × 180° = □°.
Use this method to find the angle sums of these polygons and fill in the table.

Polygon	Angle sum
pentagon	
hexagon	
heptagon	
octagon	

3 Work out the angles marked with letters.

a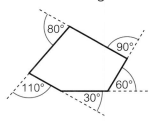
130° 150° 100° 120° a

b
100° b 130°

c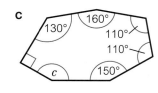
160° 130° 110° 110° c 150°

Q3a hint

Use the angle sums you found in Q2.
a = sum – □° – □° – □° – □° – □°

4 Jess measured the exterior angles of this pentagon and added them together.

80° 90° 110° 30° 60°

Explain how you know her measurements are wrong.

Q4 hint

What should the exterior angles add up to?

5 Problem-solving The exterior angle of a regular polygon is 30°.

30°

a How many exterior angles does the polygon have?
b How many sides does the polygon have?

Q5a hint

The exterior angles add up to 360°.
□ × 30° = 360°

Enrichment

1 a Draw two parallel lines on squared paper.
Cross the lines with a third line.

co-interior angles

b Measure the two marked angles. They are called **co-interior angles**.
c Repeat part **b** with two more diagrams.
d Add the co-interior angles together. What do you notice?

2 Reflect These strengthen lessons cover the topics:
 • Angles and parallel lines
 • Triangles and quadrilaterals
 • Interior and exterior angles
Which topic did you find easiest?
Write down one thing about this topic you fully understand and you are sure about.
Which topic did you find hardest?
Write down one thing about this topic you still do not understand, or you are not sure about.

Q2 hint

Show what you have written down to a friend or your teacher. Ask them to help you with the topic you are not sure about.

Reflect

5 Extend

You will learn to:

- Extend your understanding with problem-solving.

1 **Problem-solving** This pattern is made up of three identical red rhombus tiles and three identical blue rhombus tiles.
   a Work out angle x.
   b Work out angle y. Show your working.

2 **Work in pairs.**
   a On squared paper draw a pair of axes numbered from 0 to 10.
   b Together, choose a quadrilateral to draw.
   c Take turns to plot the vertices of the quadrilateral.
   d Join the points and check that this is the correct quadrilateral.
   e Repeat the activity with different quadrilaterals.

3 **Real** The diagram shows a ship S and a lighthouse L on a map.
   The arrows both point to north.
   They are parallel.
   Work out the angle marked x.

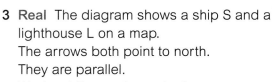

> **Q3 hint**
>
> Extend the line SL.

4 **Problem-solving / Reasoning**
   a Measure angles to decide which triangles in the diagram are isosceles, scalene and right-angled.
   b What shape is
      i EGCF
      ii ABCD?

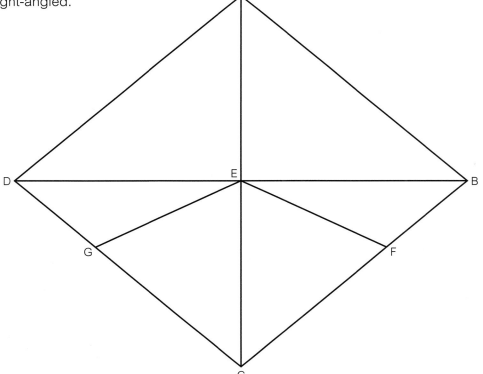

5 Reasoning Work out all of the angles.
Give reasons for your answer.
  a ABCD is a parallelogram.
  AFE is a straight line.
  Angle BFA = 30°
  Angle CDA = 140°

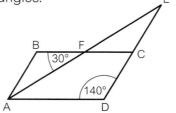

Q5 Strategy hint
Copy the diagram. Mark any parallel lines. Write in each angle as you work it out. Describe the angles using 3 letters.

  b ABCD is a kite. ABE and DCE
  are both straight lines.
  Angle BCE = 85°
  Angle ADC = 65°

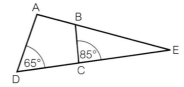

6 Reasoning The diagram shows four identical quadrilaterals.
  a Write down the angle sum of the quadrilateral.
  $a + \square + \square + \square = \square°$
  b Use your answer to part **a** to explain why the quadrilaterals fit exactly together at the point marked with a red dot.

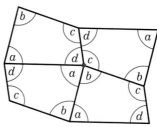

7 Problem-solving a Draw two identical equilateral triangles joined together along one of their sides. What shape have you made?
  b Repeat part **a** for two identical
    i isosceles triangles   **ii** right-angled triangles.
  Discussion How many different quadrilaterals can you make in part **b i**?

8 Reasoning Show that the sum of the interior angles of a dodecagon (12-sided shape) is 1800°.

Q8 Strategy hint
'Show that' means work out the answer and show it is the same as the one given.

9 Work out the angles marked with letters. Give a reason for each step in your answer.

  a

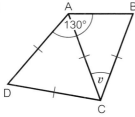

  b

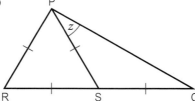

10 Work out angle x. Give a reason for each step in your answer.

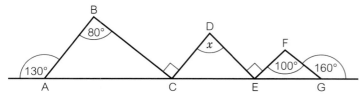

11 Work out the angles marked with letters.
Give reasons for your working.

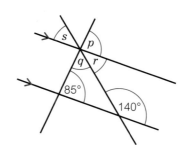

12 Reasoning If two lines are both perpendicular to a third line what can you say about the two lines?

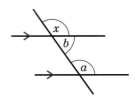

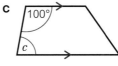

13 In the diagram, angles a and b are called **co-interior angles**.
Copy and complete this proof that
co-interior angles sum to 180°.
$a = \square$ because (_____ angles)
$b = \square - \square°$ (angles on a straight line)
$a + b =$ ___ + _____
    = _____

14 Work out angles a, b and c.

a
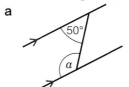

b
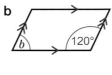

c

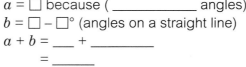

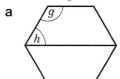

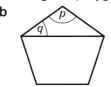

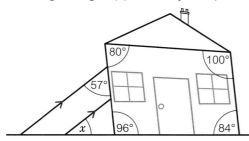

15 Real / Problem-solving / Reasoning The diagram shows an old building being supported by two parallel wooden beams.

a Work out the angle x that the beams make with the ground.
b Are the floor and ceiling parallel? Give a reason for your answer.

16 Reasoning / Problem-solving The diagram shows an adjustable ladder on a horizontal surface.
a The ladder has two equal legs held together by DE. DE is horizontal.
What does this tell you about lines AC and DE?
b What shape is ADEC?
c Work out
   i the angle that leg BC makes with the ground
   ii the angle ABC between the two legs.

17 Reasoning Here are some regular polygons.

a   **b**   **c**

   i Work out the angles marked with letters.
   ii Give a reason for each answer.

18 A hectogon is a polygon with 100 sides.
For a regular hectogon, work out the
   a exterior angle
   b interior angle.

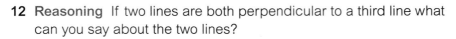

Q12 Strategy hint
Draw a diagram.

Q13 hint
You must prove that $a + b = 180°$.
Find the expressions for a and b and then add them together.

Q14 hint
Look at Q13.

Q17 hint
Use line symmetry.

Investigation

The centre of this regular pentagon has been joined to its vertices.

1   The lines from the centre are all equal. Explain why.
2   a   How many angles at the centre are there?
    b   Work out the size of each angle at the centre.
    c   Work out the angle marked x.
    d   How can you use x to work out the interior angle?
3   Repeat step 2 for a regular hexagon.
4   Write a rule to work out the interior angle from the angle at the centre.

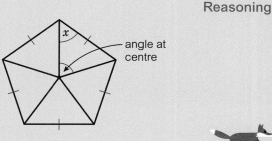

19 **Reasoning** These red shapes are made from regular polygons.

The centre of each polygon is marked using a dot.
Work out the angles marked with letters.

20 **Problem-solving** Work out the angle between the hands of
a clock at
    a   5 o'clock
    b   7 o'clock
    c   half past 8
    d   half past 4.

21 **Reasoning** The diagram shows a polygon in the shape of a star.

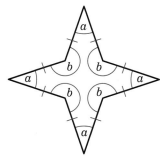

Angle a is 40°. Work out angle b.

> **Q21 hint**
>
> Work out the sum of the interior angles.

22 **Reflect** Look back at the questions you answered in these
extend lessons.
Find a question that you could not answer straightaway, or that
you really had to think about.
While you worked on this question:
   • What were you thinking about?
   • How did you feel?
   • Did you keep trying until you had an answer? Did you give up
     before reaching an answer, and move on to the next question?
   • Did you think you would get the answer correct or incorrect?
Write down any strategies you could use to help you stay calm
when answering tricky maths questions. Compare your strategies
with others.

Master
P107

Check
P119

Strengthen
P121

Extend
P125

TEST

5 Unit test

Log how you did on your
Student Progression Chart.

1 Work out the angles marked with letters.
Give a reason for each answer.

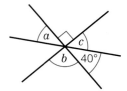

2 Work out angle x.

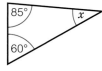

3 The diagram shows an arrowhead.
a Copy the diagram.
Mark any equal sides, angles and parallel lines.
b How many lines of symmetry does an arrowhead have?
c Describe the rotational symmetry of an arrowhead.

4 The diagram shows three vertices of the kite ABCD.
Find the coordinates of vertex D.

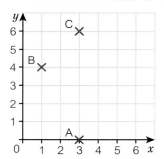

5 Work out angle x.

6 A quadrilateral has two pairs of equal sides and one pair of equal angles.
What is its name?

7 Work out angle x.

8 Work out the angles marked with letters.
Give a reason for each answer.

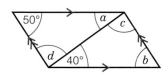

9 The diagram shows the exterior angles of a polygon.

   a Work out angle x.

   b Work out the sum of the interior angles.

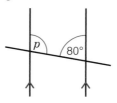

10 Copy the diagram.

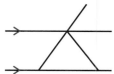

   a Mark a pair of alternate angles with the letter a.

   b Mark a pair of corresponding angles with the letter c.

11 Work out angle p.

   Give a reason for your answer.

12 Work out angle a.

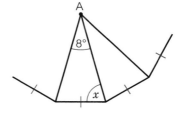

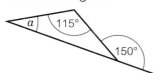

13 a Work out the exterior angle of a regular 15-sided polygon.

   b Work out the interior angle of a regular 15-sided polygon.

14 A regular polygon has an exterior angle of $12°$.

   How many sides does the polygon have?

15 The diagram shows part of a regular polygon.

   The point marked A is the centre of the polygon.

   a Work out the number of sides the polygon has.

   b Work out angle x.

   c Work out the interior angle of the polygon.

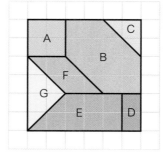

Challenge

16 A **tangram** is a puzzle made of seven shapes that fit together to make another shape.

   Here is a tangram drawn on squared paper.

   a Name each shape.

   b Draw your own tangram on a similar square grid.

     Try to include as many different shapes as possible.

     Label each shape from A to G.

     List the names of the shapes.

   c Make a tangram that includes an arrowhead, kite and pentagon.

   d Challenge a classmate to make a tangram that includes three shapes of your choice.

17 **Reflect** Which of these statements best describes your work on lines and angles in this unit.

     I did the best I could   I could have tried harder

   Why did you choose that statement?

   Was it true for every lesson?

   Write down one thing you will do to make sure you do the best you can in the next unit.

6.1 Ordering decimals

You will learn to:
- Write decimals in ascending and descending order.

CONFIDENCE

Why learn this?
You can work out who finished first in a race.

Fluency
How many tenths are in
- 2
- 5
- 6
- 10?

Explore
Which element has the lowest boiling point?

Exercise 6.1

Warm up

1 Write these numbers in order from smallest to largest.
  a −3, 5, −2, 0, 7   **b** −2, 0, 2, −5, −3   **c** −5, −3, −8, −7

2 Write < or > between each pair of numbers.
  a −4 ☐ 2   **b** 5 ☐ 3   **c** −7 ☐ −8

Worked example

Write these **decimals** in order from smallest to largest.
6.5, 6.23, 6.55

H	T	U	•	$\frac{1}{10}$	$\frac{1}{100}$	$\frac{1}{1000}$
		6	•	5	0	
		6	•	2	3	
		6	•	5	5	

On a place value table, the numbers look like this. Write a **zero place holder** when ordering decimals with different numbers of decimal places.

6.23, 6.5, 6.55

The units are all 6. $\frac{23}{100}$ is the smallest fraction and $\frac{55}{100}$ is the largest.

Key point
Digits after the decimal point are fractions.
$0.1 = \frac{1}{10}$
$0.01 = \frac{1}{100}$
$0.001 = \frac{1}{1000}$

3 Write these decimals in order from smallest to largest.
  0.6, 0.006, 0.06

4 Reasoning   Carly says, '10.42 is greater than 10.5 because 42 is greater than 5.' Is Carly correct? Explain.

5 Write these decimals in **ascending** order.
  a 0.7124, 0.73, 0.7241, 0.724, 0.703
  b 12.874, 12.8475, 12.92, 12.9
  c −0.203, −0.291, −0.2, −0.24, −0.29
  d −0.43, −0.491, −0.45, −0.405, −0.49

Q5 Literacy hint

Ascending means increasing in value from small to large.

Topic links: Tables

6 Write these decimals in **descending** order.
  a 0.3516, 0.37, 0.3105, 0.315, 0.376
  b 18.429, 18.9142, 18.49, 18.4
  c −0.13, −0.107, −0.7, −0.17, −0.73
  d −0.52, −0.514, −0.55, −0.502, −0.56

Q6 Literacy hint

Descending means decreasing in value from large to small.

7 Reasoning These were the top three athletes in the women's javelin at the 2012 Summer Olympics.

Athlete	Distance (m)
Christina Obergföll	65.16
Barbara Špotáková	69.55
Linda Stahl	64.19

  a Who won gold, silver and bronze?
  b Did you place the distances in ascending or descending order?

These were the top three athletes in the women's 400 m at the 2012 Summer Olympics.

Athlete	Time (s)
Christine Ohuruogu	49.70
Sanya Richards-Ross	49.55
DeeDee Trotter	49.72

  c Who won gold, silver and bronze?
  d Did you place the times in ascending or descending order?

Q7a hint

The longest distance wins gold.

Q7c hint

The quickest time wins gold.

8 Real These are the qualifying times from the British Grand Prix in 2013.
In what order were the drivers placed in the qualifying heats?

Driver	Time (min : s)
Lewis Hamilton	1:29.607
Daniel Ricciardo	1:30.757
Nico Rosberg	1:30.059
Sebastian Vettel	1:30.211
Mark Webber	1:30.220

Q8 hint

The driver with the fastest time is placed first.

9 STEM A car part needs to measure between 0.095 cm and 0.105 cm. The first five parts off the production line measure 0.098 cm, 0.1 cm, 0.15 cm, 0.09 cm, 0.0955 cm
Which of these parts are acceptable?

10 Real The data shows the times (in seconds) of 10 students in the 100 m. Copy and complete the grouped frequency table.
12.34 14.85 12.50 13.07 11.97 15.43 12.56 13.48 12.03 14.61

Time (seconds)	Tally	Frequency
$11.5 \leqslant t < 12.5$		
$12.5 \leqslant t < 13.5$		
$13.5 \leqslant t < 14.5$		
$14.5 \leqslant t < 15.5$		

11 Write < or > between each pair of numbers.
  a 2.6 ☐ 2.9   b 3.6 ☐ 3.54   c 12.043 ☐ 12.009
  d −2.14 ☐ −2.41   e −9.09 ☐ −9.088

12 **Explore** Which element has the lowest boiling point?
What have you learned in this lesson to help you answer this question? What other information do you need?

13 **Reflect** In this lesson you have been working with decimals.
Imagine someone had never seen a decimal point before.
How would you define it? How would you describe what it does?
Write a description in your own words. Compare your description with others in your class.

6.2 Rounding decimals

You will learn to:
- Round to decimal places.

Why learn this?
In the 2014 Sochi Olympics, the women's downhill ended in a tie, but only because the times were rounded to 2 decimal places.

Fluency
Round these numbers to the nearest 10.
- 58
- 385
- 396

Explore
Which is the most crowded city in the world?

Exercise 6.2

1 Write down the digit in the second decimal place of each number.
 a 5.64
 b 37.25
 c 8.0532
 d 146.265

2 Round to the nearest whole number.
 a 12.3
 b 2.7
 c 6.5
 d 11.29
 e 37.14

3 **Round** these numbers to one decimal place.
 a 5.64
 b 3.89
 c 0.65
 d 8.96
 e 9.98

4 **Real** Devon scores 53, 26, 3, 7, 19 and 85 in 6 cricket matches. Calculate his mean score. Round your answer to 1 decimal place.

5 **Problem-solving** Toni writes an answer of 3.4 correct to 1 decimal place.
 What could her number have been correct to 2 decimal places?

6 Round these numbers to 2 decimal places.
 a 2.947
 b 0.803
 c 12.996
 d 14.017

 7 Use a calculator to write these fractions as decimals correct to 2 d.p.
 a $\frac{5}{7}$
 b $\frac{9}{11}$

8 **Reasoning** Frank says that 6.998 rounded to 2 decimal places is 7.
 a Explain why Frank is wrong.
 b What is the correct answer?
 Discussion Explain the difference between 8, 8.0 and 8.00. Which is the more accurate and which is the less accurate?

9 **Finance** Jilna buys four drinks for £4.39. How much does each drink cost? Round your answer to the nearest penny.

Key point

To **round** a decimal to one decimal place (**1 d.p.**), look at the digit in the second decimal place. If the digit is less than 5, round down. If the digit is 5 or more, round up.

Q3 hint

Write the number in the first decimal place, even if it is 0.

Key point

To round to two decimal places (2 d.p.), look at the digit in the third decimal place.

Q7a hint

Work out 5 ÷ 7

Topic links: Mean

10 a Copy and complete the table showing populations of different countries around the world.

Country	Population (numbers)	Population (numbers and words)
Italy	60 000 000	60 million
Canada	34 300 000	
Sri Lanka		20.4 million
Norway		5.1 million
Fiji	900 000	

b The population of Sweden is 9 658 301 and of Barbados is 285 000. Write these populations in both forms, correct to the nearest 100 000.

11 Rory works out $\sqrt{7}$. The number on his calculator is 2.645751311. Round this number to 3 decimal places.

> **Key point**
>
> To round a decimal to 3 decimal places, look at the digit in the fourth decimal place.

12 Athlete A runs the 100 m in 9.7528 seconds. Athlete B runs the same race in 9.7456 seconds.
  a Which athlete has the faster time?
  b The times are reported to 3 decimal places. Does the result change?
  c The times are reported to 2 d.p. Does the result change?

13 Problem-solving Emily writes down an answer of 4.29 correct to 2 decimal places.
  Which two of these could have been her unrounded answer?
  a 4.286   **b** 4.296   **c** 4.2845   **d** 4.293

14 Problem-solving Write down a number with 3 decimal places that would round to:
  a 3 to the nearest whole number and 3.2 to the nearest tenth
  b 3 to the nearest whole number and 2.5 to the nearest tenth
  c 2 to the nearest whole number and 2.5 to the nearest tenth
  d 3.2 to the nearest tenth and 3.25 to the nearest hundredth
  e 3.3 to the nearest tenth and 3.25 to the nearest hundredth.

15 The numbers of a beetle are recorded in 4 woods. The bar chart shows the results.
  a Work out the mean number of beetles in a wood.
  b What is the mean to the nearest 100?

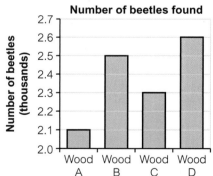

16 Explore Which is the most crowded city in the world?
  What have you learned in this lesson to help you answer this question?
  What other information do you need?

17 Reflect Lee and Ethan are discussing Q13.
  Lee says, 'I rounded all the numbers to 2 decimal places to see which ones rounded to 4.29'
  Ethan says 'I looked at the third decimal place of all the numbers to see which ones would round up or down.'
  How did you decide which numbers could have been rounded to 4.29?
  Which method is most efficient?

Explore

Reflect

6.3 Adding and subtracting decimals

You will learn to:
• Add and subtract decimals.

CONFIDENCE

Why learn this?
You can keep track of how much money you have saved.

Fluency
What is 5 230 000 as millions to 1 d.p.?

Explore
How much change would you have from £20 after buying a burger and a milkshake?

Exercise 6.3

Warm up

1 Work out
  a 45 + 186
  b 387 − 35

2 Work out
  a
```
   1 9 0
 −  7 3
 ───────
```
  b
```
   1 0 0 0
 −   3 6 7
 ─────────
```

3 a 0.4 + ☐ = 1
  b 0.3 + ☐ = 1
  c 0.42 + ☐ = 1
  d ☐ + 0.67 = 1

4 Work out
  a 3 − 0.2
  b 7 − 0.4
  c 10 − 6.34
  d 100 − 8.59

Q4a hint

Count up

0.8   2

0.2   1   3

5 Work out
  a 3.45 + 2.51
  b 4.56 + 7.88
  c 13.4 + 9.83
  d 2.02 + 7.9

6 Reasoning Jody says, '4.3 + 2.15 = 6.18, because 2 + 4 = 6 and 3 + 15 = 18.' Explain why Jody is wrong.

7 Work out these. Use an **estimate** to check your answer.
  a 4.96 − 2.13
  b 5.11 − 4.39
  c 14.45 − 7.6

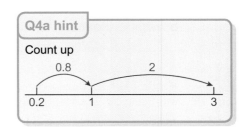

Q7 Strategy hint

Estimate by rounding the values to the nearest whole number to do the calculation.

Topic links: Rounding   **Subject links:** Geography (Q12)

8 **Real / Problem-solving / Finance** Varsha orders:

Lasagne	£6.95
Ice cream	£1.99
Cola	£1.45

How much change does Varsha get from £20?
Use an estimate to check your answer.

9 **Finance** Kelly has £503.62 in her bank account. She spends £206.87.
   a Approximately how much money does Kelly have left?
   b Work out exactly how much money Kelly has left.

Q9 Literacy hint

Working out 'approximately' is the same as estimating.

10 **Real** Debbie has 3.25 m of fabric. She cuts a piece 1.47 m long.
   How long is the remaining fabric?

Worked example

Work out 4.7 − 2.24

$$4.\overset{6}{\cancel{7}}\overset{1}{0}$$
$$-2.2\ 4$$
$$\overline{2.4\ 6}$$

Line up the units, tenths and hundreds.
Write the **zero place holder**.

Check: 4.7 ≈ 5 and 2.24 ≈ 2, 5 − 2 = 3, 2.46 is close to 3.

Key point

You can use a **zero place holder** when subtracting decimals with different numbers of decimal places.

11 Work out using ~~the column~~ *written* method.
   a 8.5 − 3.13 + 6.9
   b 3.45 + 8.7 − 2.96
   c 4.26 − 3.94 + 8.53

12 The population of a city was 7 546 231 in 2010.
   In 2014 it was 8 235 965. Estimate the population increase.

Q12 hint

Write the population as millions to 1 d.p.

13 **Problem-solving** Work out
   a 0.45 + 0.28 − 0.61 = ☐
   b 0.45 − 0.61 + 0.28 = ☐
   Discussion Will this always happen? Explain your answer.
   c Use this strategy to work out 0.75 − 0.96 + 0.25

14 **Explore** How much change would you have from £20 after buying
   a burger and a milkshake?
   Look back at the maths you have learned in this lesson.
   How can you use it to answer this question?

15 **Reflect** Look back at the work you have done this lesson.
   In what way is adding and subtracting decimals the same as adding
   and subtracting integers?
   In what way is it different?

6.4 Multiplying decimals

You will learn to:
- Multiply a decimal by an integer
- Use place value to multiply decimals.

CONFIDENCE

Why learn this?
You can work out the total cost of vegetables by knowing the price per kg and weighing the item.

Fluency
$5.5 \times \square = 550$
$4 \div 10 = \square$
$\square \div 1000 = 0.78$

Explore
Does multiplying always make a number bigger?

Exercise 6.4

Warm up

1 a
$$\begin{array}{r} 83 \\ \times\ \ 4 \\ \hline \end{array}$$

b
$$\begin{array}{r} 97 \\ \times\ 13 \\ \hline \end{array}$$

c
$$\begin{array}{r} 402 \\ \times\ \ 29 \\ \hline \end{array}$$

2 Work out
  a $4 \times 56 = 4 \times 50 + 4 \times 6 = \square + \square = \square$
  b $9 \times 27 = \square \times \square + \square \times \square = \square + \square = \square$
  c $83 \times 7 = \square \times \square + \square \times \square = \square + \square = \square$

3 Round each number to the nearest 10 to estimate.
  a $19 \times 23 \approx 20 \times 20 = \square$ **b** $34 \times 44 \approx \square$
  c $195 \times 32 \approx \square$

Worked example

Work out 8.9×7.

Estimate: $8.9 \approx 9$, $9 \times 7 = 63$

$$\begin{array}{r} 89 \\ \times\ \ 7 \\ \hline 623 \\ {\scriptstyle 6} \end{array}$$

Ignore the decimal point and work out 89×7.

$8.9 \times 7 = 62.3$

Use your estimate to see where to put the decimal point.

Key point

You can use the column method to multiply a decimal by a whole number.

4 Use the column method to work out these. Use an estimate to check your answers.
  a 4.6×8 **b** 7×7.34 **c** 6×24.76
  d 12.4×1.3 **e** 3.72×14

Discussion For each part, count the number of digits after the decimal point in both numbers in the question. Count the number of digits after the decimal point in the answer. What do you notice?

5 Real / Finance It costs £4.75 for one person to go bowling.
How much does it cost for 8 people?

6 Finance The cost of one share in a company is £1.76.
Louise buys 12 shares. How much does this cost?

7 Work out
  a 6×7 **b** 6×0.7 **c** 0.6×7 **d** 6×0.07

Q7 hint

Your answer will have the digits 4
and 2. Where do you put the decimal
point?

8 Work out
  a 6×0.3 **b** 7×0.2 **c** 20×0.09
  d 0.8×0.3 **e** 0.1×0.06 **f** 0.07×0.08

9 Use the multiplication facts given to work out the answers.
  a $42 \times 10 = 420$ Work out
     i 42×0.1 **ii** $42 \div 10$
  b $37 \times 10 = 370$ Work out
     i 370×0.1 **ii** $370 \div 10$
  Discussion What do you notice?

10 a Copy and complete.
     $72 \times 1 = \square$ $72 \times 0.1 = \square$ $72 \times 0.01 = \square$
  b Reasoning What division calculation is equivalent to $\times 0.01$?

Key point

You can use **partitioning** to work
out decimal multiplications.
You can check your answer using
an estimate.

11 Work out these. Check your answer using an estimate.
  a $22 \times 3.3 = 20 \times 3.3 + 2 \times 3.3 = \square + \square = \square$
  b $27 \times 1.2 =$ **c** $19 \times 5.1 =$

12 Real / Finance Harry changes £50 to euros. The exchange rate is
£1 = €1.20. How many euros does he get?

Q12 hint

$\times \square$ (£1 = €1.20) $\times \square$
         £50 = $\square$

13 Work out
  a 1×30 **b** 2×15 **c** 4×7.5
  Discussion What do you notice about the three answers?
  Explain why this happens.
  d Use this strategy to calculate
     i 2.8×50 **ii** 250×4.8

Q14 hint

Round to 1 d.p.

14 A metal rod measures 0.357 m. Estimate the length of metal
needed to make 6 of these rods.

15 Use the fact $0.83 \times 3.5 = 2.905$ to calculate:
  a 0.083×3.5 **b** 8.3×35 **c** 830×0.035
  d Write down two other multiplications that will have an answer of 2.905.
  e Explain why $83 \times 35 \neq 2915$.

Q15a hint

How many digits are there after the
decimal point in both numbers in the
question?

Q15 Literacy hint

$\neq$ means 'not equal to'

16 Explore Does multiplying always make a number bigger?
Choose some sensible numbers to help you explore this situation.
Then use what you've learned in this lesson to help you answer the
question.

17 Reflect In this lesson you multiplied decimals using:
the **column method** and **multiplication facts**.
For each method, make up your own calculation to show how it works.
Work out the answer to each calculation and show how you worked out each step.
Explain how you chose the numbers for your calculations.

Explore

Reflect

6.5 Dividing decimals

You will learn to:
- Divide a decimal by a whole number
- Divide a number by a decimal.

Why learn this?
Compare different quantities of an item in a supermarket to work out which represents the best value.

Fluency
- 6 × 10
- 0.8 × 100
- 0.03 × 10
- 95.24 × 100

Explore
Does dividing one number by another always make it smaller?

Exercise 6.5

1 Work out
  a 30 ÷ 6   **b** 300 ÷ 6

2 Work out
  a $7\overline{)903}$ **b** $6\overline{)339}$ **c** $12\overline{)348}$

3 Copy and complete these equivalent fractions.

  a

$$\frac{3}{8} = \frac{\Box}{16} = \frac{60}{\Box}$$

  b $\frac{19}{25} = \frac{\Box}{250} = \frac{1900}{\Box}$

Worked example

Work out 74.8 ÷ 4

```
      1 8 . 7
4 | 7³4 .²8
```
First write the decimal point for the answer above the decimal point in the question. Then divide as normal, starting from the left.

74.8 ÷ 4 = 18.7

Key point
You can use short or long division to divide a decimal by a whole number.

4 Work out
  a 58.4 ÷ 4
  b 41.52 ÷ 6
  c 198.64 ÷ 8
  d 183.84 ÷ 12

5 Finance 5 friends share the bill for a meal equally.
The bill comes to £64.25.
How much do they each pay?

5 Real / Finance It costs £4.75 for one person to go bowling.
How much does it cost for 8 people?

6 Finance The cost of one share in a company is £1.76.
Louise buys 12 shares. How much does this cost?

7 Work out
  a 6 × 7   **b** 6 × 0.7   **c** 0.6 × 7   **d** 6 × 0.07

Q7 hint

Your answer will have the digits 4
and 2. Where do you put the decimal
point?

8 Work out
  a 6 × 0.3   **b** 7 × 0.2   **c** 20 × 0.09
  d 0.8 × 0.3   **e** 0.1 × 0.06   **f** 0.07 × 0.08

9 Use the multiplication facts given to work out the answers.
  a 42 × 10 = 420   Work out
    i 42 × 0.1   **ii** 42 ÷ 10
  b 37 × 10 = 370   Work out
    i 370 × 0.1   **ii** 370 ÷ 10
  Discussion What do you notice?

10 a Copy and complete.
    72 × 1 = ☐   72 × 0.1 = ☐   72 × 0.01 = ☐
  b Reasoning What division calculation is equivalent to × 0.01?

Key point

You can use **partitioning** to work
out decimal multiplications.
You can check your answer using
an estimate.

11 Work out these. Check your answer using an estimate.
  a 22 × 3.3 = 20 × 3.3 + 2 × 3.3 = ☐ + ☐ = ☐
  b 27 × 1.2 =   **c** 19 × 5.1 =

12 Real / Finance Harry changes £50 to euros. The exchange rate is
£1 = €1.20. How many euros does he get?

Q12 hint

×☐(£1 = €1.20)×☐
£50 = ☐

13 Work out
  a 1 × 30   **b** 2 × 15   **c** 4 × 7.5
  Discussion What do you notice about the three answers?
  Explain why this happens.
  d Use this strategy to calculate
    i 2.8 × 50   **ii** 250 × 4.8

14 A metal rod measures 0.357 m. Estimate the length of metal
needed to make 6 of these rods.

Q14 hint

Round to 1 d.p.

15 Use the fact 0.83 × 3.5 = 2.905 to calculate:
  a 0.083 × 3.5   **b** 8.3 × 35   **c** 830 × 0.035
  d Write down two other multiplications that will have an answer of 2.905.
  e Explain why 83 × 35 ≠ 2915.

Q15a hint

How many digits are there after the
decimal point in both numbers in the
question?

Q15 Literacy hint

≠ means 'not equal to'

16 Explore Does multiplying always make a number bigger?
Choose some sensible numbers to help you explore this situation.
Then use what you've learned in this lesson to help you answer the
question.

17 **Reflect** In this lesson you multiplied decimals using:
the **column method** and **multiplication facts**.
For each method, make up your own calculation to show how it works.
Work out the answer to each calculation and show how you worked out each step.
Explain how you chose the numbers for your calculations.

MASTER

Check
P147

Strengthen
P149

Extend
P153

Test
P157

6.5 Dividing decimals

You will learn to:

- Divide a decimal by a whole number
- Divide a number by a decimal.

CONFIDENCE

Why learn this?
Compare different quantities of an item in a supermarket to work out which represents the best value.

Fluency
- 6 × 10
- 0.8 × 100
- 0.03 × 10
- 95.24 × 100

Explore
Does dividing one number by another always make it smaller?

Exercise 6.5

Warm up

1 Work out
  a 30 ÷ 6
  b 300 ÷ 6

2 Work out
  a 7)903
  b 6)339
  c 12)348

3 Copy and complete these equivalent fractions.

  a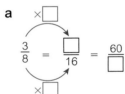
  $$\frac{3}{8} = \frac{\square}{16} = \frac{60}{\square}$$

  b $\frac{19}{25} = \frac{\square}{250} = \frac{1900}{\square}$

Worked example

Work out 74.8 ÷ 4

$$\begin{array}{r} 1\,8\,.\,7 \\ 4\overline{)\,7^3 4\,.^2 8} \end{array}$$

74.8 ÷ 4 = 18.7

First write the decimal point for the answer above the decimal point in the question. Then divide as normal, starting from the left.

Key point
You can use short or long division to divide a decimal by a whole number.

4 Work out
  a 58.4 ÷ 4
  b 41.52 ÷ 6
  c 198.64 ÷ 8
  d 183.84 ÷ 12

5 Finance 5 friends share the bill for a meal equally.
The bill comes to £64.25.
How much do they each pay?

Worked example

Calculate $30 \div 0.06$

$$\overset{\times 10}{\underset{\times 10}{\frac{30}{0.06}}} = \overset{\times 10}{\underset{\times 10}{\frac{300}{0.6}}} = \frac{3000}{6} = 500$$

> Multiply the numerator and denominator by 10 until you have a whole number in the denominator.

6 Work out

    a $4 \div 0.1$ **b** $113 \div 0.1$ **c** $0.9 \div 0.1$

    d $8 \div 0.01$ **e** $7.2 \div 0.01$ **f** $0.83 \div 0.01$

    Discussion What multiplication is equivalent to $\div 0.1$? $\div 0.01$?

7 Work out

    a $200 \div 0.4$ **b** $150 \div 0.2$ **c** $300 \div 0.6$

    d $250 \div 0.02$ **e** $1800 \div 0.06$ **f** $48 \div 0.08$

8 Estimate the answers.

    a $2.5 \div 6 \approx 2.4 \div 6 = \square$ **b** $7.3 \div 8$

    c $85 \div 1.2$ **d** $68 \div 1.1$

9 James works out $3.02 \div 0.49$ on his calculator. His answer is $3.35555\ldots$
    Use an approximate calculation to show that James must be wrong.

 10 Work out

    a $44 \div 11$ and $4.4 \div 1.1$ **b** $56 \div 8$ and $5.6 \div 0.8$

    c $396 \div 3$ and $3.96 \div 0.03$ **d** $570 \div 15$ and $5.7 \div 0.15$

    Discussion What do you notice? How does this help you work
    out $6.3 \div 0.7$ and $0.81 \div 0.09$ without a calculator?

11 Work out

    a $0.6 \div 0.2$ **b** $0.18 \div 0.3$ **c** $0.24 \div 0.8$

    d $0.06 \div 0.03$ **e** $0.9 \div 0.02$ **f** $0.15 \div 0.05$

12 Continue the pattern to work out the answers.

    a $6862 \div 94 = 73$

        $6862 \div 9.4 = 730$

        i $6862 \div 0.94 =$ **ii** $6862 \div 0.094 =$ **iii** $6862 \div 0.0094 =$

    b $945 \div 35 = 27$

        i $94.5 \div 35 =$ **ii** $9.45 \div 35 =$ **iii** $0.945 \div 35 =$

13 $7.8 \times 54 = 421.2$

    Use this multiplication fact to work out

    a $421.2 \div 54$ **b** $421.2 \div 7.8$ **c** $421.2 \div 5.4$

    d $42.12 \div 54$ **e** $421.2 \div 78$

> **Q13 hint**
>
> Use number patterns similar to Q12 to help.

14 **Explore** Does dividing one number by another always make it smaller?
    Look back at the maths you have learned in this lesson.
    How can you use it to answer this question?

15 **Reflect** Look back at the work you did in lesson 6.4 and this lesson.
    What happens if you divide a positive number by a number between 0 and 1?
    What happens if you multiply a positive number by a number between
    0 and 1? Write your own 'What happens if___' question and answer it.

Explore

Reflect

6.6 Fractions, decimals and percentages

You will learn to:
- Convert between fractions, decimals and percentages
- Compare different proportions using percentages.

CONFIDENCE

Why learn this?
In speed calculations, we often need to convert hours and minutes into a decimal number of hours.

Fluency
What fraction of an hour is
- 30 minutes
- 15 minutes
- 45 minutes
- 20 minutes
- 36 minutes?

Explore
What does 'up to 50% off' actually mean?

Exercise 6.6

Warm up

1 Write the value of
 a the tenths digit in 2.3
 b the hundredths digit in 34.96.

2 Convert to a decimal.
 a $\frac{4}{5}$
 b $\frac{7}{8}$
 c $\frac{2}{25}$

3 Copy and complete the table by finding the missing fractions, decimals or percentages.

Fraction	$\frac{1}{10}$				$\frac{1}{2}$			$1\frac{3}{5}$
Decimal		0.25		0.4			1.5	
Percentage			30%			75%		

4 Look at the Decimal and Percentage rows in the table in Q3.
 Copy and complete.
 To convert a decimal to a percentage, × ☐
 To convert a percentage to a decimal, ÷ ☐

5 Convert these decimals to %.
 a 0.72
 b 0.23
 c 0.09
 d 1.08

6 Lois says that 0.58 = 5.8%.
 a What mistake has Lois made?
 b What is the correct answer?

7 Convert these percentages to decimals.
 a 42%
 b 191%
 c 6%
 d 1.3%
 e 29.4%

8 Write these percentages and decimals in ascending order.
 a 0.6, 6%, 0.66, 63%, 0.606
 b 80%, 0.88, 0.85, 8%, 8.8%

Q5 hint
×100
decimal → percentage
0.5 → 50%

Q7 hint
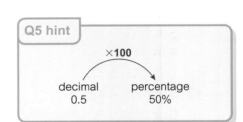
decimal ← percentage
0.5 ← 50%
÷100

Q8 hint
Convert all to decimals or all to percentages to compare.

9 Write each time as a decimal number of hours.

   a 1h 30 min   **b** 5h 15 min

   c 3h 45 min   **d** 2h 12 min

   e Show that 1 hour 25 min ≠ 1.25 hours.

Q9 hint

Write as a mixed number first.

Q9e hint

Convert 1 hour 25 min to a decimal.

10 Write these decimals as fractions. Simplify the fractions where possible.

   a 0.3

   b 0.8

   c 0.39

   d 1.85

   e 5.48

   f 2.529

Q10a, c hint

$0.3 = 3 \text{ tenths} = \frac{3}{\square}$

$0.39 = \frac{39}{\square}$

11 **Reasoning** Harry says that $0.6 = \frac{6}{10}$. Sophie says that 0.6 is $\frac{3}{5}$.

   a Explain why they are both correct.

   b Write another fraction equivalent to 0.6.

Investigation   **Problem-solving**

Evie uses her calculator to convert $\frac{1}{9}$ and $\frac{2}{9}$ to decimals.
She writes down:

$\frac{1}{9} = 0.111...$ $\frac{2}{9} = 0.222...$

  1 Continue Evie's pattern up to $\frac{9}{9}$.

  2 Write $\frac{13}{9}$ as a decimal.

  3 Investigate fractions with 99 as the denominator.

Use your answers to write these **recurring decimals** as fractions:

    a 0.373 737...   **b** 0.656 565....   **c** 0.060 606...

> **Key point**
>
> In a **recurring decimal**, a dot over the beginning and end of a sequence shows it recurs.
> For example 0.111111111 is $0.\dot{1}$ and 4.185185185 is $4.\dot{1}8\dot{5}$

12 Match each fraction to its recurring decimal.

    $\frac{5}{6}$ $\frac{2}{9}$ $\frac{7}{15}$ $\frac{3}{11}$ $\frac{5}{12}$

    $0.\dot{2}$ $0.4\dot{6}$ $0.8\dot{3}$ $0.\dot{2}\dot{7}$ $0.41\dot{6}$

13 Write these recurring decimals using dots.

   a 0.777...

   b 0.333...

   c 0.282828...

   d 0.145145145...

   e 0.0767676...

   f 0.09111...

14 **a** Convert these fractions to decimals. Write your answers to 2 d.p.

     i $\frac{1}{3}$

    ii $\frac{2}{3}$

   b Write $\frac{1}{3}$ and $\frac{2}{3}$ as percentages.

15 Put these quantities in ascending order.

   a $\frac{1}{3}$, 35%, 0.38, $\frac{2}{5}$, 25%, 0.39

   b $\frac{7}{10}$, 73%, 79%, $\frac{17}{20}$, 0.74, 0.86

   c 0.56, 84%, $\frac{5}{6}$, 86%, $\frac{4}{5}$, 0.08

Q15 Strategy hint

Convert all the values to decimals first.

16 Copy and complete.

Fraction	Decimal	Percentage
$\frac{27}{50}$		
$\frac{5}{8}$		
$\frac{19}{25}$		

17 Convert these percentages to fractions.

    a 23%

    b 9%

    c 1%

    d 16%

    e 12%

    f 45%

 18 Rewrite these statements giving the proportions as **percentages**.
Round your answer to 1 decimal place where necessary.

    a 19 out 40 students are vegetarian.

    b 11 out of 50 people own a dog.

    c 77 out of 80 people own a mobile phone.

    d 31 out of 45 people watched TV last night.

    e 16 out of 29 people read a daily newspaper.

 19 Between 2005 and 2008, Tiger Woods won 25 out of 58 golf
tournaments.
Over the same period Roger Federer won 35 out of 77 tennis
tournaments.
Which player won a higher proportion of the tournaments they
entered?

20 Write these percentages as decimals and fractions.

    a 3.5%

    b 25.5%

    c 32.5%

    d 62.5%

21 **Explore** What does 'up to 50% off' actually mean?
Look back at the maths you have learned in this lesson.
How can you use it to answer this question?

22 **Reflect** After this lesson, Harriet says, 'Fractions and decimals are
numbers but percentages show proportions.' Luc says, 'Fractions,
decimals and percentages all show proportions.'
Who do you agree with?
Write down a situation where you would use a fraction, a decimal
and a percentage.

Q17a hint

Per cent means out of 100.

23% = $\frac{\square}{\square}$

Q17d hint

Give your answer in its simplest form.

Q18 Strategy hint

Write as a fraction, then a decimal,
then a percentage.

Q19 hint

Write as percentages.

Q20 Strategy hint

First convert the percentage to a
decimal. Then write the decimal as
a fraction.

6.7 FINANCE: Working with percentages

You will learn to:
* Calculate percentages with and without a calculator
* Calculate percentage increases and decreases
* Work backwards to solve a percentage problem.

Why learn this?
Urban planners calculate population growth so they know how many houses to build.

Fluency
What is
* 50% as a fraction
* 10% as a fraction
* 1% as a fraction?
Work out 50%, 10% and 1% of £250.

Explore
How much money are you likely to make in one year if you invest £1000?

Exercise 6.7: Percentages of amounts

1 Work out 50% of
  a 12 m
  b 42 kg
  c 326 g

2 Work out
  a 10% of 60 g
  b 20% of 60 g
  c 70% of 60 g
  d 5% of 60 g
  e 1% of 60 g

3 Work out 80% of £30.

4 Finance Work out
  a 21% of £120
  b 35% of £320
  c 94% of £810

5 Finance Anish earns £1400 per month. He donates 6% of his monthly salary to charity. How much money does he donate each month?

6 Finance Molly buys a new mp3 player. There is 30% off the original price of £75. How much does Molly pay?

7 Finance David puts £350 into a savings account. The account pays 5% interest per year. How much money is in the account after 1 year?

Q2b hint
$\times 2 \left(\begin{array}{l} 10\% = \square \\ 20\% = \square \end{array} \right) \times 2$

Q2d hint
$\div 2 \left(\begin{array}{l} 10\% = \square \\ 5\% = \square \end{array} \right) \div 2$

Q3 hint
Work out 10% first.

Q4a hint
21% = 20% + 1%

Q6 hint
First work out 30% of £75. Then subtract the answer from £75.

Q7 hint
First work out 5% of £350. Then add the answer to £350.

Warm up

8 Problem-solving / Finance Sophia wants to buy a new computer.
She sees the same computer for sale in three different stores.

Computer World
Was £650. 15% off.

Plenty of PCs
Pay only £70 today. Then 10
monthly payments of £49

Computers for You
Was £800. 10% off
Special reduction – further
20% off all items

Which shop should she buy it from?

9 Problem-solving / Finance Remi invests £2000.

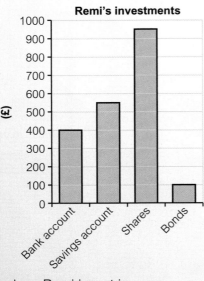

Remi's investments

What percentage does Remi invest in
a bonds   **b** shares   **c** bank or savings account?

Worked example

Use a calculator to work out 5.4% of £206.47.

5.4% = 0.054 ——— First convert 5.4% to a decimal.

5.4% of £206.47 = 0.054 × £206.47 = £11.14938

£11.15 ——— Always round money to the nearest penny.

Key point

You can use a **multiplier** to work out
a percentage, by using the decimal
equivalent of the percentage.

 10 Finance Ella has £326.43 in her savings account. The account pays
4.3% interest **annually**. How much money will Ella earn after 1 year?
Discussion How many decimal places should you round the
answer to?

Literacy hint

Annually means once a year.

11 Finance / Problem-solving
a Work out 15% of £300.
b Add your answer to part **a** to £300.
c Work out £300 × 1.15.
d What do you notice about your answers to parts **b** and **c**?
e Copy and complete.
To increase by 5%, multiply by ☐
To increase by 10%, multiply by ☐
To increase by 50%, multiply by ☐

12 Write down the multiplier for each percentage increase or decrease.

a 16% increase   b 5% increase

c 3.7% increase   d 14% decrease

e 4.9% decrease

Q12d hint

Decrease by 14% = 100% − 14%

= ☐%

13 **Finance** Jen wants to invest £800. She sees these rates offered.

Savings R Us — 4.3%

Gold Savings — 5.1%

Investor's Delight — 4.8%

Strategy hint

To calculate **simple interest** work out the interest in year 1, then add on the same amount each year after that.

Copy and complete the table to show the simple interest she would earn in each bank.

Year	Savings R Us		Gold Savings		Investor's Delight	
	Interest	Total savings	Interest	Total savings	Interest	Total savings
1						
2						
3						

Discussion What do you notice about the difference in the total amounts as the years progress?

14 **Finance** Luke buys shares for £15.26 each. They decrease in value by 3.5%. Work out the new share price.

15 **Finance** In his first year at university, Josh pays 60% of his tuition fees. He pays £4800.
How much are his total tuition fees?

16 In a '30% off' sale, Brett saved £146 on a TV.
What was the full price of the TV?

Q15 hint

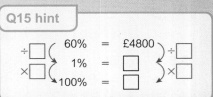

÷☐ ×☐ { 60% = £4800, 1% = ☐, 100% = ☐ } ÷☐ ×☐

Q16 hint

30% = £146

10% = ☐

100% = ☐

Investigation   Problem-solving

Emily earns £20 000 per year, Gary earns £40 000 per year and Simra earns £100 000 per year.
The Government proposes three different tax policies.
• Policy A: Everyone pays 15% on all the money they earn.
• Policy B: Everyone pays 20% on any money earned above £10 000.
• Policy C: Everyone pays 30% on any money earned above £30 000.
Which policy is the best for each person?
Which policy is the best for the Government in this case?

---

17 **Explore** How much money are you likely to make in one year if you invest £1000?
What have you learned in this lesson to help you answer this question? What other information do you need?

18 **Reflect** Write down the steps you take to use a multiplier to calculate:
• a percentage increase
• a percentage decrease.
Can you use these to write one set of steps that work for percentage increase and percentage decrease?

Explore

Reflect

6 Check up

Log how you did on your Student Progression Chart.

Ordering and rounding decimals

1 Which number is smaller, 52.4 or 52.13?

2 Write these numbers in ascending order.
6.6, 6.53, 6.05, 6.535, 6.015

3 A pack of 6 lollies costs £2.95.
How much does each lolly cost to the nearest penny?

 4 Work out 2 ÷ 7. Give your answer to 2 decimal places.

5 Write these numbers in descending order.
–2.1, –2.43, –2.03, –2.203, –2.5

Add and subtract decimals

6 Work out
   a 5.4 + 7.9   b 3.19 + 8.7   c 10.7 – 3.8
   d 4.8 – 2.93   e 100 – 39.2

7 Adam has £273.20. He pays a bill of £65.85.
Approximately how much money does he have left?
Show how you work out your estimate.

8 A carpenter has a piece of wood measuring 1.8 m.
He cuts a piece 0.95 m long.
How long is the remaining piece?

Multiply and divide decimals

9 A crate of vegetables weighs 1.352 kg.
Estimate how much 7 crates weigh.

10 Work out
   a 5.3 × 7   b 69.2 ÷ 4   c 8 × 9.13

11 Work out
   a 46 × 0.2   b 0.9 × 0.9
   c 0.04 × 0.7   d 0.03 × 0.06

12 Work out
   a 180 ÷ 0.06   b 0.9 ÷ 0.3
   c 0.4 ÷ 0.01   d 0.06 ÷ 0.2

13 0.92 × 14 = 12.88
Use this fact to work these out. Check your answers using an approximate calculation.
   a 9.2 × 14   b 0.92 × 140   c 0.092 × 1.4

Fractions, decimals and percentages

14 Copy and complete this table. Write fractions in their simplest form.

Fraction	$\frac{1}{4}$		$\frac{1}{3}$			
Decimal		0.75			0.7	1.8
Percentage				66.$\dot{6}$%		

15 Will asks 25 people whether they own a tablet. 7 people say yes.
   a What fraction of people say yes?
   b What percentage of people say yes?

16 A supermarket currently sells 9000 different products.
   They increase this by 30%.
   a How many extra products do they now sell?
   b What is the total number of products they now sell?

17 Write these in ascending order.
   25%, $\frac{2}{5}$, 0.04, 44%, $\frac{3}{8}$, 38%

18 Copy and complete this table. Write fractions in their simplest form.

Fraction	Decimal	Percentage
$\frac{13}{40}$		
	0.245	
		17.5%

19 A course of swimming lessons costs £80. There is a 15% discount for paying in advance. Work out the price for paying in advance.

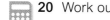 **20** Work out 3.2% of £128.40. Round your answer to the nearest penny.

21 The cost of entry to a theme park is reduced by 30%.
   The new price is £5.70 less. What was the original price?

22 **How sure are you of your answers? Were you mostly**
   😣 **Just guessing**   😐 **Feeling doubtful**   🙂 **Confident**
   What next? Use your results to decide whether to strengthen or extend your learning.

Challenge

23 You start with £100. You have these 6 percentage cards.

| 10% increase | 20% increase | 25% increase |
| 10% decrease | 20% decrease | 25% decrease |

   a Which of these percentage calculations return you to your starting value?
      i A 10% increase followed by a 10% decrease
      ii A 25% increase followed by a 20% decrease
      iii A 25% decrease followed by a 20% increase
   b Which 2 cards would you use if you wanted to end with:
      i £99   **ii** £112.50   **iii** £96?
   c What is the smallest amount you could end with after using 2 cards?
   d What is the largest amount you could end with after using 2 cards?

Handwritten notes:
10% decrease × 25% increase
1.2 × 0.8   0.8 × 0.75
1 × 1.1 × 0.9 = 0.99
1 × 1.25 × 0.8 = 1
1 × 0.75 × 0.2 = 0.9

6 Strengthen

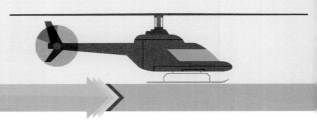

You will:
- Strengthen your understanding with practice.

Ordering and rounding decimals

1 a Copy this number line. Mark on the line the number 1.33.

1.3   1.4

b Which is larger, 1.4 or 1.33?

c Which is smaller, 1.4 or 1.39?

2 Write these numbers in order from smallest to largest.

a 7.2, 6.3, 6.5, 7.4

b 4.6, 4.06, 4.4, 4.44, 4.5

c 0.04, 0.33, 0.004, 0.404, 0.033

3 Which of these numbers are rounded to 2 decimal places?

2.471   12.6   9.34   0.01   102.8

4 Round each number to 2 decimal places.

a 0.354

b 0.3654

c 0.3449

5 Poppy works out £3.96 ÷ 5 = £0.792.
Write her answer to the nearest penny.

6 Work out to the nearest penny.

a £5.80 ÷ 7

b £35 ÷ 3

Add and subtract decimals

1 Work out these. Use an estimate to check your answers.

a 15 − 1.3

b 100 − 6.4

c 200 − 102.1

2 Work out these. Use an estimate to check your answers.

a 3.5 + 6.8

b 4.7 + 2.5

c 9.4 + 4.63

d 3.1 + 7.92

e 19.2 − 6.7

f 6.03 − 4.8

Q2c hint

Use a number line to help you.

Q3 hint

Which numbers have 2 digits after the decimal point?

Q4a hint

Use the number line to help you.
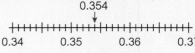
0.34   0.35   0.36   0.37
0.354
Is 0.354 closer to 0.35 or 0.36?

Q5 hint

£□.□□

Q1a hint

First subtract the whole number.
Then subtract the decimal.

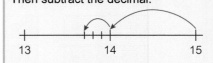

13   14   15

Q2a hint

```
    3 . 5
  + 6 . 8
  ─────────
   □ . 3
      1
```

Q2c hint

Line up the decimal points.

3 Work out these. Use an estimate to check your answers.

   a 1.6 − 0.43

   b 12.9 − 5.32

   c 2.4 − 0.982

4 Sammy is 0.85 m tall. His dad is 1.7 m tall. Work out the difference in their heights.

Q3a hint

   1 . $\overset{5}{\cancel{6}}\overset{1}{0}$ ←——— Write a zero
− 0 . 4 3   to make the
□ . □□   calculation easier.

Multiply and divide decimals

1 Work out these multiplications.
Use an estimate to check your answers.

   a 4.3 × 2

   b 12.3 × 8

   c 10.92 × 3

Q1a hint

Use a number pattern.
43 × 2 = 86, 4.3 × 2 = □

2 Copy and complete these number patterns.

   a 4 × 30 = 120   4 × 3 = 12   4 × 0.3 = 1.2   4 × 0.03 = □

   b 7 × 60 = 420   7 × 6 = □   7 × 0.6 = □   7 × 0.06 = □

3 Use a mental method and the multiplication facts you know to work out

   a 7 × 0.2

   b 40 × 0.2

   c 0.09 × 5

   d 60 × 0.03

Q3a hint

Use a number pattern.
7 × 2 = 14, 7 × 0.2 = □

4 Work out

   a 0.6 × 0.6

   b 0.08 × 0.6

   c 0.05 × 0.04

Q4a hint

Use a number pattern.
6 × 6 = 36, 6 × 0.6 = □,
0.6 × 0.6 = □

5 Work out

   a 1.4 × 0.23

   b 0.81 × 2.5

   c 0.28 × 1.43

Q5a hint

Use a pattern to work out 1.4 × 0.23

     1 4
  × 2 3
  ‾‾‾‾

6 Copy and complete these number patterns.

   a 300 ÷ 5 = 60   30 ÷ 5 = 6   3 ÷ 5 = 0.6   0.3 ÷ 5 = □

   b 738 ÷ 6 = 123   73.8 ÷ 6 = 12.3   7.38 ÷ 6 = □

7 Work out

   a 41.5 ÷ 5

   b 65.7 ÷ 9

   c 21.08 ÷ 4

Q7a hint

5)‾4‾1‾5‾

415 ÷ 5 = □
41.5 ÷ 5 = □

8 Work out

   a 6 ÷ 0.3

   b 36 ÷ 0.4

   c 82 ÷ 0.02

Q8a hint

Use a number pattern.
6 ÷ 3, 6 ÷ 0.3

9 Work out

   a 0.9 ÷ 0.03

   b 0.08 ÷ 0.02

   c 0.15 ÷ 0.2

   d 0.04 ÷ 0.2

Q9a hint

Use a number pattern.
9 ÷ 3, 0.9 ÷ 3, 0.9 ÷ 0.3, 0.9 ÷ 0.03

Fractions, decimals and percentages

1 Copy and complete these number lines showing percentages, decimals and fractions. Write each fraction in its simplest form.

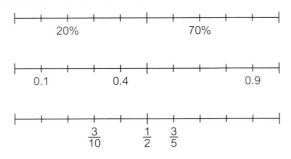

Q1 hint

First complete the percentages number line, then the decimals, then the fractions. Write the fractions as tenths and simplify.

2 Match the equivalent cards.

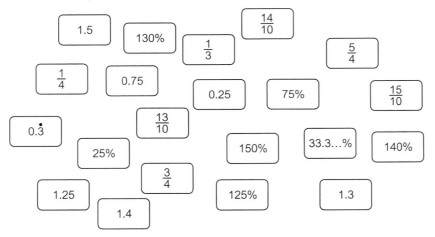

3 Write these decimals as percentages.

  a 0.24

  b 1.98

  c 1.345

Q3a hint

To convert a decimal to a percentage multiply by 100.

4 Write these percentages as decimals.

  a 27%

  b 85.5%

  c 132%

Q4 hint

To convert a percentage to a decimal divide by 100.

Q5 hint

H	T	U	.	$\frac{1}{10}$	$\frac{1}{100}$	$\frac{1}{1000}$
		0	.	2	4	

$0.24 = \frac{24}{100} = \frac{\square}{50} = \frac{\square}{25}$

5 Change each decimal in Q3 into a fraction in its simplest form.

6 Change each percentage in Q4 into a fraction in its simplest form.

Q6 hint

Convert the percentage to a decimal first.

7 a Write these in ascending order.

  i $\frac{3}{10}$, 23%, $\frac{4}{5}$, 0.45, 40%, 0.79

  ii $\frac{7}{20}$, 75%, 0.72, 0.6, $\frac{2}{5}$, 27%

  b Write these in descending order.

    $\frac{4}{5}$, 90%, 0.08, $\frac{3}{25}$, $\frac{3}{10}$, 9%

Q7 Literacy hint

Ascending means smallest → largest
Descending means largest → smallest

Q7a hint

Convert them to decimals first.

8 Convert these fractions to percentages.
  a $\frac{3}{8}$
  b $\frac{7}{40}$
  c $\frac{8}{25}$

Q8 hint

Fraction	→	decimal	→	percentage
$\frac{1}{8}$	→	$1 \div 8 = 0.125$	→	12.5%

9 Work out 1% of
  a 30
  b 150
  c 75

Q9a hint

$1\% = \frac{1}{100}$

$\frac{1}{100} \times 30 = 30 \div 100 = \square$

10 Work out
  a 12% of 60
  b 48% of 80
  c 71% of 120

Q10a hint

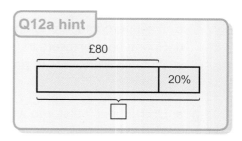

 11 Work out
  a 37% of 79
  b 24% of £60
  c 81% of 500 km

12 **a** Increase £80 by 20%.
  b Increase 48 kg by 30%.
  c Decrease 60 m by 25%.
  d Decrease 300 students by 5%.

Q12a hint

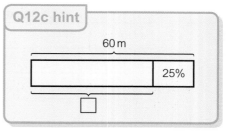

 13 **a** Increase 82 m*l* by 57%.
  b Decrease 105 m by 13%.

14 Use the information given to work out the value of 100%.
  a 25% = 45
  b 80% = 72
  c 150% = 60

Q12c hint

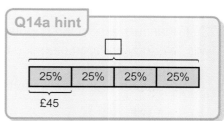

Enrichment

1 The value of shares can increase or decrease.
  a Copy and complete the table showing the share price of a
  company over a 5-year period.

Year	Value at start of year	Percentage change	Value at end of year
1	£50	30% increase	£50 × 1.3 = £65
2	£65	20% decrease	
3		20% decrease	
4		10% increase	
5		5% increase	

  b What can you say about the share price over the 5-year period?

Q14a hint

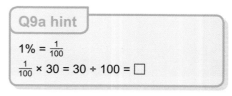

2 **Reflect** This lesson used number lines to help solve problems with
  decimals.
  Did the numbers lines help you? Explain why or why not.
  Would you use number lines to help you solve mathematics problems
  in future? Explain why or why not.

Reflect

6 Extend

You will:
- Extend your understanding with problem-solving.

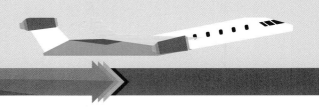

1 **a** Write a formula to convert percentages to decimals.
   b Write a formula to convert decimals to percentages.

 2 **Problem-solving** On an activity week each student selected one activity.
   a How many students took part in the activity week?
   b What percentage of students chose to build a campfire?
   c What percentage of students chose beach walk or crazy golf?
   d Round your answers to parts **b** and **c** to 1 decimal place.
   e Write your answers to parts **b** and **c** as a recurring decimal.

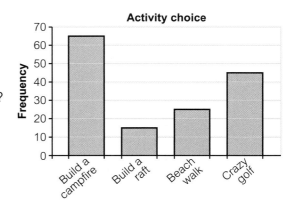

3 **a** Use your calculator to work out these.
   Then round your answer to 2 decimal places.

	Full calculator display	Rounded to 2 decimal places
$\sqrt{2}$		
$\sqrt{3}$		
$\sqrt{5}$		
$\sqrt{6}$		

   b Why was $\sqrt{4}$ not included in this table?

 4 Planners expect the population of a town to grow by 20% every 10 years.
   a Copy and complete the table to show the population at the end of each **decade**.
   Round your answers to the nearest whole number.

> **Q4 Literacy hint**
> **Decade** = 10 years

Year	2010	2020	2030	2040	2050	2060	2070
Population (thousands)	10	12					

   b Plot this data on a graph with 'Year' on the horizontal axis and 'Population (thousands)' on the vertical axis.
   Plot your points and join them with a smooth curve.
   c Use your graph to estimate the population in 2045.
   d Describe what happens to the population between 2010 and 2070.

5 **Problem-solving** **a** Find two possible original numbers.

Original number	Rounded to 1 d.p.	Rounded to nearest whole number
	6.5	6
	6.5	7

   b Compare your answers with someone else in your class.
   Are you both correct?

6 Problem-solving Here are Carl Lewis's reaction times and race times for the 100 m sprint.

Race	Reaction time (seconds)	Race time (seconds)
1987 (Rome)	0.193	9.93
1988 (Seoul)	0.136	9.92
1991 (Tokyo)	0.140	9.86

Using this rule, Actual time = Race time – Reaction time, which was Carl Lewis's fastest race?

7 An acute angle is increased by 20%. The new angle is obtuse. Write a possible size for the acute angle.

Q7 hint

Try some different acute angles.

8 This wooden door expands 3% in the damp weather. Will it still close in the doorway?

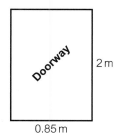
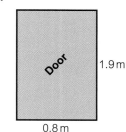

2 m

1.9 m

0.85 m   0.8 m

9 Jenny jogs 2 km in 30 minutes. After 6 weeks' training, she has reduced her time by 30%.
How long does she take to jog 2 km now?

10 Copy and complete this number pattern.
a 588.8 ÷ 92 = 6.4
588.8 ÷ 9.2 = 64
588.8 ÷ 0.92 =
588.8 ÷ 0.092 =
588.8 ÷ 0.0092 =
b Work out 58.88 ÷ 9.2. Use estimates to check your answer.

11 4.4 × 63 = 277.2
Use this number fact to work out these.
Check your answers using estimates.
a 0.44 × 63   **b** 0.44 × 6.3
c 0.0044 × 630   **d** 277.2 ÷ 63
e 277.2 ÷ 6.3   **f** 27.72 ÷ 6.3

12 Sam converts some fractions to decimals.
$\frac{28}{99} = 0.\dot{2}\dot{8}$ $\frac{29}{99} = 0.\dot{2}\dot{9}$

Use this information to write these fractions as recurring decimals.
a $\frac{30}{99}$ **b** $\frac{1}{99}$
c $\frac{100}{99}$ **d** $\frac{33}{99}$
e What decimal is equivalent to $\frac{33}{99}$?
f Write $\frac{234}{999}$ as a recurring decimal. Check your answer using a calculator.

13 **Finance** Faith is quoted £836.47 for 1 year's car insurance.
   a How much does this cost per month?
   b How much does this cost per quarter (4 equal payments)?
   She is offered a 5% discount for paying all at once.
   c How much will she save by choosing this option?
   d How much will she pay if she chooses this option?

14 In an archery competition Tara scores 8, 3, 5, 9, 4 and 8.
   a Work out her mean score. Write down all the numbers on your calculator display.
   b Write down her mean score correct to 2 decimal places.
   c Write down her mean score as a recurring decimal.

15 Work out
   a $0.75 - 0.2 \times 0.4$
   b $5 \times (1 - 0.3)$
   c $0.2 \times 0.6 + 0.9 \times 0.4$
   d $0.6 - 0.4^2$

> **Q15 hint**
>
> Remember the priority of operations.

16 Let $x = 0.2$, $y = 0.3$ and $z = -0.4$. Work out
   a xy
   b $y - z$
   c z^2
   d $3x^2 + y$
   e Jose says, '$xyz = -0.24$, because $2 \times 3 \times -4 = -24$.'
   Explain why Jose is wrong. What is the correct answer?

17 **Finance** Ankit invested £600. He earned 5% simple interest per year.
   a How much money will Ankit have after 1 year?
   b How much money will Ankit have after 51 months?

> **Q17b hint**
>
> First write 51 months in years and months.
> Then convert this to a decimal number of years.

18 **Finance / Problem-solving** Simra invested £180. She earned simple interest over 5 years. At the end of 5 years, her investment was worth £225. It increased by the same amount every year. What interest rate did she receive?

19 **Finance / Problem-solving** Brian invests £300 in an account that pays 4.35% simple interest per year.
   a How much money will he have after the first year?
   b How much money will he have after 5 years?
   c Most banks pay **compound interest**. Copy and complete this table to show how much money Brian will have after 5 years of compound interest.

> **Q19 Literacy hint**
>
> In **compound interest** the interest earned in the first year is added and then earns interest in the next year.

Year	Money at start of year	Interest rate	Money at end of year
1	£300	4.35%	£300 × 1.0435 = £313.05
2	£313.05	4.35%	£313.05 × 1.0435 =
3		4.35%	
4		4.35%	
5		4.35%	

> **Q19c Strategy hint**
>
> Keep the exact answer in your calculator.
> Write down the amount to the nearest penny.

Discussion Compare the final amount after 5 years with simple interest and with compound interest. What do you notice?

20 Write these in ascending order.

0.3%, $\frac{7}{90}$, 4.51%, 0.79, 7.7%, $\frac{9}{200}$

21 The bar chart shows the percentage of adults in a country who are illiterate.

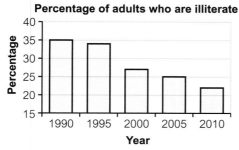

Percentage of adults who are illiterate

a In 1990 there were about 20 000 000 adults. About how many were illiterate?

b Between 1990 and 2010, the adult population increased by 27%. What was the adult population in 2010?

c About how many adults were illiterate in 2010?

d How many fewer adults were illiterate in 2010 than in 1990?

e What was the percentage decrease in adults who were illiterate between 1990 and 2010?

Discussion The country received a large fund from the UN during this time period. In what year does the data suggest they received the money? Explain your answer.

Q21e hint

$$\text{Percentage decrease} = \frac{\text{actual decrease}}{\text{original value}} \times 100$$

22 Work out

a 7.4 × 0.63   **b** 0.92 × 1.9   **c** 0.37 × 1.64

23 **Reasoning**

a Write < or > between each pair of numbers.

i 0.8 ☐ 0.4   **ii** −0.8 ☐ −0.4

b Repeat with these two pairs of numbers.

i 0.35 ☐ 0.42   **ii** −0.35 ☐ −0.42

Discussion Will this always happen? Explain your answer.

24 **Problem-solving** Harvey gets the answer 9.7 correct to 1 decimal place. Write down all the 2 decimal place numbers that round to 9.7.

25 **Problem-solving** John is thinking of a number. Write down a possible value for John's number at each step.

a His number has 3 digits after the decimal point.

b His number rounds to 10 to the nearest whole number.

c His number rounds to 10.2 to the nearest tenth.

d His number rounds to 10.25 to the nearest hundredth.

Q24 hint

Use the number line to help you.

9.6   9.7   9.8

26 **Reflect** Write a definition of a decimal, in your own words. Be as accurate as you can.

Remember to explain decimal **notation** in your definition.

Check your definition against some of the decimal numbers in this unit. Does your definition fully describe them?

Q26 Literacy hint

Mathematical **notation** means the symbols used in maths.

For example, the notation = means 'equals' and the symbol < means 'less than'.

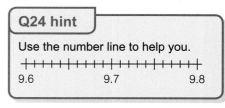

Reflect

6 Unit test

Log how you did on your Student Progression Chart.

1 **a** Work out 10% of 84.

   b Work out 1% of 84.

   c Use your answers to parts **a** and **b** to work out 29% of 84.

2 John has a piece of wood 2.4 m long. He cuts off a piece 0.84 m long. How long is the remaining piece?

3 Copy and complete this table of fractions, decimals and percentages. Write all fractions in their simplest form.

Fraction	$\frac{3}{10}$			$1\frac{1}{3}$		
Decimal			0.25		1.2	
Percentage		40%				175%

4 A figure skater scores 74.92 in her first skate and 144.19 in her second skate. What is her total score?

5 There are 20 questions in a test. Faye answers 17 correctly.

   a What fraction of questions does Faye answer correctly?

   b What percentage of questions does Faye answer correctly?

6 Use the fact that $27 \times 1.09 = 29.43$ to work out

   a 2.7×1.09

   b 2.7×109

   c $29.43 \div 2.7$

7 Write these decimals in ascending order.
   5.78, 5.08, 5.8, 5.287, 5.078

8 Round 4.389 to 2 decimal places.

9 Colin says, '4.997 rounded to 2 decimal places is 5.'
   Is Colin correct? Explain your answer.

10 John's salary is £375 per week. He pays 20% of that money in tax.

   a How much money does John pay in taxes?

   b How much does he keep each week?

11 Work out

   a 7×0.4

   b 0.06×50

   c $400 \div 0.02$

   d $0.48 \div 0.06$

12 The same pool table is on sale in two different shops.

Pool Table World
Price: Pay £70 today
Then 8 monthly payments
of £60

Sporting Store
15% off original
price of £650

   a What is the cost of the pool table in Pool Table World?
   b What is the cost of the pool table in the Sporting Store?

13 20% of an amount is 3.2. Work out the original amount.

14 Work out
   a 0.14 × 0.87
   b 0.52 × 6.57
   c 0.36 × 5.24

15 Lara invested £500. She earned 4% simple interest per year.
   a How much money will Lara have after 1 year?
   b How much money will Lara have after 45 months?

16 Write < or > for each pair of numbers.
   a −6.9 ☐ −6.85   **b** −7.02 ☐ −7.2

Challenge

17 Work out the missing digits in each of these.

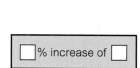

   a
```
  4 [Ø] . 8 3
- 2 5 . [9] 4
 ─────────────
  [1] 6 . 8 9
```
   b
```
  7 [3] . 6
- [5] 6 . 5 4
 ─────────────
  1 7 . [Ø] 6
```

18 Write some possible percentages that would give an answer of £24.

☐% of ☐

☐% of ☐

£24

☐% increase of ☐

☐% decrease of ☐

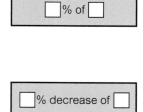

10% of 240
50% of 48
20% of 120

19 Reflect Put these topics in order, from easiest to hardest.
(You could just write the letters.)
   A Writing decimals in order
   B Rounding decimals
   C Multiplying and dividing decimals
   D Adding and subtracting decimals
   E Converting between fractions, decimals and percentages
   F Finding percentages of amounts
   G Increasing by a percentage
   H Decreasing by a percentage

Think about the two topics you said were hardest.
What made them hard?
Write at least one hint to help you for each topic.

7.1 Solving one-step equations

You will learn to:
- Write and solve simple equations
- Solve problems using equations.

Why learn this?
Police collision investigators use an equation to work out the speed a car was travelling before it crashed. The equation uses the length of skid and the final position of the car.

Fluency
Work out
- $3 + -6$
- $-5 + 2$
- -2×7
- $12 \div -6$

Explore
How far can a car travel in 10 seconds?

Exercise 7.1

1 When $x = 6$ and $y = 3$, what is

  a $x - y$ **b** $3x$ **c** $2y$

  d $\dfrac{x}{y}$ **e** $\dfrac{2y}{x}$ **f** xy

2 Jack is 3 years older than Adele. Write an expression for Jack's age when Adele is x years old.

3 Write an expression for the cost of 5 cinema tickets at £y each.

> **Key point**
>
> A **function** is a rule.
> The function +3 adds 3 to a number.
> The **inverse function** is −3, because it reverses the effect of the function +3.
>
> $2 \rightarrow \boxed{+3} \rightarrow 5$
>
> $2 \leftarrow \boxed{-3} \leftarrow 5$

4 Work out the outputs for each **function** machine.

  a input   output

    $0 \rightarrow$
    $1 \rightarrow \boxed{+6}$
    $2 \rightarrow$
    $3 \rightarrow$

  b input   output

    $0 \rightarrow$
    $1 \rightarrow \boxed{\times 5}$
    $2 \rightarrow$
    $3 \rightarrow$

5 Use the **inverse function** to find each missing input.

  a $\square \rightarrow \boxed{\times 2} \rightarrow 16$

    $\leftarrow \boxed{} \leftarrow 16$

  b $\square \rightarrow \boxed{\div 5} \rightarrow 4$

    $\leftarrow \boxed{} \leftarrow 4$

  c $\square \rightarrow \boxed{-8} \rightarrow 12$

    $\leftarrow \boxed{} \leftarrow 12$

Topic links: Negative numbers, Angles in a right angle and on a straight line

Subject links: Science (Q9, Q16)

CONFIDENCE

Warm up

6 Copy and complete the function machines to solve these **equations**.

a $x - 6 = 4$

$$x \rightarrow \boxed{-6} \rightarrow 4$$
$$\square \leftarrow \big(\quad \big) \leftarrow 4$$
$$x = \square$$

b $4x = 12$

$$x \rightarrow \boxed{\times 4} \rightarrow 12$$
$$\square \leftarrow \big(\quad \big) \leftarrow 12$$
$$x = \square$$

c $\dfrac{x}{3} = 7$

$$x \rightarrow \boxed{\div 3} \rightarrow 7$$
$$\square \leftarrow \big(\quad \big) \leftarrow 7$$
$$x = \square$$

d $x + 11 = 8$

$$x \rightarrow \boxed{+11} \rightarrow 8$$
$$\square \leftarrow \big(\quad \big) \leftarrow 8$$
$$x = \square$$

7 Draw function machines to solve these equations.

a $3x = 18$ **b** $n + 15 = 21$ **c** $\dfrac{m}{5} = 2$ **d** $p - 0.7 = 2.1$

Discussion Do you always need to draw a function machine to solve an equation?

Worked example

Solve the equation $x + 5 = 12$

$x + 5 - 5 = 12 - 5$

$x = 7$

Check: $7 + 5 = 12$ ✓

Visualise the function machines to decide which inverse to use.

$$x \rightarrow \boxed{+5} \rightarrow 12$$
$$\square \leftarrow \big(-5 \big) \leftarrow 12$$

Check by replacing x in the equation with your solution.

Balance the equation by subtracting 5 from each side.

8 Solve these equations.

a $z + 15 = 27$ **b** $4x = 36$ **c** $\dfrac{y}{7} = 3$

d $1.2 + c = 4.6$ **e** $3a = 2.7$ **f** $\dfrac{k}{0.5} = 6$

g $x + 5 = 1$ **h** $7 + y = -10$ **i** $-5n = 15$

j $3p = 0$ **k** $-2 + x = -3$ **l** $-x = 7$

9 STEM Substitute the values given into each formula.
Solve the equation to find the unknown value.

a $x - 2 = e$ Find x when $e = 9$

b $\dfrac{m}{4} = d$ Work out m when $d = 2$

c $6t = u$ Work out t when $u = 30$

d $d = \dfrac{m}{v}$ Work out m when $d = 7$ and $v = 2$

e $V = IR$ Find R when $V = 6$ and $I = 3$

f $s = \dfrac{d}{t}$ Find d when $s = 4$ and $t = 10$

Discussion What is the difference between an equation and a formula?

Key point

An **equation** contains an **unknown** number (a letter) and an '=' sign. To solve an equation means to work out the value of the unknown number.

Q7 hint

You can use any letter to stand for an unknown value.

Key point

In an equation, the expressions on both sides of the equals sign have the same value. You can visualise them on balanced scales.

$$\underline{\; x + 3 \;} \quad = \quad \underline{\; 8 \;}$$

To stay balanced, do the same operation to both sides.

$$\underline{\; x + 3 - 3 \;} \quad = \quad \underline{\; 8 - 3 \;}$$

This is called the **balancing method**.

Q8 hint

Remember to check each solution.

Q8l hint

$-x = -1x$

10 Real / Modelling An online retailer adds £3 post and packing to each order.

   a Write a formula for the total cost C for an order of £x.

   b Work out the value of the order £x when the total cost is £36.50.

Q10a hint

$C = \square + \square$

11 Modelling

   a Write an equation for these three angles.

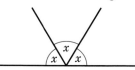

   b Solve your equation to find the value of x.

Q11a hint

What do the angles on a straight line add up to?

12 Modelling

   a Work out the value of m.

   b Work out the sizes of the three angles.

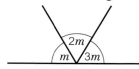

Q12a Strategy hint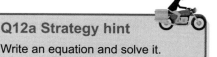

Write an equation and solve it.

13 Modelling

   a Use the formula $S = 180°(n - 2)$ to work out the sum of the interior anges of a pentagon.

   b Work out the size of the missing angles.

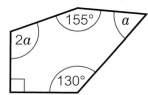

14 Problem-solving / Modelling One week Craig spent 12 hours on his PlayStation.

   He spent the same length of time each weekday, and twice as much each day at the weekend.

   How long did he spend on his PlayStation on Saturday?

   Give your answer in hours and minutes.

Q14 hint

Use n to stand for the number of hours each weekday.

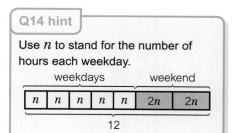

15 Problem-solving / Modelling Tickets for 2 adults and 3 children at the zoo come to £28. An adult ticket costs twice as much as a child ticket.

   Work out the price of an adult ticket. $4x + 3x$

16 Explore How far can a car travel in 10 seconds?

   Is it easier to explore this question now you have completed the lesson? What further information do you need to be able to answer this?

17 Reflect Write down the steps you take to solve equations like the ones in this lesson.

   Beside each step, show if you found that step OK (☺) or difficult (☹).

   Ask a friend or your teacher to help you with any difficult steps.

Q17 hint

Look at the equations you solved for Q6, 7 and 8.

7.2 Solving two-step equations

You will learn to:
- Write and solve two-step equations
- Write and solve equations that have brackets.

Why learn this?
By writing and solving equations, John Couch Adams and Urbain Le Verrier both, independently, calculated the position of Neptune, which was first seen by telescope in 1846.

Fluency
$t = 5$
Work out
- $3t$
- $4t + 3$
- $3(t + 1)$
- t^2
- $2t^2$

Explore
Is there a polygon whose angles add up to $3000°$?

Exercise 7.2

1 Solve these equations.

a $y - 8 = 6$ **b** $\dfrac{a}{4} = -2$ **c** $-x = 3$

2 Expand the brackets.

a $2(x + 4)$ **b** $3(y - 2)$ **c** $5(3 - z)$

3 Work out the outputs for these two-step function machines.

a input ... output
1 →, 3 →, 5 → [×2] → [+4] →

b input ... output
3 →, 9 →, 12 → [÷3] → [−1] →

Discussion Does it matter which function you use first?

4 Use inverse function machines to find the value of the input of each two-step function machine.

a $x →$ [×2] → [−3] → 7
□ ← ( ) ← (+3) ← 7
$x = □$

b $y →$ [÷2] → [+4] → 9
□ ← ( ) ← ( ) ← 9
$y = □$

c $z →$ [×5] → [+2] → 32

d $m →$ [÷4] → [−1] → −6

Discussion How could you write these as equations?

5 Draw function machines to solve each equation.

a $2x + 3 = 11$ **b** $3y - 4 = 17$ **c** $\dfrac{r}{2} - 1 = -4$

Discussion What do you notice about the order of the operations in the function machine and the order in the inverse function machine?

Warm up

Worked example

Solve $4x + 7 = 27$

$4x + 7 - 7 = 27 - 7$ ← Balance the equation by subtracting 7 from each side.

$4x = 20$

$x = 5$ ← Balance again by dividing both sides by 4.

Check: $4 \times 5 + 7 = 27$ ✓ ← Check by replacing x in the equation with your solution.

Visualise the function machines to decide which inverses to use.

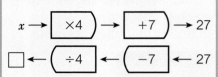

6 Solve these equations.

a $2x + 11 = 19$ b $3x - 2 = 10$ c $8 + 4x = 16$

d $12 + 2x = 24$ e $\frac{x}{3} - 2 = 2$ f $\frac{9x}{2} = 36$

g $\frac{5x}{4} = 10$ h $2(x - 1) = 8$ i $\frac{x + 5}{2} = 4$

Q6f hint

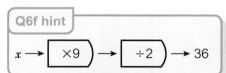

Q6h hint

Expand the brackets first.

Investigation

Reasoning

Here are two ways of solving the equation $6(x + 2) = 30$

Method 1

Balancing the equation by dividing both sides by 6:

$6(x + 2) = 30$

$x + 2 = \frac{30}{6}$

$x + 2 = 5$

$x = 3$

Method 1 hint

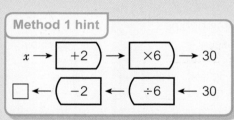

Method 2

Expanding the brackets, then balancing:

$6(x + 2) = 30$

$6x + 12 = 30$

$6x = 30 - 12$

$6x = 18$

$x = 3$

1 Use both methods to solve $4(x + 5) = 28$.
   Which method do you prefer? Why?

2 Which method would you use to solve $2(x - 3) = 7$? Explain why.

Discussion When is it easiest to expand the brackets first?

---

7 STEM Substitute the values given into each formula. Solve the equation to find the unknown value.

a $P = 2v + r$ Find v when $r = 6$ and $P = 28$

b $y = mx + c$ Work out x when $y = 11$, $m = 3$ and $c = -1$

c $D = \frac{w}{8} + v$ Work out w when $v = 5$ and $D = 15$

d $A = \frac{(a + b)h}{2}$ Work out h when $a = 3$, $b = 4$ and $A = 10.5$

e $v = u + at$ Find a when $u = 0$, $t = 10$ and $v = 45$

f $s = ut + \frac{1}{2}at^2$ Work out u when $t = 2$, $a = 10$ and $s = 30$

8 Solve

a $-3x + 5 = -7$ b $8 - x = -2$ c $\frac{-x}{5} + 11 = 7$

Q8b hint

Addition can be done in any order.
You could rewrite this as $-x + 8 = -2$

Subject links: Science (Q7)

9 **Modelling** Pia says, 'I think of a number, multiply it by 6 and add 3. My answer is 21.'

    a Write an equation to show Pia's calculation. Use n for the number she thinks of.

    b Solve your equation to find Pia's number.

10 **Modelling** Write and solve equations for these 'think of a number' problems.

    a I think of a number, divide it by 4 and subtract 10. My answer is 1.

    b I think of a number, add 7 and multiply by 6. My answer is 54.

    c I think of a number, double it and add 12. My answer is 42.

    d I think of a number, subtract 3 and then halve it. My answer is 5.

11 **Modelling** **a** Use the formula $S = 180°(n - 2)$ to work out the number of sides of a polygon with angle sum 1980°.

    b Work out the exterior angle of a regular nonagon.

    c Write a formula to work out the exterior angle of a regular n-sided polygon.

    d Use your formula from part **c** to work out the number of sides of a regular polygon with exterior angle 18°.

> **Q11c hint**
>
> $E = \square$

12 **Modelling** Work out the value of each letter.

    a 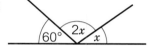   **b**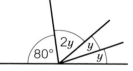

> **Q13c hint**
>
> What do you know about the blue angle?

13 **Modelling** Work out the sizes of the angles.

    a    **b** 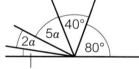   **c**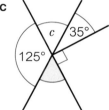

14 **Modelling / Real** Theatre tickets for 2 adults and 1 senior citizen cost a total of £31. A senior citizen ticket is £5 less than an adult ticket.

    a Write an equation for the cost of the tickets.

    b Work out the cost of an adult ticket.

> **Q14a hint**
>
> An adult ticket costs £x. Write an expression for the cost of a senior citizen ticket.

15 **Explore** Is there a polygon whose angles add up to 3000°? Look back at the maths you have learned in this lesson. How can you use it to answer this question?

16 **Reflect** Look back at the steps you wrote down for solving equations at the end of lesson 7.1.
In this lesson you have solved more complex equations.
Choose an equation from this lesson.
Do the steps solving equations that you wrote at the end of lesson 7.1 work for this equation too? If not, rewrite your steps.
Check that they work for another equation from this lesson.

Explore

Reflect

7.3 More complex equations

You will learn to:
- Write and solve equations with letters on both sides.

Why learn this?
To work out the path for the Rosetta spacecraft to intercept a comet in August 2014, NASA scientists wrote and solved equations for the motion of both objects.

Fluency
Find the angles marked with letters.

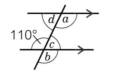

Explore
When do two expressions have the same value?

Exercise 7.3

1 Write an expression for each 'think of a number' problem.

  a I think of a number and add 5.

  b I think of a number, double it and add 10.

  c I think of a number, add 4 and multiply by 7.

> **Q1 hint**
> Use n for the number each time.

2 Solve these equations.

  a $5x - 2 = 18$ **b** $3 + 6x = 21$ **c** $4x + 11 = -5$

Worked example

Solve the equation $3x - 1 = 2x + 5$

$$3x - 1 = 2x + 5$$
$$3x - 2x - 1 = 2x - 2x + 5$$
$$x - 1 = 5$$
$$x - 1 + 1 = 5 + 1$$
$$x = 6$$

Check: $3 \times 6 - 1 = 17$
$$2 \times 6 + 5 = 17 ✓$$

> You need to end up with $x = \square$, so start by subtracting $2x$ from both sides, which leaves an x term on the left-hand side and no x term on the right.

> Simplify.

> Add 1 to both sides.

> Substitute $x = 6$ into both sides to check they have the same value.

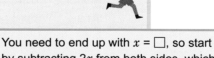

3 Solve these equations.

  a $3x - 2 = 2x + 1$ **b** $8x - 10 = 6x$

  c $5y - 3 = 2y + 18$ **d** $6m + 11 = 5m + 8$

  e $3(x - 4) = 2x$ **f** $8(x - 3) = 7x - 13$

  g $5(x + 4) = 4(x + 7)$ **h** $7(m - 5) = 2(m + 5)$

  i $4(r + 3) = 2(r + 9)$

> **Q3 hint**
> Remember to check your solutions.

> **Q3e hint**
> Expand the brackets first.

Topic links: Angles in parallel lines

4 Modelling Solange says, 'I think of a number, double it and add 4. When I start again with the same number, multiply it by 5 and subtract 20, I get the same answer.'

  a Write an expression for each of Solange's calculations.

  b Write an equation to show that both calculations give the same answer.

  c Solve your equation to find the number Solange was thinking of.

5 Reasoning Write a 'think of a number' problem like Q4 for one of the equations in Q3.

> **Key point**
>
> The **coefficient** of x is the number that is multiplying x.
> In the term $4x$, the coefficient of x is 4.

> **Investigation**   **Reasoning**
>
> Solve the equation $3x + 6 = 7x - 2$ in two ways.
>
> **1** $3x + 6 = 7x - 2$ **2** $3x + 6 = 7x - 2$
>   First subtract $7x$ from both sides   First subtract $3x$ from both sides
>
> Did you get the same answer both ways?
> Was one way easier than the other? If so, explain which one was easiest and why.
> What would you do first to solve $2x + 6 = 9x - 8$?
>
> **Discussion** How does looking at the **coefficients** of x help you to decide which step to do first?

6 Solve these equations.

  a $2x + 5 = 3x - 1$

  b $5x + 8 = 7x - 4$

  c $3(y + 6) = 5y + 12$

  d $6(x - 5) = 3(x - 2)$

  e $12(m + 3) = 10(m + 4)$

  f $5(y + 6) = 3(y + 12)$

> **Q6a hint**
>
> Subtract $2x$ from each side first, as it has the smallest coefficient of x.

> **Q7a hint**
>
> What do you know about the two angles?

7 Modelling / Problem-solving Write an equation and solve it, to find the size of each angle.

  a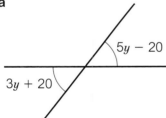

  b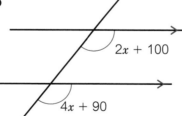

  c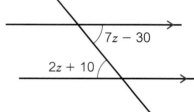

8 Reasoning / Problem-solving

  a Look at this equation: $x + 5 = y - 3$
    Which is larger, x or y? How much larger?

  b Look at this equation: $5 - r = 7 - s$
    Which of r and s is greater? By how much?

> **Q8a Strategy hint**
>
> Rearrange the equation so that one letter is 'on its own' on one side of the equals sign.

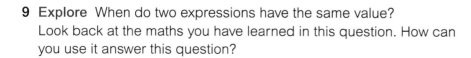

9 Explore When do two expressions have the same value? Look back at the maths you have learned in this question. How can you use it answer this question?

10 Reflect Do the steps you wrote for solving equations at the end of lesson 7.2 work for equations with an unknown (a letter) on both sides of the = sign?
If not, rewrite them.

Explore

Reflect

7.4 Trial and improvement

You will learn to:

- Solve equations that include x^2 and x^3
- Use trial and improvement to find solutions to 1 decimal place.

CONFIDENCE

Why learn this?
Trial and improvement is a useful method for solving equations that do not have an exact solution.

Fluency
What are the positive and negative square roots of
- 16   • 36   • 81?

What is the **cube root** of
- 8   • 64   • −27?

Explore
What is the shortest length of chicken wire needed to fence a rectangular play area?

Exercise 7.4

1 Which two numbers do these values lie between?

   a $\sqrt{45}$ **b** $\sqrt{72}$ **c** $\sqrt[3]{20}$ **d** $\sqrt[3]{-4}$

 2 a Work out the value of $x^2 + 5$ when

     i $x = 3$ **ii** $x = 2.8$

   b Work out the value of x^3 when

     i $x = 4$ **ii** $x = 3.5$

   c Work out the value of $x^2 + x$ when $x = 3.7$

3 Which is closer to 12?

   a 11.6 or 12.3   **b** 11.72 or 12.38   **c** 11.971 or 12.019

4 Solve these equations.

   a $x^2 = 25$ **b** $x^3 = 125$ **c** $5a^2 = 405$

   d $3x^2 = 300$ **e** $2x^3 = 128$ **f** $3x^3 = -81$

5 Modelling / Problem-solving

4 square tiles cover 10 000 cm² of floor.

   a Write an expression for the area of 1 tile.

   b Write an equation for the area of 4 tiles.

   c Solve your equation to find the side length of one square tile, in cm.

   Discussion Do you need to give the positive and negative solutions to the equation?

Q3a hint

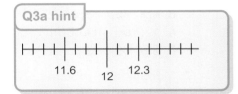

11.6   12   12.3

Q4a hint

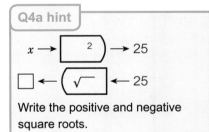

$x \rightarrow \boxed{^2} \rightarrow 25$

$\square \leftarrow \boxed{\sqrt{}} \leftarrow 25$

Write the positive and negative square roots.

Q4c hint

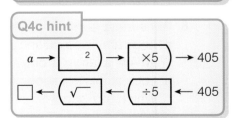

$a \rightarrow \boxed{^2} \rightarrow \boxed{\times 5} \rightarrow 405$

$\square \leftarrow \boxed{\sqrt{}} \leftarrow \boxed{\div 5} \leftarrow 405$

Investigation   Problem-solving

Find three values of n that **satisfy** this equation by trying different values of n.

$n(n - 1) =$ a multiple of 10

Work systematically and show your working in a list.
You could start with:

$1 \times 0 =$

$2 \times 1 =$

Literacy hint

A value that **satisfies** an equation makes the equation true.

    Topic links: Area

Worked example

Solve the equation $x^3 = 54$ using **trial and improvement**.
Give your answer to 1 decimal place.

Draw a table for your working.

x	x^3	Comment
3	27	too small
4	64	too big
3.5	42.875	too small
3.7	50.653	too small
3.8	54.872	too big

54 is between the cube numbers 27 (3^3) and 64 (4^3)
So $\sqrt[3]{54}$ is between 3 and 4.

3^3 ——————————————— 4^3
27   54   64

Try the value halfway between 3 and 4. Cube the value.
Decide if it is too big or too small.

The value of x lies between 3.7 and 3.8

3.8^3 (54.872) is closer to 54
than 3.7^3 (50.653)

$x = 3.8$ (to 1 decimal place)

Try another value.

Find two values to 1 decimal place
that x lies between. Decide which
gives the answer closer to 54.

Key point

To use **trial and improvement** to
solve an equation:
- Estimate a value. Try your value in
  the equation. Is your answer too
  big or too small?
- Use this to help you improve your
  estimate and try again.
- Keep improving your estimate until
  you get very close to the value.

6 Solve these equations using trial and improvement.
Give your answers to 1 decimal place.
a $x^2 = 42$
Discussion How many solutions are there to $x^2 = 42$?
b $x^3 = 39$

7 Modelling / Problem-solving A square has area 20 cm².
Work out the length of one side, to 1 decimal place.

8 Solve these equations using trial and improvement.
Give your answers to 1 decimal place.
a $x^2 + 2 = 50$
b $x^3 - 7 = 15$
c $x^2 + x = 40$
d $x^3 - x = 90$

9 Explore What is the shortest length of chicken wire needed to
fence a rectangular play area?
Choose some sensible numbers to help you explore this situation.
Then use what you've learned in this lesson to help you answer the
question.

10 Reflect Look back at the work you have done in this lesson.
How have you used estimating?
How have you used your knowledge of decimals?
What other maths topics have you used in this lesson?

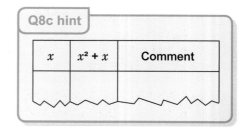

Q6a hint

6^2 ——————————————— 7^2
36   42   49

Q8c hint

x	$x^2 + x$	Comment

Explore

Reflect

Master
P159

CHECK

Strengthen
P171

Extend
P175

Test
P179

7 Check up

Log how you did on your
Student Progression Chart.

Solving equations

1 Solve these equations.

a $x - 7 = 12$

b $4 + n = 15$

c $\frac{s}{3} = 5$

d $6y = 24$

e $8m = 0$

f $-2p = 8$

2 a $V = IR$ is a formula used in science. Work out I when $V = 18$ and $R = 9$

b Use the formula $s = \frac{d}{t}$ to find the value of d when $s = 7$ and $t = 3$

3 Solve these equations.

a $3x + 5 = 17$

b $4x - 1 = 19$

c $\frac{n}{3} + 2 = 4$

d $5(m + 4) = 30$

e $4x + 15 = 3$

f $13 - 2x = 7$

4 A taxi driver uses this formula to work out the cost of a journey:

$C = 5 + 3m$

where C is the cost of a journey in £ and m is the number of miles.
A journey costs £29. Work out how many miles it was.

5 Solve the equation $2x + 5 = 3x - 3$

6 Solve $4(n + 2) = 5(n + 1)$

7 Find both solutions of these equations.

a $x^2 = 64$

b $2x^2 = 98$

8 Solve $2x^3 = 250$

Writing equations

9 a Write an equation for these angles.

b Solve your equation to find the value of a.

10 Work out

a the value of x

b the size of each angle.

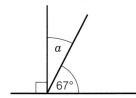

11 Work out the size of the angles.

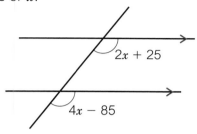

12 Find the value of x.

2x + 25

4x − 85

13 Theatre tickets for 4 adults and 7 children cost a total of £45.
An adult ticket is twice the price of a child's ticket.
a Write an equation for the cost of the tickets.
b Work out the cost of an adult ticket.

14 Zoe thinks of a number. She multiplies it by 3 and adds 4.
She gets the same answer when she adds 5 on to the number
and then multiplies by 2.
a Write an equation, using n for Zoe's number.
b Solve your equation to find Zoe's number.

Trial and improvement

15 Solve the equation $x^3 = 97$ using trial and improvement.
Give your answer to 1 decimal place.

x	x^3	Comment

16 **How sure are you of your answers? Were you mostly**
😟 **Just guessing**   😐 **Feeling doubtful**   🙂 **Confident**
**What next? Use your results to decide whether to strengthen or
extend your learning.**

Challenge

17 To write an equation with solution $x = 6$
• Write a calculation that includes 6 and work out the answer.
  $4 \times 6 + 2 = 26$
• Replace 6 with x.
  $4x + 2 = 26$
Write four more equations with solution $x = 6$.
You can use +, −, ×, ÷ and brackets.

18 Choose another value for x. Write two equations for it – one easy one
and one difficult one. Swap with a partner and solve each other's.

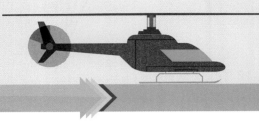

7 Strengthen

You will:

- Strengthen your understanding with practice.

Solving equations

1 Work out the value of each symbol.

a $3 + \square = 8$

b $5 \times \triangle = 30$

c $10 - \lozenge = 7$

d $\dfrac{\bigcirc}{2} = 9$

Q1 hint

Use number facts and times tables.

2 Problem-solving Which of these is the correct solution to $3x - 2 = 16$?

$x = 4$ $x = -5$ $x = 6$

Q2 hint

Substitute each value into $3x - 2$ to check.

3 Solve these equations.
Check each answer by substituting back into the equation.

a $x + 7 = 11$ **b** $m + 15 = 29$

c $28 = 12 + n$ **d** $x - 3 = 6$

e $y - 9 = 2$ **f** $13 = s - 22$

Q3a hint

Draw a bar model.
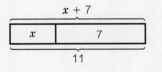

4 Solve these equations.
Check each answer by substituting back into the equation.

a $5x = 35$ **b** $6y = 48$

c $9p = 63$ **d** $36 = 4q$

e $5s = -15$ **f** $\dfrac{n}{4} = 10$

g $4 = \dfrac{h}{2}$ **h** $\dfrac{y}{3} = 5$

i $\dfrac{m}{4} = -2$

Q4f hint

Draw a bar model.
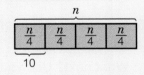

5 Substitute the values given into each formula.
Solve the equation to find the value of the **unknown**.

a $L = m - 5$ Find m when $L = 17$

b $y = x + 4$ Find x when $y = 13$

c $R = A + B$ Find A when $R = 7$ and $B = 2$

d $y = 3x$ Find x when $y = 21$

e $y = kx$ Find x when $y = 27$ and $k = 9$

f $v = at$ Find a when $v = 30$ and $t = 10$

g $T = \dfrac{P}{2}$ Find P when $T = 11$

h $m = \dfrac{d}{r}$ Find d when $m = 5$ and $r = 4$

Q5 Literacy hint

The **unknown** is the letter in an equation.

Q5a hint

$L = m - 5$
$\square = m - 5$

Q5f hint

$\square = a \times \square$

Topic links: Angles on a straight line, Rectangles, Negative numbers

6 a Shireen solves the equation $4m - 3 = 5$ like this.

$4m - 3 = 5$

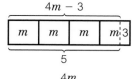

$4m - 3$

| m | m | m | m | 3 |

5

+3 on both sides

$4m$

| m | m | m | m |

$5 + 3 = 8$

$4m = 8$
÷ 4 on both sides

| m |
| m |

$8 ÷ 4 = 2$

$m = 2$

Substitute $m = 2$ into $4m - 3 = 5$
Did Shireen get the correct solution?

b Solve these equations.
Check each answer by substituting back into the equation.

   i $7x - 10 = 32$ **ii** $8n + 9 = 25$

   iii $\frac{x}{5} + 3 = 7$ **iv** $\frac{y}{6} - 4 = 1$

7 Solve these equations.
   a $15 - 2x = 5$ **b** $11 - 3x = 2$ **c** $6x + 7 = -5$

8 Use the formula $m = vt - g$ to find the value of v when $t = 3$, $g = 7$
and $m = 5$

9 a Copy and complete the balance to solve the equation.
   $2x + 5 = 3x - 3$

| $(2x) + 5$ | = | $3x - 3$ |

Subtract $2x$ from both sides.

| $\square$ | = | $x \ominus 3$ |

Add 3 to both sides.

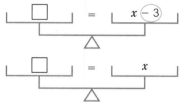

| $\square$ | = | x |

b Solve these equations.
   i $5x + 4 = 6x + 1$ **ii** $6x - 7 = 2x + 1$

10 a Expand the brackets on both sides of the equals sign.
   $4(n + 2) = 5(n + 1)$

   b Solve your equation.

   c Solve $3(x - 2) = 7(x - 6)$

11 Work out
   a 2^2 **b** 7^2 **c** $(-3)^2$
   d $(-6)^2$ **e** $\sqrt{49}$ **f** $\sqrt{36}$

12 Work out
   a 2^3 **b** $(-3)^3$ **c** 3^3
   d $(-1)^3$ **e** $\sqrt[3]{8}$ **f** $\sqrt[3]{-27}$

> **Q6bi hint**
>
> You don't have to draw the bar model.
> Add 10 to both sides.
> Divide both sides by 7.

> **Q6biii hint**
>
> Subtract $\square$
> Multiply by $\square$

> **Q7a hint**
>
> $\frac{-10}{-2} = +\square$

> **Q9bii hint**
>
> Subtract $2x$ from both sides first.

> **Q11e hint**
>
> $\square \times \square = 49$, $-\square \times -\square = 49$

13 Find both solutions of these equations.
 a $x^2 = 81$
 b $2x^2 = 200$

14 Solve $2x^3 = 54$

Q13b hint

$2x^2 = 200$
$x^2 = \square$
$\square \times \square = \square$

Writing equations

1 Modelling **a** Copy and complete: $x + 95 = \square$

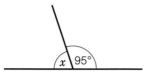

 b Solve to find x.

2 Modelling Write an equation for these angles:

Work out the size of the two missing angles.

Q2 hint

Find n. Then work out $3n$. Make sure you write down the sizes of both angles.

3 Problem-solving / Modelling Here is Billy's answer to the question, 'Work out the lengths of the sides of this rectangle.'

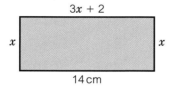

$3x + 2 = 14$
$3x = 12$
$x = 4$

Tisha said, 'You haven't answered the question.'
Finish Billy's working to answer the question.

4 Problem-solving / Modelling Work out the lengths of the sides of this rectangle.

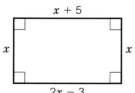

Q4 hint

Write an equation. Find x, then use this value to find the length of each side.

Trial and improvement

1 a Write down the first 10 square numbers.
 b Write down the first 5 cube numbers.

2 Follow these steps to solve $x^2 = 57$ to 1 decimal place.
 a Which two square numbers is 57 between?
 b Copy and complete this number line, using your square numbers from part **a**.

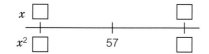

Q1a hint

The 1st square number is $1^2 = 1$, the 2nd square number is $2^2 = 4$ and so on.

Q2a hint

Use your list of square numbers from Q1.

c Copy this table and fill in the top two rows. Use the values from your number line.

x	x^2	Comment
7		too small
	64	

d Write the value halfway between the first two values of x in line 3. Work out x^2.

e Which two values does x lie between now? Choose a value between them. Write it in your table and work out x^2.

f Keep trying values of x between 7 and 8. You should end up with these values:

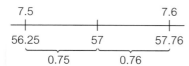

Write down the value that gives x^2 closer to 57.

3 Solve $x^3 = 34$ to 1 decimal place.

x	x^3	Comment
3	27	
4		

Q3 hint

The table has been started for you.

Enrichment

1 The sum of two numbers is 20 and their difference is 6.
Use x and y for the two numbers:
the sum is $\quad\quad x + y = 20$
the difference is $\quad x - y = 6$
Follow the flow diagram to find x and y.

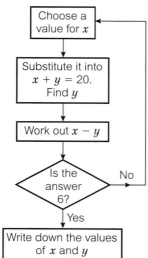

2 Reflect In these strengthen lessons you solved equations using the balancing method and bar models. You may also have used other methods.
Which method do you prefer for solving equations?

7 Extend

You will:
- Extend your understanding with problem-solving.

1 Modelling

a What do the external angles of a polygon add up to?

b A 10-sided regular polygon has exterior angle $x°$.
Copy and complete this equation for the polygon:
$\Box x = \Box°$

c Solve your equation to work out the size of one exterior angle.

2 Modelling

a Work out the size of an exterior angle of a regular polygon with 12 sides.

b What is the size of an interior angle of a regular polygon with 12 sides?

3 Modelling One exterior angle y of a regular polygon is 15°.
How many sides does it have?

4 Problem-solving The formula for the angle sum of a polygon is
$S = 180°(n - 2)$ where n is the number of sides.
A polygon has angle sum 900°.
What is the name of the polygon?

5 Problem-solving / Modelling Work out the sizes of the angles marked with letters.

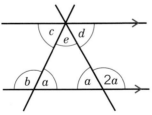

6 Solve these equations.

a $\dfrac{x + 17}{3} = 9$

b $\dfrac{2x + 6}{4} = 5$

7 Modelling The mean of five numbers 21, 25, x, 23, 18 is 20.

a Write an expression for the sum of the five numbers.

b Divide your expression by 5, to give an expression for the mean.

c Write an equation for the mean.

d Solve the equation to find x.

8 Modelling / Problem-solving The mean of 6 numbers 11, 10, 15, y, 19, 8 is 13.
What is the value of y?

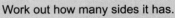

Q2a hint
Write an equation and solve it, like in Q1.

Q2b hint
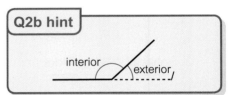
interior   exterior

Q4 Strategy hint
Work out how many sides it has.

Q5 hint
Write and solve an equation for a first.

Topic links: Angles of polygons, Mean, Area and perimeter of rectangles, Angles on a straight line, Angles in a triangle, Area of a trapezium, Square numbers

9 **Modelling / Problem-solving** The perimeter of this rectangle is 36 cm.

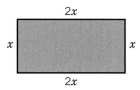

Work out the length and the width.

10 **Modelling / Problem-solving** The length of a rectangle is 3 times its width.

  a Sketch the rectangle. Label its width w.
    What is the length of the rectangle **in terms of** w?

  b The perimeter of the rectangle is 24 cm.
    Work out the length and the width.

Q10a Literacy hint

An expression **in terms of** w includes the letter w.

11 **Problem-solving** $x = 3$. Pair up the cards to make three equations.

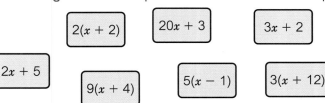

$2(x + 2)$ $20x + 3$ $3x + 2$

$2x + 5$ $9(x + 4)$ $5(x - 1)$ $3(x + 12)$

12 **Modelling / Problem-solving** Work out the size of each angle in this isosceles triangle.

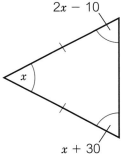

$2x - 10$

x

$x + 30$

Q12 Strategy hint

Write and solve an equation for the two equal angles.
Substitute the value of x into the expressions for the angles.
Check: Make sure your angles add up to 180°.

13 **Modelling / Problem-solving** Work out

  a the perimeter of this rectangle

  b the area of the rectangle.

Q13 Strategy hint

Write and solve an equation for two equal sides.
Use the value of x to work out the length of each side.

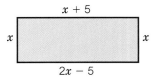

$x + 5$

x x

$2x - 5$

14 **Modelling** Two **consecutive integers** add to make 315.
Jamal writes expressions for the two integers:

1st number n, 2nd number $n + 1$

  a Add Jamal's expressions together.

  b The two integers add to make 315. Write this as an equation using your answer to part **a**.

  c Solve your equation to find the value of n.

  d Write down the two integers.

Q14 Literacy hint

An **integer** is a whole number.
Two **consecutive** integers come one after the other on a number line.

15 Modelling / Problem-solving The sum of two consecutive integers is 523.
What are the two integers?

16 Modelling / Problem-solving Three consecutive integers sum to 63.
What are the three integers?

17 Modelling / Real I am 25 years older than my son.

   a My son is m years old. Write an expression for my age.

   b Write an expression for our total age.

   c Our total age is 57.

      Write an equation and solve it to find m.

   d How old is my son?

   e How old am I?

18 Modelling / Real Rose is 28 years younger than her mother.
Their total age is 112.
What are their ages?

19 Modelling / Problem-solving Write a problem like Q17 for a friend to solve.
Make sure you know the answer.

20 Modelling / Real Train tickets to London for 3 adults and 1 child cost £95.
An adult ticket costs £25 more than a child's ticket.
Work out the cost of each ticket.

21 Problem-solving The formula for the area of a trapezium is

$$\text{area} = \frac{(a + b)h}{2}$$

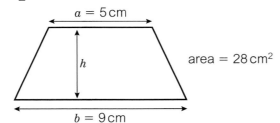

$a = 5\,\text{cm}$

h

$\text{area} = 28\,\text{cm}^2$

$b = 9\,\text{cm}$

What is the height h of this trapezium?

Q21 Strategy hint

Substitute the values for area, a and b into the formula. Solve to find h.

22 Modelling I think of a positive number, square it, add 14 and the answer is 63.

   a Write an equation to represent this problem.

   b Solve it to find my number.

23 Modelling A rectangular patio is twice as long as it is wide.
Its area is 26 m² to the nearest m².

   a Write an equation for the area.

   b Solve it to find the width of the patio. Give your answer to 1 decimal place.

24 Use trial and improvement to find the solution to $x^3 + 3x - 5 = 70$, to 1 decimal place.

Q24 Strategy hint

You could use a spreadsheet to do the calculations.

25 A square card of side x cm has a rectangle 3.5 cm by $0.5x$ cm cut from it.
The area of remaining card is 220 cm².
Find x, to 1 decimal place.

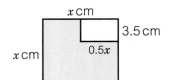

Q25 hint

Write an equation.
Use trial and improvement.

26 Continue this table to use trial and improvement to find the solution to $x^3 - 6 = 80$, to 2 decimal places.

x	$x^3 - 6$	Comment
4	58	too small
5	119	too big
4.5	85.125	too big
4.4	79.184	too small
4.45		
4.41		
4.42		

Which of 4.41 and 4.42 gives $x^3 - 6$ closer to 80?

27 Use trial and improvement to find the solution to $x^3 + x = 100$, to 2 decimal places.

28 **Modelling / Problem-solving** In a rectangular field, the shorter sides are 2 m shorter than the longer sides.

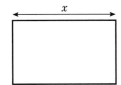

 a A longer side is x metres long.
 Write an expression using x for the length of the shorter side.
 b Write an expression for the area of the field.
 c The area of the field is 400 m².
 Write an equation for the area of the field.
 d Solve your equation using trial and improvement to find the lengths of the sides in metres, to the nearest centimetre.

29 **Reflect** Look back at Q15–20.
How did you decide what letter to use when you wrote the equation?
Did it make a difference to your final answer?

Reflect

7 Unit test

Log how you did on your Student Progression Chart.

1 Solve these equations.

   a $x - 8 = 15$ **b** $5x = 45$ **c** $\frac{x}{7} = 2$

2 Solve these equations.

   a $4x - 5 = 23$ **b** $\frac{x}{6} + 4 = 6$

   c $17 - 3x = 9$ **d** $5(x + 8) = 55$

   e $\frac{5x}{4} = -10$

3 Work out the size of each angle in this triangle.

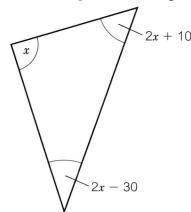

   $2x + 10$

   x

   $2x - 30$

4 Solve $\dfrac{3x - 1}{5} = 4$

5 Use the formula
$m = \frac{1}{2}sv - 3s^2$
to work out the value of v when $s = 4$ and $m = 62$

6 Solve these equations.

   a $5m + 2 = 7m - 10$

   b $3(n - 4) = 2(n - 1)$

   c $2(x + 5) = 4(x - 2)$

7 The sum of three consecutive numbers is 48.
What are the three numbers?

8 These two rectangles have the same area.

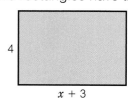
4

$x + 3$

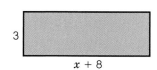
3

$x + 8$

Work out the value of x.

9 Solve
   a $5x^2 = 245$
   b $4x^3 = -108$

10 Use trial and improvement to find the solution to $x^2 + x = 75$

x	$x^2 + x$	Comment

11 Maria has started to use trial and improvement to find the solution to
$x^3 - x = 80$
Complete her workings to find an approximate solution to $x^3 - x = 80$
to 2 decimal places.

x	$x^3 - x$	Comment
4	60	too small
5	120	too big
4.5	86.625	too big
4.2	69.888	too small

Challenge

12 **Problem-solving / Modelling** In this magic square, each row, column
and diagonal adds to make a cube number.

$4a + 2$	$2c$	$5a + 8$
$4a + 2b + 8$	$3a + 6$	$2a$
5	$b + 8$	$2a + 10$

Work out the values of a, b and c.

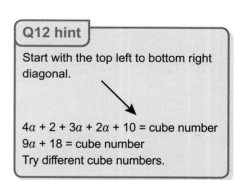

Q12 hint

Start with the top left to bottom right
diagonal.

$4a + 2 + 3a + 2a + 10$ = cube number
$9a + 18$ = cube number
Try different cube numbers.

13 **Reflect** In this unit you have learnt some new vocabulary.
List the new words you have learned, and write a description next
to each.
Ask your friend or teacher to help if you aren't sure what some of the
words mean.

8.1 STEM: Metric and imperial units

You will learn to:
- Convert between metric and imperial units
- Use metric units.

CONFIDENCE

Why learn this?
Different units of measurement are used in different parts of the world.

Fluency
Copy and complete.
- 1 cm = ☐ mm
- 1 m = ☐ cm
- 1 km = ☐ m
- 1 kg = ☐ g
- 1 litre = ☐ ml

Explore
What mass in kg could you pull with your teeth?

Exercise 8.1: Using measures

Warm up

1 Copy and complete these sentences with the most suitable metric units.

I would use centimetres to measure the length of a pencil.

  a I would use _____ to measure the height of a door.

  b I would use _____ to measure the length of a drill bit.

  c I would use _____ to measure the liquid in a bottle.

2 Copy and complete.

  a 1400 g = ☐ kg   **b** 350 cm = ☐ m

  c 73 cm = ☐ m   **d** 2.8 litres = ☐ ml

  e 0.03 litres = ☐ ml **f** 2.04 km = ☐ m

3 Copy and complete.

  a 3 ha = ☐ m^2 **b** ☐ ha = 5000 m^2

  c 2.5 t = ☐ kg   **d** ☐ t = 10 000 kg

4 A woodland charity is planting 8 hectares of woodland.
Each tree needs 4 m^2 to grow. How many trees should be planted?

5 **Problem-solving** Harry buys 1.5 litres of orange concentrate for his party. On the side of the bottle it says, 'Enough for 50 glasses'. Approximately how much orange juice should be put into each glass?

6 **STEM / Modelling** The average mass of a car is 1175 kg.

  a Write this mass in tonnes.

  b An old bridge has a safety limit of 7.5 tonnes.
How many cars can it safely hold at one time?

Key point

Some more metric units that you need to know:
1 tonne (t) = 1000 kg
1 hectare (ha) = 10 000 m^2

Q4 hint

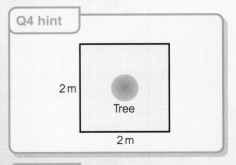

2 m   Tree   2 m

Q5 hint

1 litre = 1000 ml

Topic links: Rounding, Decimals, Fractions, Ratio/Proportion   **Subject links:** Science (Q8, 9), Geography (Q10)

7 Copy and complete these metric to **imperial** conversions.

 a 5 miles ≈ ☐ km
 b $\frac{1}{2}$ mile ≈ ☐ km = ☐ m
 c 6 ft ≈ ☐ cm = ☐ m
 d $\frac{1}{2}$ ft ≈ ☐ cm
 e 2 lbs ≈ ☐ g = ☐ kg
 f $\frac{1}{2}$ lb ≈ ☐ g = ☐ kg
 g 4 pints ≈ ☐ litres = ☐ ml
 h $\frac{1}{2}$ pints ≈ ☐ litres = ☐ ml
 i 4 gallons ≈ ☐ litres
 j $\frac{1}{5}$ gallon ≈ ☐ litres = ☐ ml

8 **STEM** A US biologist collected data on people's masses.
Convert these masses to kg.
Give your answers to the nearest kg.
 a 210 lb
 b 118 lb
 c 140 lb
 d 127 lb

9 **STEM** An electric car can travel between 50 and 100 miles.
 a What is this range in kilometres?
You plan to visit a friend 75 kilometres away and then return.
 b Will you have enough charge to make this journey?

10 **Real** A US airline has a maximum size for carry-on luggage of
9 in × 14 in × 22 in.
Can you carry-on a bag with dimensions 50 cm × 30 cm × 25 cm?

11 **STEM / Modelling** Formulae for predicting the adult heights of
girls and boys are:
 Girl: (father's height − 13 + mother's height) ÷ 2
 Boy: (father's height + 13 + mother's height) ÷ 2
All the measurements must be in centimetres.
Mr Howard is 6 ft 1 in tall and Mrs Howard is 5 ft 4 in tall.
Work out the predicted adult heights of their son and daughter.

 Discussion Audrey and Louis have two sons.
Would you expect them to be the same height?

12 **STEM / Modelling** A US car company is opening a plant in the UK.
An engine component is 3 inches long. In the UK, they decide to
make this piece 7.5 cm long.
Is this a good idea?

13 **Explore** What mass in kg could you pull with your teeth?
Is it easier to explore this question now you have completed the
lesson?
What further information do you need to be able to answer this?

14 **Reflect** Look back at Question 6. What steps did you take to work
out the answer? Is there just one way to work it out?
What assumptions did you make?

STEM

Q7a hint

×1.6
1 mile ╲ 1.6 km
×☐ ( ) ×☐
5 miles ─── km
÷ ☐

Key point

You need to know these conversions
between metric and **imperial** units.
1 foot (ft) ≈ 30 cm
1 mile ≈ 1.6 km
1 kg ≈ 2.2 pounds (lb)
1 litre ≈ 1.75 pints
1 gallon ≈ 4.5 litres

Q10 hint

1 inch ≈ 2.5 cm

Explore

Reflect

8.2 Writing ratios

You will learn to:
- Write a ratio in its simplest form
- Simplify a ratio expressed in fractions or decimals.

Why learn this?
We can judge the performance of football players by comparing the ratio of goals scored to matches played.

Fluency
Simplify:
- $\frac{5}{10}$
- $\frac{9}{12}$
- $\frac{30}{50}$

Explore
What is the ratio of males to females in your school? In the UK? What about in the world?

Exercise 8.2

1 Find the highest common factor of these pairs of numbers.
   a 10 and 15   **b** 40 and 24   **c** 63 and 72

2 Copy and complete.

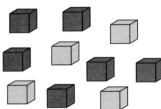

There are ☐ red cubes for every ☐ blue cubes.

3 Copy and complete these conversions.
   a 1 m = ☐ cm   **b** 1 cm = ☐ m   **c** 1 km = ☐ m   **d** 1 kg = ☐ g

4 Write the **ratio** of red beads to white beads for each of these necklaces.

   a
   b
   c

Discussion Is the ratio 3:2 the same as 2:3?

5 Decide whether each statement is sensible.
   a The ratio of your hand length to face length is 1:1.
   b The ratio of height to width of a car is 5:1.
   c The ratio of width to height of a computer screen is 3:4.

Key point

A **ratio** is a way of comparing two or more quantities.

Q4a hint

There are 3 red beads for every 2 white beads. Write the ratio 'red':'white' using numbers.

red : white
☐ : ☐

6 A necklace has 2 black beads for every 5 white beads.

  a What is the ratio black beads : white beads?

  b Copy these 10 white beads.

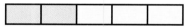

    Draw 2 black beads for every 5 white beads.

    Write the ratio black beads : white beads ☐ : 10

    Discussion Are the ratios in parts **a** and **b** the same?

Q6 Strategy hint

Sketch a diagram.

Worked example

Find the missing value in these equivalent ratios.

$4 : 5 = 24 : \square$

$$\times 6 \overbrace{\begin{array}{ccc} 4 & : & 5 \\ 24 & : & 30 \end{array}}^{} \times 6$$

> Find the multiplier.
> Multiply each part.

$4 : 5 = 24 : 30$

Key point

The ratios 2 : 5 and 4 : 10 are called **equivalent ratios**. Equivalent ratios show the same proportion. Both sides of a ratio are multiplied or divided by the same number to give an equivalent ratio.

---

7 To make green paint, you mix 2 cans of blue paint with 3 cans of yellow paint. The ratio of blue to yellow is 2 : 3.

I have 4 cans of blue paint. How many cans of yellow paint do I need?

8 Which of these ratios are equivalent to the ratio 1 : 2?

  a 2 : 4   **b** 8 : 12

  c 6 : 12   **d** 5 : 10

9 **STEM** 10 g of copper reacts with 5 g of sulfur.

  a Write the ratio of copper to sulfur.

  b How much sulfur is needed to react with 20 g of copper?

  c How much copper is needed to react with 25 g of sulfur?

Worked example

Write 8 : 12 in its simplest form.

$$\div 4 \overbrace{\begin{array}{ccc} 8 & : & 12 \\ 2 & : & 3 \end{array}}^{} \div 4$$

> The HCF of 8 and 12 is 4.

Key point

You can make the numbers in a ratio as small as possible by **simplifying**. You simplify a ratio by dividing the numbers in the ratio by the **highest common factor (HCF)**.

---

10 Write each ratio in its **simplest form**.

  a 5 : 20   **b** 4 : 12

  c 6 : 30   **d** 100 : 20

  e 8 : 10   **f** 36 : 18

11 **Real** 120 students and 8 teachers go on a school trip.
The recommended ratio of adults to students is 1 : 15.
Is the ratio of adults to students correct?

Q10a hint

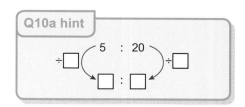

12 Simplify each ratio.

    a $4:20:36$ **b** $6:24:12$ **c** $25:20:45$

    d $27:9:36$ **e** $30:48:18$ **f** $99:77:33$

Q12a hint

The highest common factor of 4, 20 and 36 is ☐.

13 **Real** A £1 coin is made of copper, nickel and zinc in the ratio $70:5:25$. Write this ratio to its simplest form.

Key point

Ratios in their simplest form do not have units. To simplify a ratio involving measures, first convert the measures to the same unit.

14 **STEM** A molecule of water has 10 protons, 8 neutrons and 10 electrons.

Write the ratio of protons, neutrons and electrons in its simplest form.

15 Write the ratio $4\,m:200\,cm$ in its simplest form.

    Discussion Does it matter whether you convert 200 cm to m or 4 m to cm?

Q15 hint

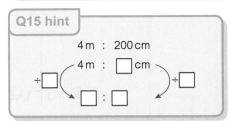

16 Simplify.

    a $2\,m:150\,cm$ **b** $250\,cm:4\,m$

    c $2\,km:1200\,m$ **d** $1.2\,cm:36\,mm$

    e $1\ day:6\ hours$ **f** $8\ hours:2\ days$

    g $63\,kg:200\,g$ **h** $2\ weeks:14\ days$

D1 U73

17 The bar chart shows the number of boys and girls at an after-school club.

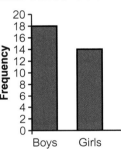

D1 U7.2

    What is the ratio of boys to girls?

Key point

For a ratio with fractions or decimals, first multiply both sides of the ratio to get whole numbers.

18 Write these ratios in their simplest form.

    a $1:2.5$ **b** $1:3\frac{1}{4}$ **c** $2:3.5$ **d** $5:1\frac{1}{10}$

Q18a hint

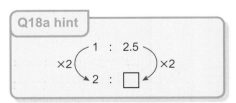

19 The ratio of the width to height of a photograph is $1:1.5$. The width of the photograph is 10 cm. What is its height?

20 **Explore** What is the ratio of males to females in your school? In the UK? What about in the world?

Is it easier to explore this question now you have completed the lesson?

What further information do you need to be able to answer this?

21 **Reflect** After this lesson, Lydia says 'Ratios are a bit like fractions because simplifying ratios is like simplifying fractions.'

Do you agree with Lydia? Explain

You could use these words in your explanation: Factor, Proportion, Divide.

Explore

Reflect

8.3 Sharing in a given ratio

You will learn to:

- Share a quantity in 2 or more parts in a given ratio.

Why learn this?
A smoothie recipe uses the correct ratio of ingredients to make it taste nice.

Fluency
Find three ratios equivalent to 4:3.

Explore
Investigate the ratio of left-handed people to right-handed people.

Exercise 8.3

1 Write down the missing values in these equivalent ratios.
   a $2:5 = 6:\square$
   b $4:7 = \square:28$
   c $3:10 = 15:\square$
   d $6:\square = 48:32$

2 The ratio of students who have school dinners to those having packed lunch in Year 7 is 72:48. Write this ratio in its simplest form.

3 Reasoning Paul and Sarah buy a £1 lottery ticket. Paul pays 20p and Sarah pays 80p. They win £1000. Is it fair that they get £500 each? Explain your answer.

Worked example

Share £30 in the ratio 1:4.
1 + 4 = 5 parts

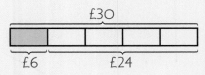

£30

£6   £24

5 parts = £30
1 part = £30 ÷ 5 = £6   4 parts = £6 × 4 = £24
£6:£24
6 + 24 = 30 ——— Check your answer by adding the parts.

4 Share these amounts in the ratios given.
   Show how you check your answers.
   a £20 in the ratio 2:3
   b £60 in the ratio 4:2
   c £35 in the ratio 3:4
   d £77 in the ratio 5:6
   e £72 in the ratio 5:4
   f £120 in the ratio 5:7

5 Peter and Catherine share £60 in the ratio 3:2.
   How much does each person receive?

Warm up

6 In a class the ratio of girls to boys is 4:5. There are 27 students in the class. How many are boys?

7 In a tennis club the ratio of men to women is 3:4.
  a In 2012 there were 14 club members. How many men were there?
  b In 2013 there were 21 club members. How many women were there?

8 Problem-solving In Year 7, the ratio of girls to boys is 5:4.
There are 110 girls.
  a How many boys are there in Year 7?
  b How many students are there in Year 7?

> **Q8 hint**
> ?
> Girls = 110   Boys = ?

9 Real There were approximately 60 million people in the UK in 2001. The ratio of under-16s to over-16s was 1:4. How many under-16s were there in 2001?

10 Problem-solving / Finance Jenny gives some of her earnings to charity. The ratio of the amount she keeps to the amount she gives to charity is 1:9.
In 2012, Jenny earned £18000. In 2013, Jenny earned £23 000.
How much more did Jenny give to charity in 2013 than in 2012?

D1 U7.3

11 Share these amounts in the ratios given.
Show how you check your answers.
  a £63 in the ratio 2:3:4
  b £108 in the ratio 5:1:6
  c £980 in the ratio 2:3:2
  d £1280 in the ratio 8:3:5

> **Q11a hint**
> £63
> 2   3   4
> How much is 1 part worth?

12 Finance In one day, the ratio of hours worked in a restaurant by three waiters, Adam, Billy and Charlie, is 3:4:2.
They split their tips in the ratio of their hours worked. The total amount in tips is £72. How much did each waiter get?

13 STEM An alloy is made from copper, tin and zinc in the ratio 6:2:1. 180 g of alloy is made.
  a How much copper is used?   **b** How much tin is used?

D2 U6.4

14 Problem-solving To make orange paint, Ally mixes red, yellow and white paint in the ratio 5:4:1.
  a Ally has 24 litres of yellow paint. How many litres of red and white paint does she need?
  b How many litres of paint does she have altogether?

15 Problem-solving The sides of a triangle are in the ratio 2:3:7.
The shortest side is 8 cm. Calculate the perimeter of the triangle.

> **Q15 hint**
> The shortest side is 8 cm. How many parts is this?

16 Explore Investigate the ratio of left-handed people to right-handed people.
Is it easier to explore this question now you have completed the lesson?
What further information do you need to be able to answer this?

17 Reflect Look back at the questions you answered on sharing an amount using ratios.
What did you do differently in Q8 and 14 than you did in Q7, 9, 11 and 12?

Explore

Reflect

Active Learn Delta 1, Section 8.3

8.4 Proportion

You will learn to:
• Understand the relationship between ratio and proportion.

Why learn this?
To make green paint, you can mix yellow and blue paint. Increasing the proportion of blue paint will make a darker shade of green.

Fluency
What is
• $\frac{1}{4}$ as a percentage
• 10% as a fraction
• $\frac{7}{10}$ as a decimal and a percentage?

Explore
How has the proportion of gold medals won by team GB changed from the 2008 Olympic games to the 2012 Olympic games?

Exercise 8.4

1 Convert these fractions to percentages.

a $\frac{3}{10} = \frac{\square}{100} = \square\%$ **b** $\frac{4}{50} = \frac{\square}{100} = \square\%$ **c** $\frac{3}{20}$ **d** $\frac{7}{25}$ **e** $\frac{4}{5}$

2 Write these fractions in their simplest form.

a $\frac{20}{50}$ **b** $\frac{12}{16}$ **c** $\frac{24}{30}$ **d** $\frac{32}{54}$

3 **Real** The Nigerian National Flag has three parts. Two parts green and one part white.
a What is the ratio of green to white?
b What is the proportion of green in the whole flag? Write your answer as a fraction.

Key point

Ratio compares part to part.
Proportion compares part to whole.
Proportions can be written as **fractions** or **percentages**.

have
KP from
Th 1 p176
first

Worked example

There are 4 male and 6 female kittens.
a Write the ratio of male to female kittens in its **simplest form**.
b What proportion of the kittens are male?
Write your answer as a fraction and a percentage.

a Male : Female

$$\div 2 \left(\begin{array}{c} 4 \\ 2 \end{array} : \begin{array}{c} 6 \\ 3 \end{array} \right) \div 2$$

b

$$\frac{4}{10} \qquad \frac{6}{10}$$

$\frac{4}{10} = \frac{2}{5}$ — Simplify the fraction.

$\frac{4}{10} = \frac{40}{100} = 40\%$ — Write as a percentage.

4 A packet of sweets has 12 chocolates and 8 mints.

   a Write the ratio of chocolates to mints.

   b What proportion of the sweets are mints? Write your answer as a fraction and as a percentage.

5 For charity art exhibition, James gave 12 paintings, Robert gave 8 and Fernando gave 5.

   a Write the numbers of paintings as a ratio.

   b What proportion of the paintings did each give?

6 **Real** In the 2012 Olympic games, the Netherlands won gold, silver and bronze medals in the ratio $6:6:8$.

   a What proportion of the medals were gold?

   b What proportion of the medals were bronze?

   Write your answers as a fraction and as a percentage.

   Discussion Why is it sometimes useful to write proportions as percentages?

7 **Problem-solving** Sam practises two stunts on his skateboard.
He has 20 attempts at the first stunt and 25 attempts at the second.
The table shows the success of his attempts.

   a In what proportion of attempts was he successful?

   b At which stunt was he more successful?

	Stunt 1	Stunt 2
Failed	5	7
Nailed it!	15	18

8 **Real / Problem-solving** Retired Brazilian footballer, Ronaldo scored 247 goals in 343 matches.
The Hungarian footballer Ferenc Puskas scored 512 goals in 528 matches.
Who is the better footballer?

9 **Problem-solving** Jennie and Claire make lemonade.
The ratio of lemon to water in Jennie's lemonade is $2:3$.
The ratio of lemon to water in Claire's lemonade is $3:4$.
Use proportions to explain which lemonade is stronger.

> **Q9 hint**
>
> Write the proportions as fractions.

10 **Real** A charity divides its budget like this:
35% for wages, 40% for resourcing and 25% for marketing
Write the ratio spent on wages to resourcing to marketing in its simplest form.

11 In a wallpaper design, $\frac{3}{5}$ of the design is squares and $\frac{2}{5}$ of the design is triangles.
Write the ratio of squares to triangles in its simplest form.

12 **Real** $\frac{7}{10}$ of the Earth is water and $\frac{3}{10}$ is land. Write this as a ratio.

Investigation   **Problem-solving**

Investigate the ratio of time you spend at school, eating, watching tv, doing homework, sleeping.
Write these as proportions.
Is this the same for other people in your class?

---

13 **Explore** How has the proportion of gold medals won by team GB changed from the 2008 Olympic games to the 2012 Olympic games?
What have you learned in this lesson to help you answer this question?
What other information do you need?

14 **Reflect** Look back at the questions you answered.
When do you think it is better to express proportions as fractions?
When would it be better to express proportions as percentages?

Active Learn   Delta 1, Section 8.4

8.5 Proportional reasoning

You will learn to:
- Solve simple word problems involving ratio and direct proportion
- Solve simple word problems involving ratio and inverse proportion.

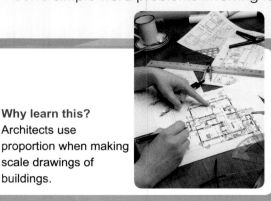

Why learn this?
Architects use proportion when making scale drawings of buildings.

Fluency
Double:
- 5, 6, 34, 70, 150
Halve:
- 10, 48, 32, 19

Explore
How would you change the ratios of a photograph to make you look taller?

Exercise 8.5

1 A comic costs £2. Work out the cost of
 a 3 comics
 b 10 comics
 c How many comics can I buy with £16?

Worked example

Alex uses 250 g of cheese to make pizzas for 4 people.
How much cheese would he need to make pizzas for 6 people?

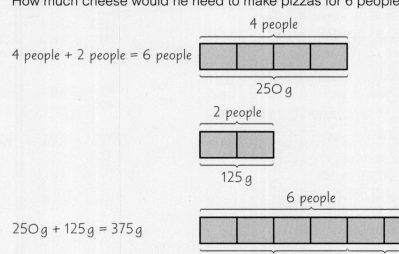

4 people + 2 people = 6 people

4 people
250 g

2 people
125 g

6 people
250 g + 125 g = 375 g
250 g   125 g

Key point

When two quantities are in **direct proportion,** as one increases or decreases, the other increases or decreases in the same ratio.

2 Two litres of lemonade costs £2.50. Work out the cost of
 a 4 litres   b 6 litres   c 1 litre   d 7 litres.

3 Downloading 30 songs from a music website costs £45.
 a How much does it cost to download 15 songs?
 b How much does it cost to download 45 songs?

Warm up

4 Problem-solving Here is a recipe for pancakes for four people.
Sophie makes pancakes for 14 people. She has 800 g of flour, 1200 ml of milk and 10 eggs.
Does she have enough ingredients?

D1 u7.1

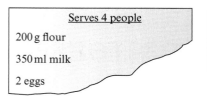

Serves 4 people

200 g flour

350 ml milk

2 eggs

Q4 hint

Show your working. Write a sentence to answer the question.

5 Fazia bought six plants for £3.60. Kunal bought three plants for £2. Who got the better deal?

Worked example

It takes 2 people 20 minutes to wash a car.
How long does it take:

a 4 people   **b** 1 person?

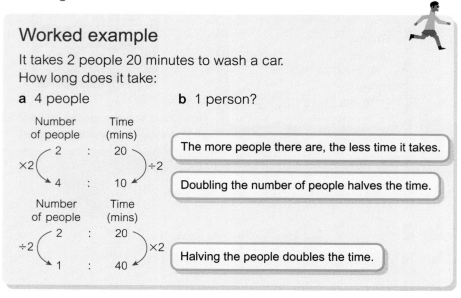

Number of people   Time (mins)

×2 (2 : 20) ÷2
     4 : 10

The more people there are, the less time it takes.

Doubling the number of people halves the time.

Number of people   Time (mins)

÷2 (2 : 20) ×2
     1 : 40

Halving the people doubles the time.

Key point

When two quantities are in **inverse proportion**, as one increases, the other decreases in the same ratio.

6 Real / Problem-solving 6 people can paint a fence in 3 hours.
a How long would it take 3 people to paint it?
b How long would it take 2 people?
c How long would it take 12 people?

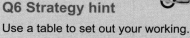

Q6 Strategy hint

Use a table to set out your working.

Number of people	Time (hours)
6	3
3	?

7 Real / Problem-solving 10 men can build a house in 8 days.
a How long will it take 20 men to build a house?
b How long will it take 5 men to build a house?

8 It costs 12 people £400 to go trekking. How much will it cost 10 people?
Discussion There are 24 people on a roller coaster. The ride takes 3 minutes. How long will it take when there are 48 people on it?

9 Problem-solving It takes 120 minutes to drive home at 60 km/h.
a How long will it take to drive home at 120 km/h?
b How long will it take to drive home at 30 km/h?
c How long will it take to drive home at 90 km/h?

10 Explore How would you change the ratios of a photograph to make you look taller?
Choose some sensible numbers to help you explore this situation. Then use what you've learned in this lesson to help you answer the question.

11 Reflect In this lesson you learnt about direct and inverse proportion. Choose 4 questions from the lesson and explain why they were about either direct or inverse proportion.

Explore

Reflect

8.6 Using the unitary method

You will learn to:

- Solve problems involving ratio and proportion using the unitary method
- Write ratios in the form $1:n$
- Solve best buy problems.

Why learn this?

You can work out the best value of products by finding out how much 1 item or 100g or 1kg costs.

Fluency

Find the missing numbers in this multiplication table

×		12	8
2	18		
		108	
			12

Explore

How much does a footballer earn in 10 minutes?

Exercise 8.6

1 Work these out
  a 125cm ÷ 5
  b 320g ÷ 8
  c £2.50 ÷ 5
  d 420m ÷ 7
  e £1.50 × 3
  f £3.85 × 2

2 Simplify these ratios
  a 20m:2m
  b 50km:5000m
  c 8 hours:1 day
  d 2p:£1

3 4 notebooks cost £1.20.
  a Work out the cost of
    i 2 notebooks
    ii 1 notebook
    iii 3 notebooks
  b Suzie has £3.00. How many notebooks can she buy?

4 Three chocolate bars cost £2.70.
  a Work out the cost of 1 chocolate bar.
  b Work out the cost of 7 chocolate bars.
  c How many chocolate bars can you buy for £7.20?

5 6 litres of petrol cost £7.50.
  How much does 40 litres cost?

6 80 mosquito nets cost £476.
  How much do 35 mosquito nets cost?

 7 Real / Problem-solving Mr Smith sells apples at £2.00 per kilogram.
  Mrs Jones sells apples at 30p per 100g.
  Who sells the cheaper apples?

8 Carly can buy 800g of pasta for £1.50, or 1kg of pasta for £1.70.
  Which is better value?

> **Key point**
>
> Using the **unitary method** means finding the value of 1 part.

> **Q5 hint**
>
> Work out the cost of 1 litre first.

> **Q7 hint**
>
> 1 kilogram = 1000 grams

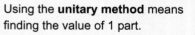
D2 U6.4

Warm up

9 **Problem-solving** Carl earns £56 for 8 hours' work.
  a Carl works for 40 hours. How much does he earn?
  b Carl is paid double for overtime. He works 5 hours of overtime in addition to his normal 40 hours work. How much does he earn?

D1 U7.1

10 **Real / Problem-solving** A supermarket sells chocolate bars at £3.00 for a 5-pack and £4.40 for an 8-pack.
  Which is better value for money?

11 **Real / Problem-solving** Jonathon's car can travel 315 miles on 35 litres of petrol.

D1 U7.1

  Sandra's car can travel 240 miles on 30 litres of petrol.
  Whose car is more economical?

Q9 hint

Find how much he gets paid for 1 hour first.

Q10 hint

Work out how much it costs to buy one chocolate bar first and then compare.

Q11 Literacy hint

'Economical' means cheaper.

Q11 hint

Work out how far each car travels on 1 litre of petrol first.

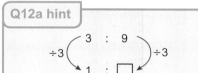

Worked example

Write the ratio 2:5 in the form 1:n

$$\div2 \overset{2\ :\ 5}{\underset{1\ :\ 2.5}{\Big(\quad\Big)}} \div2$$

---

12 Write these ratios in the form 1:n
  a 3:9   **b** 4:24
  c 8:48   **d** 12:120
  e 0.5:1   **f** 50 cm:2 m
  g 200 m:1.2 km   **h** 6 hours:1 day

Q12a hint

$$\div3 \overset{3\ :\ 9}{\underset{1\ :\ \square}{\Big(\quad\Big)}} \div3$$

13 Write these ratios in the form n:1
  a 8:4   **b** 10:2
  c 12:3   **d** 0.4:0.8
  e 0.25:0.5   **f** 0.9:0.3
  g 6 m:800 cm   **h** 43 cm:10 mm

Q13a hint

$$\div4 \overset{8\ :\ 4}{\underset{\square\ :\ 1}{\Big(\quad\Big)}} \div4$$

14 A school has 150 computers and 900 students. What is the ratio of the number of computers to the number of students?
  Give your ratio in the form 1:n.

D2 U6.4

15 A shop has two different offers on its sale of paper plates.

OFFER A
6 paper plates for 90p

OFFER B
4 paper plates for 72p

  a Write the ratio of number of paper plates to price, in its simplest form, for Offer A and Offer B.
  b Which gives better value for money?
  Discussion Why do you think it is useful to represent ratios in the form 1:n?

16 **Problem-solving** Dylan made an orange drink using the ratio of orange squash to water in the ratio 2:9. Sarah made another drink using the ratio of orange squash to water in the ratio 3:10.
  a Write each of these ratios in the form 1:n.
  b Which drink was stronger?

17 **Problem-solving** A shop-keeper wants to charge 1.5 times as much per toilet roll for offer B than offer A.

What is the cost of offer B?

Offer A
8 toilet rolls
£2.40

Offer B
3 toilet rolls
?

01 47.1

18 **Real** Here are some multipacks of crisps. Each pack is the same brand and contains the same size of smaller packs.

SMALL MULTIPACK
5 packets of crisps
£1.50

MEDIUM MULTIPACK
10 packets of crisps
£2.98

LARGE MULTIPACK
20 packets of crisps
£5.50

a Work out the price of one packet of crisps from the
  i small multipack
  ii medium multipack
  iii large multipack
b Which is best value for money?
Explain your answer.

19 **Real / Reasoning** Here are some jars of honey at different prices from different producers.

HONEY A
50 g
£1.20

HONEY B
250 g
£4.75

HONEY C
380 g
£7.80

a Work out the cost of 10 g of honey from each jar.
b Which jar of honey is the best value for money?
Explain your answer.

20 **Explore** How much does a footballer earn in 10 minutes?
Is it easier to explore this question now you have completed the lesson?
What further information do you need to be able to answer this?

21 **Reflect** Look back at the questions you answered in this lesson.
For questions 13 and 14 you broke down the ratio to solve the problems.
For questions 15, 16, 17, 18 and 19, you used the unitary method.
When do you think it is better to use the unitary method?

Master
P181

CHECK

Strengthen
P197

Extend
P201

Test
P205

8 Check up

Log how you did on your
Student Progression Chart.

Ratio and measures

1 Write these ratios in their simplest form.
a 6:15
b 28:32

2 Write this ratio in its simplest form.
22:44:55

3 Share £200 in the ratio 3:7.

4 Write these ratios in their simplest form.
a £1.50:25p
b 8m:20cm
c 3000kg:4 tonnes

5 Copy and complete.
a 4 miles ≈ ☐km
b 3 lb ≈ ☐g
c 7 pints ≈ ☐litres
d 9 gallons ≈ ☐litres
e 4 feet ≈ ☐cm = ☐m

6 Bessie the cow produces 25 pints of milk per day.
The dairy pays 30p for each litre produced.
How much does the dairy pay for Bessie's milk each day?

7 There are 210 students in Year 7. The ratio of students studying
French to students studying Spanish is 3:4.
How many students study French and how many study Spanish?

8 Kate has blue fish and yellow fish.
The ratio of blue fish to yellow fish is 4:5.
She has 15 yellow fish. How many blue fish does she have?

9 Dan is training for a swimathon. In his training session he used
butterfly, front crawl and back stroke in the ratio 2:5:3.
He swam 60 lengths of back stroke. How many lengths of front crawl
did he swim?

10 Write these ratios in their simplest form.
a 0.25:0.5
b $1:\frac{4}{5}$

11 Write 4:6 in the form 1:n.

12 Write 7:2 in the form n:1.

Direct and inverse proportion

13 In a class of 30 drama students 18 are girls.
   a Write the proportion of girls as a fraction.
   b Write the proportion of boys as a fraction.
   c Write the ratio of girls to boys in its simplest form.

14 In a bowl of fruit there are 10 bananas, 6 apples and 4 pears.
   What proportion of the fruit are apples?
   Write your answer as a fraction and as a percentage.

15 The ratio of blue cars to red cars in a car park is 3:2.
   What percentage of cars are
   a red
   b blue?

16 It takes Paul 50 minutes to walk 2 km.
   How long will it take him to walk
   a 4 km
   b 1 km
   c 3 km?

17 3 tickets to a museum cost £19.50.
   Work out the cost of 4 tickets.

18 Which is cheaper, 6 cartons of milk for £4.80, or 5 cartons
   of milk for £4.25?

19 The table shows the number of visitors to a museum one weekend.

	Adults	Children
Saturday	120	300
Sunday	180	400

   Which day had the larger proportion of children visiting?

20 It takes 6 painters 4 days to paint a large house.
   How long will it take
   a 3 painters   b 12 painters   c 1 painter?

21 It takes Simon 40 minutes to drive to work at an average speed of
   60 mph. How long would it take him at an average speed of
   a 120 mph
   b 15 mph?

22 **How sure are you of your answers? Were you mostly**
   😟 **Just guessing**   😐 **Feeling doubtful**   😊 **Confident**
   **What next? Use your results to decide whether to strengthen or
   extend your learning.**

Challenge

22 a How many people do you think can stand in a square with sides
     of 1 m?
   The dimensions of a football pitch are 1203 m by 50 m.
   b Calculate the area of the football pitch.
   c Estimate how many people can stand on a football pitch.

8 Strengthen

You will:
• Strengthen your understanding with practice.

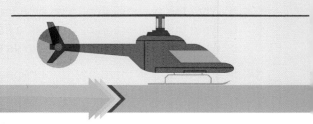

Ratio and measures

1 Copy and complete.
   a 3 miles ≈ ☐ km
   b ½ mile ≈ ☐ km
   c 8 km ≈ ☐ miles
   d 5 km ≈ ☐ miles
   e 7 pints ≈ ☐ litres
   f 5 litres ≈ ☐ pints
   g 13 litres ≈ ☐ gallons
   h 9 gallons ≈ ☐ litres
   i 4 kg ≈ ☐ lb
   j 12 lbs ≈ ☐ kg

2 a Write 2:8 in its simplest form.
   b Write 3:12 in its simplest form.

3 Match each ratio to its simplest form.

3:6	4:1
4:12	2:7
5:20	2:3
24:6	1:3
6:9	2:5
8:28	1:4
4:10	1:2

4 Write each of these ratios in their simplest form.
   a 0.1:0.5
   b 0.2:0.8
   c 0.3:0.6

5 Write each ratio in its simplest form.
   a $\frac{1}{3}:\frac{2}{3}$
   b $\frac{4}{6}:\frac{1}{6}$
   c $\frac{4}{10}:\frac{6}{10}$

6 Write these ratios in their simplest form.
   a £1.00:10p
   b 10p:£2.00
   c 20 cm:3 m
   d 400 g:3 kg

7 Bunting has red and blue flags in the ratio 3:5.
  A length of bunting has 20 blue flags.
  How many red flags are there?

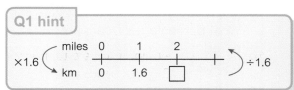

Q1 hint

miles 0 1 2
×1.6 ↘ ÷1.6
km 0 1.6 ☐

Q2a hint

2 : 8
÷2 ↘ ↘ ÷2
☐ : ☐

Q2b hint

What is the largest number you can divide 3 and 12 by?

3 : 12
÷☐ ↘ ↘ ÷☐
☐ : ☐

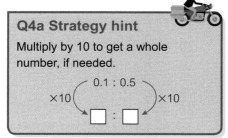

Q4a Strategy hint

Multiply by 10 to get a whole number, if needed.

0.1 : 0.5
×10 ↘ ↘ ×10
☐ : ☐

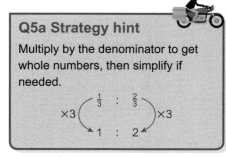

Q5a Strategy hint

Multiply by the denominator to get whole numbers, then simplify if needed.

$\frac{1}{3}$: $\frac{2}{3}$
×3 ↘ ↘ ×3
1 : 2

Q6a hint

Write both parts in the same units first.
100p:10p
☐:☐

8 Jenny buys some drinks for her birthday party.
For every one carton of apple juice, she buys three cartons of orange juice. She buys 16 cartons altogether.
a How many cartons of apple juice does she buy?
b How many cartons of orange juice does she buy?
c Do your answers to parts **a** and **b** add up to 16?

Q8 hint

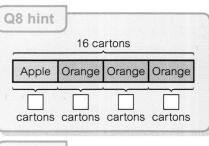

9 The ratio of boys to girls taking part in the school play is 2:3.
There are 20 students in the school play.
a How many students are boys?
b How many students are girls?

Q9 hint

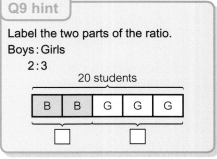

10 In a zoo, the ratio of female to male tigers is 3:1.
There are 12 tigers altogether.
How many tigers are female?

Q10 hint

11 Ally and Billie share some sweets in the ratio of their ages.
Ally is 10 years old and Billy is 11 years old.
They have 63 sweets altogether.
How many does each person get?

12 Share these amounts in the ratios given.
a £20 in the ratio 1:4
b £32 in the ratio 1:3
c £30 in the ratio 5:1

13 Share these amounts in the ratios given.
a £12 in the ratio 1:2:3
b £27 in the ratio 1:3:5
c £60 in the ratio 3:2:5

Q13a hint

14 Problem-solving The sides of a right-angled triangle are in the ratio 3:4:5.
The perimeter of the triangle is 36 cm.
Calculate the length of each side of the triangle.

Q14 Strategy hint

Draw a sketch.

Direct and inverse proportion

1 a There are 3 toffees in a pack of 10 sweets.
What proportion of the pack are toffees?
b There are 6 toffees in a pack of 10 sweets.
What proportion of the pack are toffees?
Write your answer in its simplest form and as a percentage.

Q1a hint

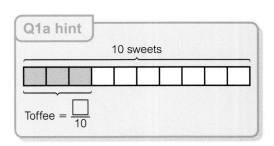

2 In May there were 12 accidents on a road. Three were serious.
a What fraction of the accidents in May were serious?
Write the fraction in its simplest form.
In June there were 15 accidents. Five were serious.
c What proportion of the accidents in June were serious?
d Which month had the higher proportion of serious accidents?

Q2 Strategy hint

Compare the proportions by comparing the fractions.

3 There are 10 girls and 15 boys in the school swimming team.
   a How many people are in the team?
   b What proportion of the team are girls?
   c Write your answer as a fraction.
   d Write the fraction in part **c** in its simplest form.

4 There are 7 apples and 3 oranges in a bowl.
   a What proportion are apples?
      Write your answer as a percentage.
   b What proportion are oranges?
      Write your answer as a percentage.

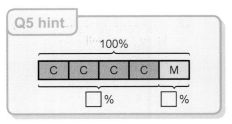

Q4a hint

How many pieces of fruit in the bowl?

5 The ratio of cars to motorcycles in a car park is $4:1$.
   What percentage are
   a motorcycles
   b cars?

Q5 hint

100%

| C | C | C | C | M |

☐ %   ☐ %

6 **Reasoning** When taking penalties in football, Anna has a ratio of goals to misses of $7:3$.
   a What percentage of penalties does Anna score?
   Bethany has a ratio of goals to misses of $1:4$.
   b What percentage of penalties does Bethany score?
   c Who should the team choose to take their penalties?

Q6 hint

Draw bar models to help you.

7 2 raffle tickets cost £4. Work out the cost of:
   a 4 tickets
   b 6 tickets
   c 1 ticket.

Q7 hint

2 raffle tickets

| | |

£4

8 5 scientific calculators cost £30. How much will it cost to buy
   a 1 calculator
   b 6 calculators
   c 14 calculators?

9 In shop A, 40 pencils cost £4.80.
   In shop B, 50 pencils cost £5.50.
   a How much does one pencil cost in shop A?
   b How much does one pencil cost in shop B?
   c Which is better value for money?

Q9 hint

Which shop has cheaper pencils?

10 In shop A 3 bottles of nail varnish cost £5.70.
   In shop B 5 bottles of nail varnish cost £9.
   Which is better value for money?

11 The Phone Box has two mobile price plans.

Plan A:
500 minutes
for £25

Plan B:
750 minutes
for £30

   a For each plan, write a ratio to show the number of minutes to price.
   b Express each ratio in the form $1:n$.
   c Which package gives the better deal?

12 Chris can type 80 words in two minutes.
How long will it take him to type
   a 40 words
   b 120 words
   c 160 words?

Q12 hint

Draw a bar model to help you.
Will Chris take more or less time?

13 If you have fewer people, does a job take
   a more time
   b less time?

14 If you have more people does a job take
   a more time
   b less time?

15 If you have twice the number of people, does a job take:
   a half the time
   b twice the time?

16 It takes one builder 8 days to build a wall.
How long will it take:
   a two builders
   b four builders?

Q16 hint

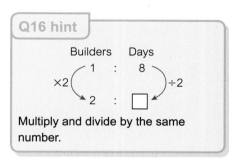

Multiply and divide by the same number.

17 It takes 2 people one day to paint a room. How long will it take one person?

18 It takes four students 10 days to build the set for a school play.
How long does it take:
   a eight students
   b two students
   c one student?

Enrichment

1 Three prizes are in the ratio 1 : 2 : 5.
The largest prize is £25. What is the smallest prize?

2 Real / Finance This table shows distances between British cities in miles.

Bristol			
168	Manchester		
142	69	Nottingham	
75	159	102	Oxford

Anu is going on a business trip. Starting in Manchester, she will visit Bristol, Oxford and Nottingham before returning home to Manchester.
   a What is the distance from Manchester to Bristol?
   b What is the total distance in:
      i miles
      ii km?
   c She gets 10p per km for expenses.
      How much will she get altogether?

Q2a hint

Read down from Bristol, across from Manchester.

3 One person takes 30 minutes to clean a car.
Write a maths question using this information. Work out the answer.

4 **Reflect** The hints in these Strengthen lessons used lots of diagrams.
Look back at the diagrams in the hints.
Which diagrams did you find most useful? Why?
Which diagrams did you find least useful? Why?

Reflect

8 Extend

You will learn to:

• Solve problems by applying your knowledge of this topic.

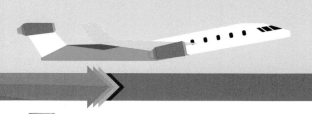

1 **Problem-solving** Karen is 12 years old. Jane is 3 years older than Karen and 3 years younger than Sarah.
Write the ratio of Karen's age to Jane's age to Sarah's age in its simplest form

D1 4 7.2

2 Michael has 240 Twitter followers. Godfrey has twice as many followers as Michael and $\frac{1}{3}$ fewer than David.
Write the ratio of the number of Michael's to Godfrey's to David's Twitter followers as a ratio in its simplest form.

3 Convert these amounts into the units shown.
   a 5 lb ≈ ☐ g = ☐ kg   b 4 ft ≈ ☐ cm = ☐ m
   c 3 miles ≈ ☐ km = ☐ m   d 5 gallons ≈ ☐ litres = ☐ m*l*
   e 3 pints ≈ ☐ litres = ☐ m*l*

4 **Real** The table shows some information about the US and GB bobsled teams at the 2014 Winter Olympics.

Times	GB	speed (km/h)	USA	speed (mph)
1st run	55.26 seconds	138.8	54.89 seconds	86.8
2nd run	55.27 seconds	137.2	55.47 seconds	85.8
3rd run	55.31 seconds	137.0	55.30 seconds	85.6
4th run	55.33 seconds	138.0	55.33 seconds	86.3

Mass	GB (kg)	USA (lbs)
Team	403	900
Sled	52	50
Total	455	950

   a Compare the top speed of the GB team with the top speed of the US team.
   b Work out the range of times for each team.
      Which team was more consistent?
   c Compare the masses of the two teams.
   d Compare the total masses.
   e What percentage of the total mass of the US bobsled is the bobsled itself?
   f What percentage of the total mass of the GB bobsled is the bobsled itself?

5 **Problem-solving** In a musical cast there are 18 singers.
There are 14 more dancers than singers.
What proportion of the cast are dancers?
Write your answer as a fraction and a percentage.

> **Q5 hint**
>
> Remember to write your fraction in its simplest form.

6 The table shows the number of matches two football teams win, lose and draw in one season.

	Win	Lose	Draw
Team A	5	8	3
Team B	3	8	4

   a Write the proportion of matches lost by each team as a percentage.

   b Which team lost the higher proportion of matches?

7 **STEM / Problem-solving** 50 g of sterling silver is made from approximately 45 g of silver and 5 g of copper.

   a Write this ratio in its simplest form.

   b A sterling silver ring contains 10 g of silver. How much does the ring weigh?

$E \quad 3E \quad \frac{1}{2}E$
$4.5E = 270$
$\Rightarrow E = £50$

8 **Problem-solving** In a group of 30 people, 1 in 5 people are left-handed and the others are right-handed.
How many more people are right-handed?

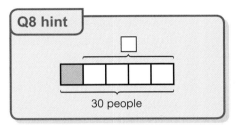

9 Three students did a sponsored silence to raise money for charity. Josh raised three times more than Emma. Emma raised twice as much as Paul.

   a Write the ratio of money raised by Josh, Emma and Paul.

   b Altogether they raised £270. How much did each person raise?

   c How much more did Josh raise than Paul?

10 Jane and Claire had an equal number of stickers.
Jane gives $\frac{1}{5}$ of her stickers to Claire.

   a Write the ratio of the number of Jane's stickers to Claire's stickers. Write the ratio in its simplest form.

   b Claire has 12 more stickers than Jane. How many stickers does Jane have now?

   c How many stickers do they have altogether?

Q10 hint

Draw a bar model to help.

Jane

Claire

11 Simon and Mark had an equal number of video games.
Simon gives $\frac{2}{5}$ of his video games to Mark.

   a Write the ratio of the number of video games that Simon has to the number Mark has now.

   b Mark has 24 more video games than Simon. How many video games does Simon have?

   c How many video games do they have altogether?

$O1 \ 47.4$

12 A 5 ha park has lawn : flowerbeds : play area in the ratio 20 : 4 : 1.
How many m² is the play area?

13 Arnie, Bob and Charlie share money in the ratio 2 : 3 : 4.
Arnie and Bob together have £20 more than Charlie.
How much did they share?

Q13 hint

A	A	B	B	B
£20	C	C	C	C

14 **Problem-solving** There are 20 coins in Julie's purse. The ratio of 50p to 20p to 10p coins is 1 : 2 : 2.

   a How many 20p coins does she have?

   b How much money does she have in total?

15 Reasoning Ratio **a** : **b** = 1 : 2 and ratio **b** : **c** = 3 : 4.
What is the ratio **a** : **b** : **c**?

16 Problem-solving A gardener plants daffodils,
roses and tulips in the ratio 5 : 3 : 2.
He plants 32 daffodils and roses altogether.
How many tulips does he plant?

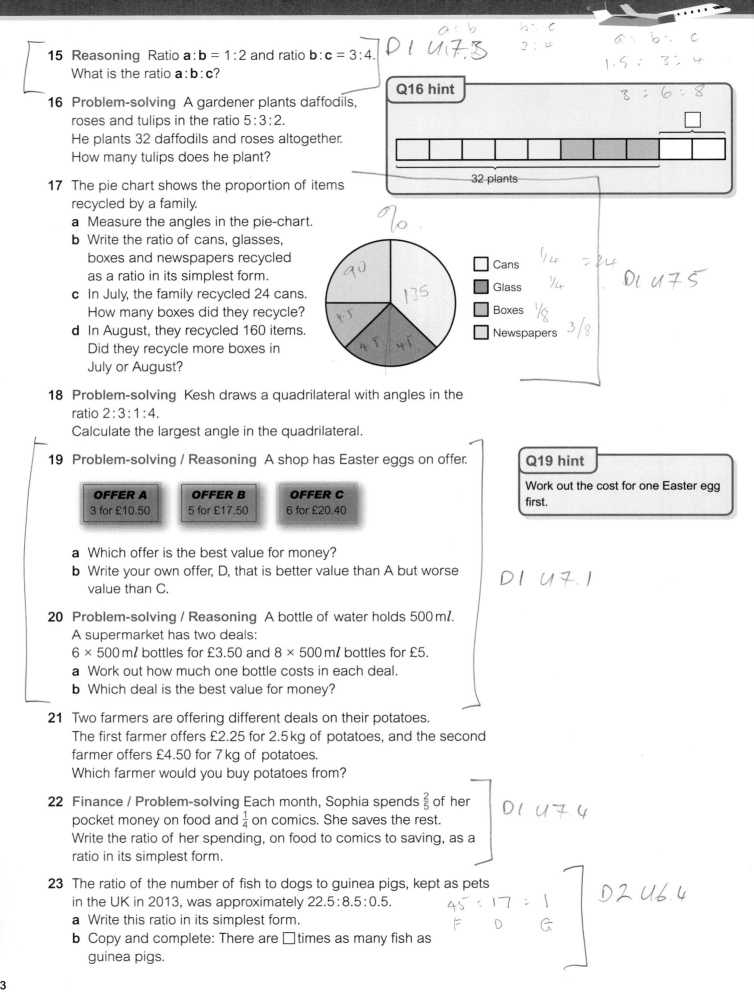

Q16 hint

32 plants

17 The pie chart shows the proportion of items
recycled by a family.
   a Measure the angles in the pie-chart.
   b Write the ratio of cans, glasses,
      boxes and newspapers recycled
      as a ratio in its simplest form.
   c In July, the family recycled 24 cans.
      How many boxes did they recycle?
   d In August, they recycled 160 items.
      Did they recycle more boxes in
      July or August?

☐ Cans
☐ Glass
☐ Boxes
☐ Newspapers

18 Problem-solving Kesh draws a quadrilateral with angles in the
ratio 2 : 3 : 1 : 4.
Calculate the largest angle in the quadrilateral.

19 Problem-solving / Reasoning A shop has Easter eggs on offer.

OFFER A
3 for £10.50

OFFER B
5 for £17.50

OFFER C
6 for £20.40

   a Which offer is the best value for money?
   b Write your own offer, D, that is better value than A but worse
      value than C.

Q19 hint

Work out the cost for one Easter egg
first.

20 Problem-solving / Reasoning A bottle of water holds 500 m*l*.
A supermarket has two deals:
6 × 500 m*l* bottles for £3.50 and 8 × 500 m*l* bottles for £5.
   a Work out how much one bottle costs in each deal.
   b Which deal is the best value for money?

21 Two farmers are offering different deals on their potatoes.
The first farmer offers £2.25 for 2.5 kg of potatoes, and the second
farmer offers £4.50 for 7 kg of potatoes.
Which farmer would you buy potatoes from?

22 Finance / Problem-solving Each month, Sophia spends $\frac{2}{5}$ of her
pocket money on food and $\frac{1}{4}$ on comics. She saves the rest.
Write the ratio of her spending, on food to comics to saving, as a
ratio in its simplest form.

23 The ratio of the number of fish to dogs to guinea pigs, kept as pets
in the UK in 2013, was approximately 22.5 : 8.5 : 0.5.
   a Write this ratio in its simplest form.
   b Copy and complete: There are ☐ times as many fish as
      guinea pigs.

24 The table shows the number of visitors to the top three attractions in London.

D1 47.6

	2011	2012
British Museum	5.8 million	5.6 million
Tate Modern	4.89 million	5.3 million
National Gallery	5.3 million	5.42 million

  a For each attraction, write the ratio of visitors in 2011 to 2012 in its simplest form.

  b Has the proportion of visitors going to the British Museum increased?

25 Problem-solving In a car-park, $\frac{1}{5}$ of the spaces are reserved for cars with children.
Write the ratio of spaces for cars with children, to cars without children, in its simplest form.   *D1 47.4*

Q25 hint
Work out the fraction of spaces for cars without children first.

26 Problem-solving In a pond, 35% of the fish are goldfish, 50% are carp and the rest are minnows.

  a Write the ratio of fish in its simplest form.   *D1 47.5*

  b There are 14 goldfish and 20 carp.
    How many minnows are there?

Q26a hint
Work out the percentage of fish that are minnows.

27 STEM The table gives the ratios of the mass and radius of three planets.

	Mass (septillion kg)	Radius (km)
Earth	5.97	6378
Mars	0.642	33 973 396
Mercury	0.330	22 402 440

Write the ratio of mass to radius for each planet in the form $1:n$.

28 The bar chart shows the number of visitors to a theme park in June and July.

  a Write the proportion of adults to children each month in the ratio $1:n$.

  b Which month had the higher proportion of children?

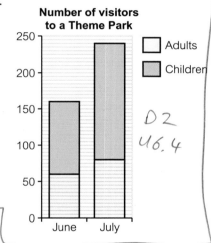

Number of visitors to a Theme Park
☐ Adults   ▨ Children

D2 46.4

29 Problem-solving It takes 12 people 40 days to build a bridge.
How many people are needed to build the bridge in 30 days?

Investigation

  1 Draw a square of side length 4 cm. Measure the diagonal.

  2 Repeat for different squares.

  3 Copy the table, and write the ratio of side length to diagonal for each square.

Side length	Diagonal length	Ratio side : diagonal		Ratio in the form 1 : n
4 cm	5.7	4 : 5.7	1.4	1 : 1.4
6 cm	8.4		1.4	
7 cm	9.9		1.4	

  4 What do you notice about the ratio of the side length to the diagonal?

  5 What do you think the length of the diagonal will be for a square of side length 10 cm?   *14 cm*

  6 What do you think the side length will be for a square with a diagonal of 14 cm?   *10 cm*

30 Reflect In these lessons you were asked questions about ratios and proportions. Are ratio and proportion the same thing or different?

Strategy hint
You could explain your answer using diagrams or real life examples.

Reflect

8 Unit test

Log how you did on your Student Progression Chart.

1 Write these ratios in their simplest form.

   a 8:12   **b** 50:20

2 Share £72 in the ratio 5:3.

3 The ratio of boys to girls in a tennis club is 3:4.
There are 12 boys in the tennis club.

   a How many girls are there?

   b How many people are there altogether?

4 Write each ratio in its simplest form.

   a 10:20:35   **b** 2 days:20 hours

   c 3000 g:2.4 kg   **d** £7.20:80p

5 Copy and complete.

   a 6 lbs ≈ ☐ g   **b** 3 ft ≈ ☐ cm

   c 10 miles ≈ ☐ km   **d** 4 gallons ≈ ☐ litres

6 A family of 4 buys 6 pints of milk on Friday.

   a Approximately how many litres is this?

   b Convert your answer into millilitres.

   One person drinks 150 ml of milk per day.

   c How many full days will the milk last the family?

7 On a school trip the ratio of teachers to students is 1:9.
Write this ratio as

   a a fraction

   b a percentage.

8 In the 2013 Wimbledon tennis final, the ratio of points won to points lost for Andy Murray was 26:11 and for Novak Djokovic was 30:22. Who won the greater proportion of points?

9 About 40% of a panda's fur is black and the rest is white.
Write the ratio of black to white fur in its simplest form.

10 8 tickets cost £360.
How much do 5 tickets cost?

11 Share 420 g in the ratio 1:2:4.

12 A yarn shop sells balls of wool in 100 g bundles. The shop has 3 different deals on wool.

| **Offer A** 2 balls for £3.25 | **Offer B** 5 balls for £7.50 | **Offer C** 8 balls for £10 |

Which offer is the best value for money?

13 Write this ratio in its simplest form:
0.6:0.8

14 One month Jamie spent $\frac{1}{4}$ of his money allowance on clothes, $\frac{1}{2}$ of his money on going out with his friends and saved the rest.
Write the ratio he spent on clothes, going out and savings as a ratio in its simplest form.

15 A gardener wants her flowerbed to be 40% pansies, 25% roses and the rest tulips.
a What percentage of flowers will be tulips?
b She plants 32 pansies and 20 roses. How many tulips does she need to plant?

16 Write these ratios in the form $1:n$.
a 5:30
b 0.2:0.8

17 Write these ratios in the form $n:1$.
a 24:3
b 5:6

18 It takes 4 people 5 hours to build a shed. How long does it take:
a 2 people
b 8 people?
c How many people are needed to build the shed in 1 hour?

Challenge

19 Here are six cards with ratios written on them.

| 3:5 | 0.1:0.3 | 1:4 | $\frac{1}{3}:\frac{2}{3}$ | 0.5:0.7 | $\frac{1}{4}:\frac{1}{5}$ |

Q19 hint

Use each ratio card once only. Only use a ratio card if it shares the amount exactly into whole numbers of pounds.

1 Start with £1000.
2 Choose a card and share £1000 in the ratio written on it.
  Circle the larger amount.
3 Choose a different card and share the circled amount in this ratio.
  Circle the smaller amount.
4 Choose a different card and share the circled amount in this ratio.
  Circle the larger amount.
  Continue these steps until you can go no further.
  a What is the smallest final amount you can find?
  b Is there a strategy you can use to try and find the smallest amount? Explain your answer.

20 **Reflect** List five new skills and ideas you have learned in this unit. What mathematics operations did you use most (addition, subtraction and division)?
Which lesson in this unit did you like best? Why?

Reflect

9.1 Triangles, parallelograms and trapeziums

You will learn to:
- Calculate the area of triangles, parallelograms and trapeziums.

CONFIDENCE

Why learn this?
Architects and engineers need to work out the areas of various shapes so they can design and construct interesting buildings.

Fluency
Work out the missing numbers.
- $\frac{1}{2} \times 8 \times 7$
- $\frac{1}{2} \times 3 \times 6$
- $7 \times \square = 35$
- $\frac{1}{2}(5 + 3) \times 10$

What does perpendicular mean?

Explore
What different shapes can you make from fitting two triangles together?

Exercise 9.1

Warm up

1 Work out the area of each shape.

a

5 cm
4 cm

b
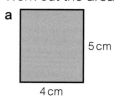
30 mm
70 mm

c
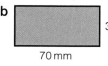
30 mm
6 cm

> **Q1c hint**
> Both sides need to be in the same units.

2 Work out the missing side length for each shape.

a

6 cm
Area 30 cm²

b
4 cm
Area 16 cm²

c

6 cm
Area 15 cm²

> **Q2 Literacy hint**
> Read 'cm²' as 'square centimetres'.

3 Substitute $a = 4$, $b = 5$ and $c = 2$ into these expressions.

a $\frac{1}{2}ab$ **b** $(c + b) \times a$ **c** $\frac{1}{2}(a + b)c$

4 Reasoning
a Copy these parallelograms on to centimetre squared paper. Label them A and B.

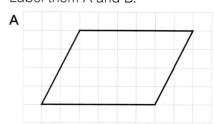
A

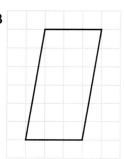
B

Topic links: Using formulae, Properties of 2D shapes

b Find the area of each parallelogram by counting squares.

c Write the measurements for each parallelogram in a table like this.

Parallelogram	Base length (cm)	Perpendicular height (cm)	Area (cm²)
A			

d What do you notice about the relationship between the base length, perpendicular height and area of a parallelogram?

e Copy and complete this formula.
Area of a parallelogram = _____

5 Work out the area of each parallelogram.

a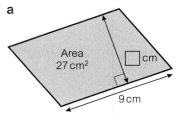

b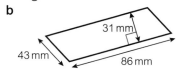

6 Work out the missing measurement for each shape.

a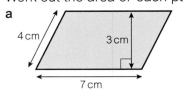

b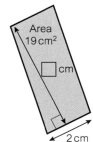

c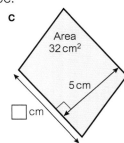

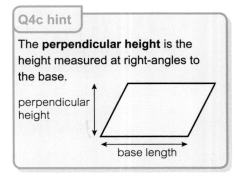

Investigation   **Reasoning**

1 Copy this parallelogram on to squared paper.
2 Calculate the area of the parallelogram.
3 Split the parallelogram in half to make two triangles.
4 What is the area of one of the triangles?
5 Complete these formulae.
 • Area of a parallelogram =
 • Area of a triangle =

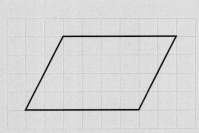

---

7 Work out the area of each triangle.

a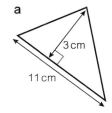

b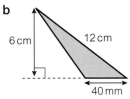

c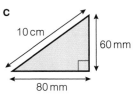

8 Work out the missing measurement for each triangle.

a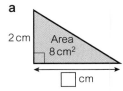

b

c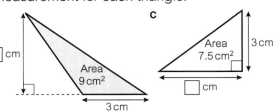

9 Real / Problem-solving Michaela is making some bunting.
Each flag is a triangle of height 40 cm and base 25 cm. She wants to
make 12 triangles.
Work out the total area of material that she needs.

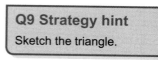
Q9 Strategy hint
Sketch the triangle.

10 Problem-solving Draw as many right-angled triangles as you can
with an area of 12 cm².
Discussion How will you know when you have drawn them all?

Q10 hint
Use whole number lengths only.

11 Reasoning Diagram A shows a trapezium. Diagram B shows two
identical trapeziums put together.

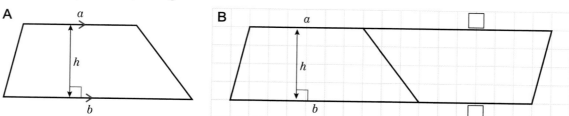

a What letters go in the two empty boxes in diagram B?
b What new shape has been made?
Copy and complete these sentences.
c The length of the base of the parallelogram is ☐ + ☐
d The area of the parallelogram is ☐ × ☐
e The area of one trapezium is ☐

12 Work out the area of each trapezium.

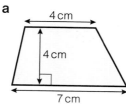
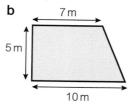
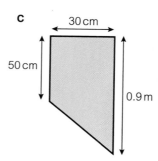
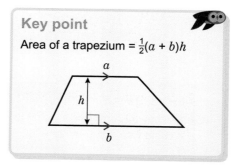

a 4 cm, 4 cm, 7 cm

b 7 m, 5 m, 10 m

c 30 cm, 50 cm, 0.9 m

Key point
Area of a trapezium = $\frac{1}{2}(a + b)h$

13 Real / Finance Car windscreen glass costs £325 per square metre.
Work out the cost of the glass for this car windscreen.

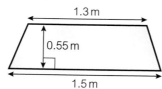

1.3 m
0.55 m
1.5 m

14 Explore What different shapes can you make from fitting two
triangles together?
What have you learned in this lesson to help you answer this
question?
What other information do you need?

15 Reflect After this lesson, Nigel says, 'Area is length × width.'
Shazia says, 'The area is the amount of space something takes up.'
Use what you have learned in this lesson to improve Nigel's definition.
Write another statement to add to Shazia's definition of area.

9.2 Perimeter and area of compound shapes

You will learn to:
- Calculate the area and perimeter of shapes made from rectangles and triangles.

Why learn this?
Carpet fitters need to calculate the area of a room in a house when they lay carpets.

Fluency
Work out
- $7 \times 3 + 4 \times 5$
- $6 \times 2 + 8 \times 4$
- $5 \times 6 - 2 \times 3$

Explore
How much would it cost to carpet an L-shaped room?

Exercise 9.2

1 Work out the area and perimeter of each shape.

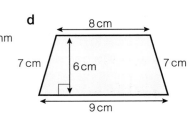

a 5 cm, 60 mm

b 30 mm, 5 cm, 40 mm

c 20 mm, 30 mm, 8 cm

d 8 cm, 7 cm, 6 cm, 7 cm, 9 cm

2 Work out each side length marked with a ☐.

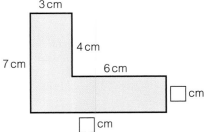

a 3 cm, 4 cm, 7 cm, 6 cm, ☐ cm, ☐ cm

b ☐ cm, 3 cm, ☐ cm, 5 cm, 7 cm, 8 cm

Q2a hint
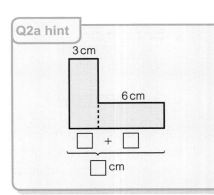
3 cm, 6 cm
☐ + ☐
☐ cm

3 Work out the perimeter of each shape.

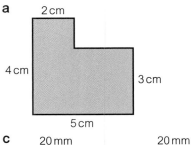

a 2 cm, 4 cm, 3 cm, 5 cm

b 5 m, 3 m, 1 m, 7 m

c 20 mm, 10 mm, 20 mm, 40 mm, 90 mm

Q3 Strategy hint
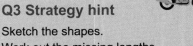
Sketch the shapes.
Work out the missing lengths.
Write them on your sketch.

Warm up

Worked example

Work out the area of this shape.

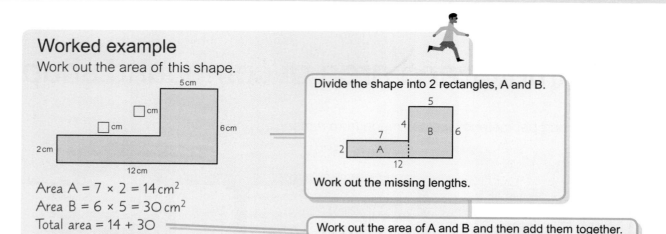

Area A = 7 × 2 = 14 cm²
Area B = 6 × 5 = 30 cm²
Total area = 14 + 30
= 44 cm²

Divide the shape into 2 rectangles, A and B.

Work out the missing lengths.

Work out the area of A and B and then add them together.

4 Real The diagram shows the dimensions of a room.
Work out the area of the floor.
Discussion How many different ways are there to work out the area of the floor?

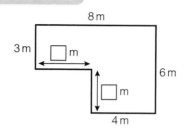

5 Reasoning / Problem-solving Karen has 20 m of fence to make the largest possible rabbit pen. She comes up with these three ideas.
a Show that each rabbit pen uses 20 m of fencing.
b Which design, A, B or C, gives the rabbits the most space?

Q5 Strategy hint
'Show that' means show working that gives 20 m as the answer.

6 Problem-solving Work out the shaded area of each shape.

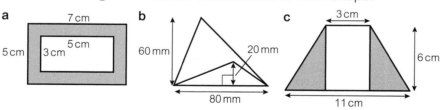

Q6 hint

Shaded area = area of whole shape − area of cut-out shape

7 Real What is the area of plastic used in this shapes stencil?

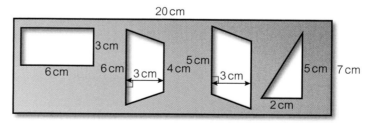

8 Explore How much would it cost to carpet an L-shaped room?
What have you learned in this lesson to help you answer this question?
What other information do you need?

9 Reflect In this lesson you split up compound shapes into more simple shapes before working out the area.
How did you decide which way to split up a shape?
Explain to a friend how you would split up this shape, and then work out its total area.
What lengths do you need to know before you can work out the area?

Topic links: Using formulae

*Active*Learn Delta 1, Section 9.2

Check P223 | Strengthen P225 | Extend P229 | Test P233

9.3 Properties of 3D solids

You will learn to:
- Identify nets of different 3D solids
- Know the properties of 3D solids.

Why learn this?
People used to think the Earth was flat, but now we know it's a sphere.

Fluency
What are the names of these 2D shapes?

Which of these shapes have parallel sides?

Explore
How could you make a 4-sided dice?

Exercise 9.3

1 Look at these solids.
   a Write the names of the solids.
   b Write the names of the 2D shapes you can see.

2 **Problem-solving**
   a Draw each **net** on squared paper and cut them out.

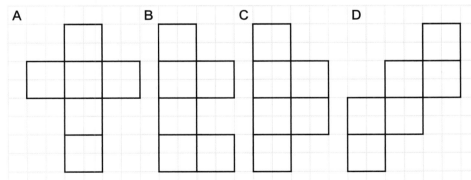

Key point
A **net** is a 2D shape that folds to make a 3D solid.

   b Fold them up.
   Do any of them form a cube?

   Discussion Predict which of E and F will form a cube.

   c Draw one more net that you think will form a cube.
   Cut it out and check that it works.

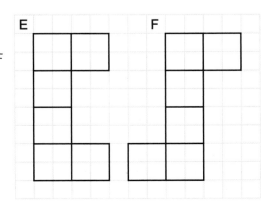

Unit 9 Perimeter, area and volume **212**

Worked example

Sketch a net of this cuboid.

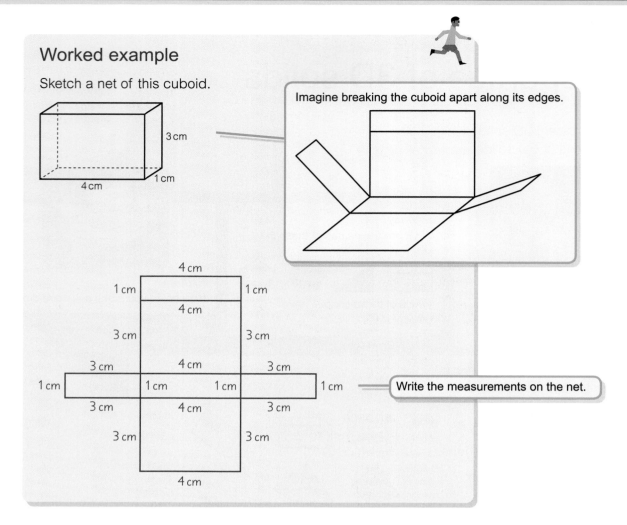

Imagine breaking the cuboid apart along its edges.

Write the measurements on the net.

---

3 Sketch a net for each cuboid.

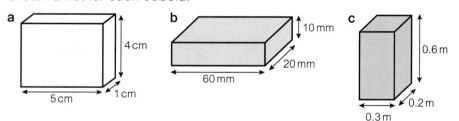

a 5 cm, 4 cm, 1 cm

b 60 mm, 20 mm, 10 mm

c 0.6 m, 0.3 m, 0.2 m

Q3 hint

For a sketch you should use a ruler and a pencil, but you don't need to measure the lengths accurately.

4 Look at these nets.

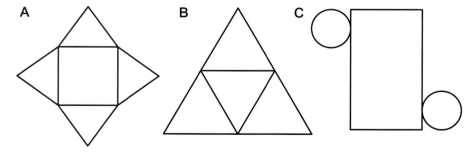

A   B   C

Which one folds to make
a a triangle-based pyramid
b a cylinder
c a square-based pyramid?

5 Write the number of **faces**, **edges** and **vertices** in this pyramid.

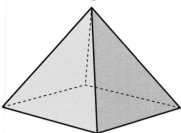

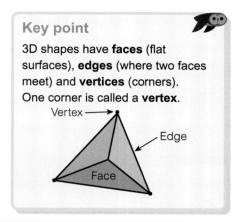
6 Problem-solving A 3D solid has 3 rectangular and 2 triangular faces. What could you call this solid?

Investigation   Reasoning

1 Record the number of faces (F), edges (E) and vertices (V) for each solid.

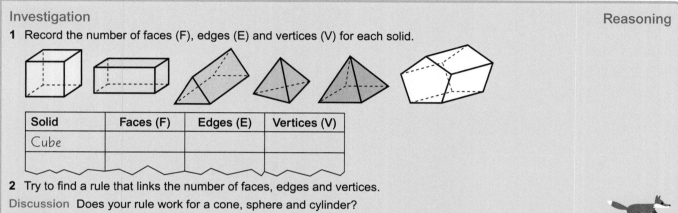

Solid	Faces (F)	Edges (E)	Vertices (V)
Cube			

2 Try to find a rule that links the number of faces, edges and vertices.

Discussion Does your rule work for a cone, sphere and cylinder?

7 Problem-solving Look at this cube. You can cut a cube into two equal parts.
What new 3D solids would you make if you cut it
   a horizontally   **b** vertically   **c** diagonally?

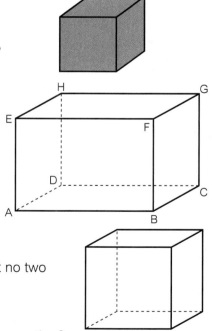

8 Look at this cuboid.
Copy and complete these sentences.
   a The edge AE is parallel to the edges DH, BF and ___.
   b The edge EF is parallel to the edges ___, ___ and ___.
   c The edge AB is perpendicular to ___ and ___.
   d The faces ABCD and _____ are parallel.
   e The faces ABFE and BCGF meet at edge ___.
   f If two edges meet, they meet at a _____.
   g If two faces meet, they meet at an _____.

9 Problem-solving This cube needs painting.
What is the smallest number of colours you must use so that no two faces that touch are the same colour?

10 **Explore** How could you make a 4-sided dice?
What have you learned in this lesson to help you answer this question?
What other information do you need?

11 **Reflect** In Q6 you worked out which solid was being described from the shape of its faces.
Describe two other solids in terms of the shape of their faces.

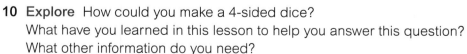
Explore

Reflect

9.4 Surface area

You will learn to:

- Calculate the surface area of cubes and cuboids.

Why learn this?
Upholsterers use surface area to work out how much fabric they need to cover sofa cushions.

Fluency
Work out

- 6 × 9 = ☐
- 6 × ☐ = 96
- 5²
- 3

Explore
How many posters can you fit on your bedroom walls and ceiling?

CONFIDENCE

Exercise 9.4

Warm up

1 Sketch a net for each shape.

a

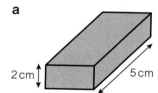

2 cm   5 cm   3 cm

b

3 cm
3 cm   3 cm

2 Work out the area of the shaded face on each shape.

a

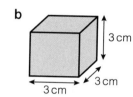

20 mm
10 mm
40 mm

b

5 cm
1.5 cm
2 cm

3 The diagrams show a cube and its net.
Work out the **surface area** of the cube.

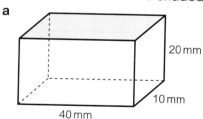

2 cm
2 cm
2 cm

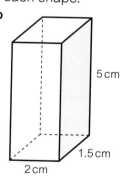

2 cm
2 cm
2 cm

Key point

The **surface area** of a 3D solid is the total area of all its faces.

Discussion You may have started by working out the area of one face of the cube. Is there a shortcut for finding the surface area of a cube?

215   **Topic links:** Formulae

4 Work out the surface area of each cube?

a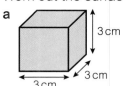
3 cm
3 cm
3 cm

b a 20 mm by 20 mm by 20 mm cube

c a cube with edge length 5 cm.

5 Reasoning Here is a cube with edge length n cm.
a What is the area of one face on this cube?
b Write a formula for the surface area of a cube with side n.
c Use your formula from part **b** to calculate the surface area of a cube with side 4 cm.

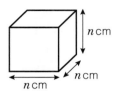
n cm
n cm
n cm

6 Work out the surface area of each cuboid.

a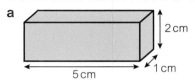
2 cm
1 cm
5 cm

b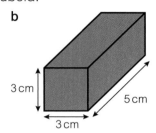
3 cm
5 cm
3 cm

Discussion Is there a shortcut for finding the surface area of a cuboid?

Q6a hint

Sketch a net. Then work out the area of each rectangle and add the areas together.

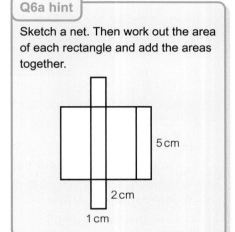
5 cm
2 cm
1 cm

Worked example

Find the surface area of this cuboid.

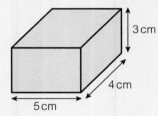
3 cm
4 cm
5 cm

Surface area
Area of top face   = 5 × 4 = 20 cm²
Area of front face = 3 × 5 = 15 cm²
Area of side face = 4 × 3 = 12 cm² +
Sum of 3 faces   = 47 cm²
Total surface area = 2 × 47 = 94 cm²

Each face has an identical pair.

7 Work out the surface area of each cuboid.

a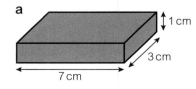
1 cm
3 cm
7 cm

b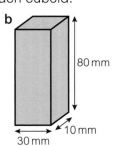
80 mm
10 mm
30 mm

c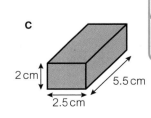
2 cm
2.5 cm
5.5 cm

Q7 hint

Use the same method as in the worked example.

8 Problem-solving A cube has a surface area of 96 cm².

   a What is the area of each face?

   b What is the length of one edge?

9 Reasoning Use the diagram to help you copy and complete:

   a The area of the front face is ☐.

   b The area of the top face is ☐.

   c The area of the side face is ☐.

   d The total area of these 3 faces is ☐.

   e The total surface area (all 6 faces) is ☐.

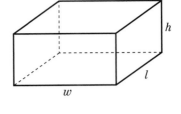

10 Real / Problem-solving Joey wants to wrap a present for his sister.

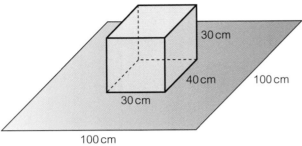

Q10 hint

Would a net of this box fit on the wrapping paper?

   Does he have enough wrapping paper?

   Discussion How does the hint help you answer the question?

11 Real / Problem-solving Kevin wants to paint the outside of this toy box. He has enough paint to cover 15 000 cm². Will this be enough?

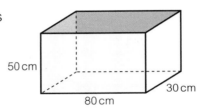

Q11 hint

The box only has 5 faces.

12 Real / Problem-solving Louise wants to make a two-step stool. Both the steps are the same size. She does not need to put wood on the base. How much wood does she need for this project?

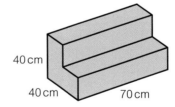

13 Explore How many posters can you fit on your bedroom walls and ceiling?

What you have learned in this lesson to help you answer this question?

What other information do you need?

14 Reflect This lesson showed you two methods for finding the surface area of a cube or cuboid.

   • Method 1 (draw then add)
     Draw a net, write the area of each face on the net, add them together (Q6)

   • Method 2 (visualise then calculate)
     Visualise pairs of opposite faces, calculate the area of each different face, add them together, double your answer (Q7)

   Which method did you prefer? Why?

Q14 hint

What are the advantages and disadvantages of your method?

Explore

Reflect

9.5 Volume

You will learn to:
- Calculate the volume of a cube or a cuboid
- Convert between cm³, m*l* and litres.

Why learn this?
The number of fish that can be put in a fish tank depends on the size (volume) of the tank.

Fluency
What is the area of these shapes?

12 cm
3 cm
7 cm
7 cm

Explore
How many fish can you put in a cuboid-shaped tank that measures 50 cm by 40 cm by 80 cm?

Exercise 9.5

1 Work out
  a $5 \times 3 \times 8$ **b** $6 \times 4 \times 3$ **c** $4 \times 2 \times 4$

2 How many 1 cm cubes make up each shape?

  a   **b**   **c**

 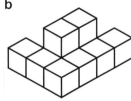 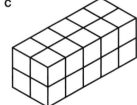

3 a How many 1 cm cubes make up each cube?

  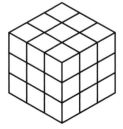

  b Work out the first three cube numbers.
    $1^3 = \square$ $2^3 = \square$ $3^3 = \square$
    What do you notice?

4 A cube has a side length of 8 cm.
  What is the **volume** of the cube?

5 Problem-solving A cube has a surface area of 54 cm³.
  a What is the area of one face?
  b What is the length of one side?
  c What is the volume of the cube?

Warm up

6 a Count the 1 cm cubes in each cuboid.

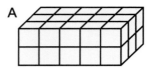 A   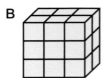 B   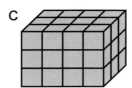 C

b Copy and complete this table for the cuboids.

Cuboid	Length	Width	Height	Length × width × height
A				

 7 a Calculate the volume of each cuboid.

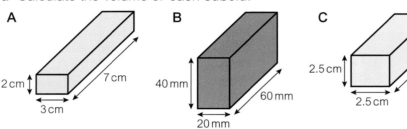

A — 2 cm, 7 cm, 3 cm

B — 40 mm, 60 mm, 20 mm

C — 2.5 cm, 5 cm, 2.5 cm

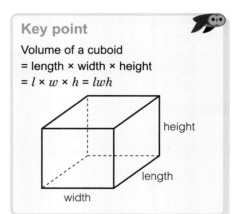

Key point

Volume of a cuboid
= length × width × height
= $l × w × h = lwh$

height
length
width

b **Reasoning** Imagine that the three cuboids are put together.
  i Will the volume of the new shape be the sum of the volumes?
  ii Will the surface area of the new shape be the sum of the surface areas?
  Explain your answers.

Investigation   **Reasoning**

Look at this cuboid.

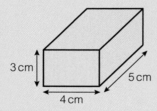

3 cm, 5 cm, 4 cm

1 What is the volume of the cuboid?
2 Write the dimensions of at least three more cuboids with the same volume.
3 Usman says the cuboid with dimensions $\frac{1}{2}$ cm by 12 cm by 10 cm has the same volume as this cuboid.
  Is he right?

Discussion Are there more cuboids with the same volume?

---

8 Copy and complete these conversions.
  a 0.45 litres = ☐ cm³
  b 6.3 cm³ = ☐ ml
  c ☐ litres = 7346 cm³

Key point

The **capacity** of a container is how much it can hold. The units of capacity are cm³, millilitres (ml) and litres (l).
• 1 millilitre (ml) = 1 cm³
• 1 litre (l) = 1000 cm³

 9 **Real / Reasoning** For a long-distance camping trip, students need a rucksack that has a **capacity** of at least 65 litres. Peter buys a rucksack measuring 34 cm by 26 cm by 75 cm.
  a Work out the capacity in cm³.
  b Work out the capacity in litres.
  c Is Peter's rucksack big enough?

    Topic links: Properties of 3D shapes, Factors, Multiplying decimals   **Subject links:** Science (Q15)

10 Problem-solving The volume of this cuboid is 168 cm³. Find the missing length.

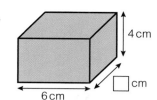

4 cm

□ cm

6 cm

11 Problem-solving

A 3 cm by 3 cm by 3 cm cube has a 1 cm by 1 cm square hole cut through it.
What is the volume of the remaining solid?

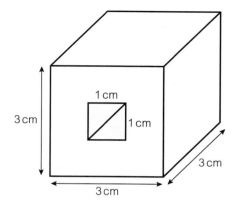

1 cm

3 cm

1 cm

3 cm

3 cm

Q11 hint

What is the volume of the piece cut out of the cube?

12 Problem-solving Look at this triangular prism.

a How many of these triangular prisms would make a 3 cm by 4 cm by 12 cm cuboid?

b Use your answer to part **a** to calculate the volume of the triangular prism.

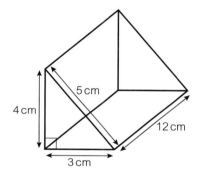

4 cm

5 cm

12 cm

3 cm

13 Problem-solving Here are the areas of three faces of the same cuboid.

A

Area = 30 cm²

B

Area = 42 cm²

C

Area = 35 cm²

a What are the dimensions of each rectangle?

b What is the volume of the cuboid?

c What is the surface area of the cuboid?

14 Explore How many fish can you put in a cuboid-shaped tank that measures 50 cm by 40 cm by 80 cm?
Is it easier to explore this question now you have completed the lesson?
What further information do you need to be able to answer this?

15 Reflect Maths is not the only subject where you use volume.
You use it in science too.
Describe how you have used volume in science.
In what ways is volume the same or different in science as in this maths lesson?
Do you think volume means the same in all subjects?
Explain your answer.

Explore

Reflect

9.6 STEM: Measures of area and volume

You will learn to:
- Convert between metric measures for area and volume.

Why learn this?
Ecologists use measures of area and volume when studying plants and animals in hedgerows.

Fluency
How many m² in one hectare?
Multiply each number by 100
- 7
- 7.5
- 7.53

Explore
How much land is needed to support a herd of deer?

CONFIDENCE

Exercise 9.6: Ecology

Warm up

1 Work out
  a $2.5 \times 10 \times 10$
  b $0.04 \times 100 \times 100$
  c $450 \div 10 \div 10$
  d $9045 \div 100 \div 100$

2 Work out the missing numbers.
  a $2 \times \square = 20\,000$
  b $760 \div \square = 7.6$
  c $\square \div 100 = 0.03$

3 Which unit of area would be sensible for measuring
  a the area of a school pond
  b the area of Scotland
  c the area of an oak leaf?

4 STEM / Modelling   A conservation trust has been given a 5.3 **hectare** piece of land. It plans to use $18\,750\,\text{m}^2$ for woodland and $28\,125\,\text{m}^2$ for a wildlife meadow.
  a Is the area they have been given big enough for their planned use?
  b They estimate that they will need $2.4\,\text{m} \times 5\,\text{m}$ sections for every 10 oak seedlings they plant. How many seedlings can they plant?
  Discussion Is this a good model for working out the number of trees? Will they need any other space in the woodland?

5 Real A rectangular reservoir measures 1.2 km by 1.6 km. How many hectares is this?

6 Copy and complete these conversions.
  a $4\,\text{cm}^2 = \square\,\text{mm}^2$
  b $\square\,\text{cm}^2 = 0.58\,\text{m}^2$
  c $17\,000\,\text{m}^2 = \square\,\text{km}^2$
  d $\square\,\text{m}^2 = 3.5\,\text{km}^2$

7 a i Work out the area of this rectangle in cm².
    ii Convert the area to mm².
  b Convert the lengths to mm and work out the area in mm².
  Discussion Which method was easier, the one in part **a** or part **b**?

36 cm

11.2 cm

Key point

It is important to be able to choose the most suitable metric units for measuring. Some of the metric units that you already know are
- mm, cm, m, km (length)
- mm², cm², m², km², hectares (area)

Q4 hint

Convert km to m and then m² to hectares. A **hectare** is $10\,000\,\text{m}^2$.

Q6a hint

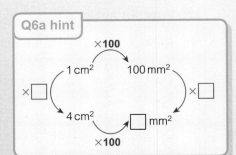

Topic links: Powers of 10   **Subject links:** Science (Q3, Q4, Q8, Q11)

8 **STEM / Problem-solving** Ann is surveying the plants growing in some wasteland, measuring 7.5m by 3.2m. She places **quadrats** at random within the survey area. Each quadrat is a 50cm × 50cm square.
   a What is the maximum number of quadrats that would fit?
   b She **samples** the plants in 12 quadrats randomly. What proportion of the wasteland has she sampled?

Q8 Literacy hint

A **quadrat** is a square frame used to **sample** organisms, such as plants, in a large area.

9 a These cubes are the same size.
   Copy the diagrams and write in the measurements.

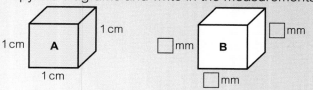

Q9 Strategy hint

You might find it easier to convert the units first and then find the volume.

   b Find the volume of
      i A in ☐cm³   **ii** B in ☐mm³
   c Copy and complete these sentences.
      i To convert from cm³ to mm³ _____ by ☐
      ii To convert from mm³ to cm³ _____ by ☐
   d These cubes are also the same size. Copy the diagrams and write in the measurements.

   e Find the volume of
      i C in ☐m³   **ii** D in ☐cm³
   f Copy and complete these sentences.
      i To convert from m³ to cm³ _____ by ☐
      ii To convert from cm³ to m³ _____ by ☐

Key point

To convert from
• cm³ to mm³ you multiply by 10³ or 1000
• mm³ to cm³ you divide by 10³ or 1000
• m³ to cm³ you multiply by 100³ or 1 000 000
• cm³ to m³ you divide by 100³ or 1 000 000

10 Copy and complete these conversions.
   a 8cm³ = ☐mm³   b ☐cm³ = 95mm³
   c 73.4m³ = ☐cm³   d ☐m³ = 250 000cm³

11 **STEM / Problem-solving** Earthworms have been called 'ecosystem engineers'. They improve soil structure and help release important nutrients to growing plants.
   Fred reads that healthy soil should have 5600 earthworms per cubic metre. He finds 40 earthworms in a 20cm × 20cm × 20cm sample. Is his sample healthy soil? Explain your answer.

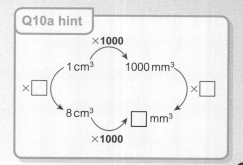

Q10a hint

12 **Explore** How much land is needed to support a herd of deer? What have you learned in this lesson to help you answer this question? What other information do you need?

13 **Reflect** Jan says, '1cm is 10mm so 1cm² is 10mm².'
   Choose two questions from this lesson that will help Jan understand her mistake.
   Using your knowledge from the previous two lessons, draw a diagram or write an explanation to show Jan how many mm³ are equal to 1 litre.

Explore

Reflect

Master
P207

CHECK

Strengthen
P225

Extend
P229

Test
P233

9 Check up

Log how you did on your
Student Progression Chart.

Area and perimeter of 2D shapes

1 Find the perimeter of this shape.

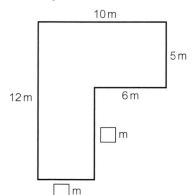

2 Work out the area of this shape.

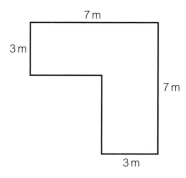

3 Work out the area of this triangle.

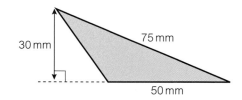

4 Work out the area of each shape.

a

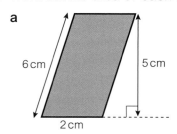

b

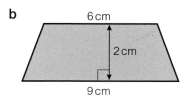

Working with 3D solids

5 Work out the surface area of this cuboid.

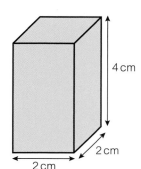

6 Sketch a net of this 3D solid.

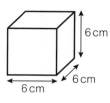

7 Calculate the volume of these solids.

a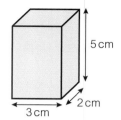

b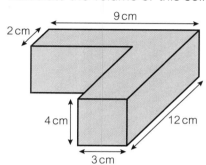

8 Calculate the volume of this solid.

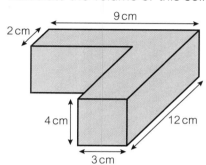

Measures of area and volume

9 What is the area of this rectangle in mm²?

3 cm

6 cm

10 Copy and complete these conversions.

    a $6 \text{cm}^2 = \square \text{mm}^2$ **b** $0.9 \text{cm}^2 = \square \text{mm}^2$

    c $350 \text{mm}^2 = \square \text{cm}^2$ **d** $3 \text{m}^2 = \square \text{cm}^2$

    e $5.02 \text{m}^2 = \square \text{cm}^2$ **f** $2590 \text{cm}^2 = \square \text{m}^2$

11 Copy and complete these conversions.

    a $18 \text{cm}^3 = \square \text{mm}^3$ **b** $\square \text{cm}^3 = 265 \text{mm}^3$

    c $0.7 \text{m}^3 = \square \text{cm}^3$ **d** $\square \text{cm}^3 = 931\,000 \text{m}^3$

    e $42 \text{m}^3 = \square \text{m}l$ **f** $3 \text{ litres} = \square \text{cm}^3$

12 **How sure are you of your answers? Were you mostly**

    😟 **Just guessing**   😐 **Feeling doubtful**   🙂 **Confident**

    What next? Use your results to decide whether to strengthen or extend your learning.

Challenge

13 A shape has an area of 10cm^2.

    Sketch and label the lengths of a possible

    a triangle   **b** rectangle

    c parallelogram   **d** trapezium.

Reflect

Master
P207

Check
P223

STRENGTHEN

Extend
P229

Test
P233

9 Strengthen

You will:
• Strengthen your understanding with practice.

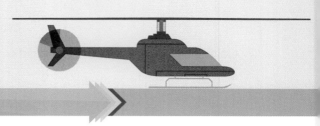

Area and perimeter of 2D shapes

1 For each pair of shapes, find the area of the rectangle and the area of the triangle.

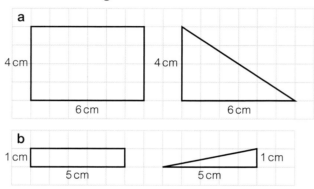

a

4 cm   6 cm   4 cm   6 cm

b

1 cm   5 cm   1 cm   5 cm

2 a For each triangle write
   i base length = ☐ cm   **ii** perpendicular height = ☐ cm

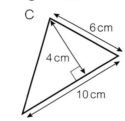

A
2 cm
6 cm

B
7 cm
3 cm

C
6 cm
4 cm
10 cm

> **Q2 hint**
>
> Area of a triangle
> = $\frac{1}{2}$ × base length × perpendicular height

b Work out the area of each triangle.

3 Work out the perimeter and area of each shape.
They have been started for you.
Copy and complete the working below.

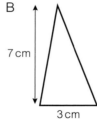

a   ☐ cm
2 cm   ☐ cm
     10 cm

b   ☐ cm
3 cm
7 cm   ☐ cm
2 cm
     10 cm

a Perimeter = 10 + 2 + ☐ + ☐ = ☐ cm
   Area = ☐ × ☐ = ☐ cm²
b Perimeter = 10 + 2 + 7 + 3 + ☐ + ☐ + ☐ = ☐ cm
   Area = ☐ × ☐ + ☐ × ☐ = ☐ cm²

> **Q3b hint**
>
>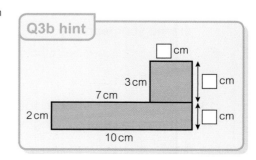
>
> ☐ cm
> 3 cm   ☐ cm
> 7 cm
> 2 cm   ☐ cm
> 10 cm

Topic links: Using formulae

4 Work out the perimeter and area of each shape.

a
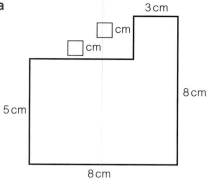
3 cm
□ cm
□ cm
8 cm
5 cm
8 cm

b
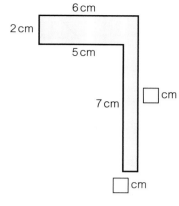
6 cm
2 cm
5 cm
7 cm
□ cm
□ cm

Q4 hint

First find each missing side length marked with a □

5 Calculate the area of each parallelogram.

a
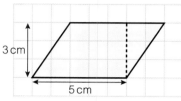
3 cm
5 cm

b
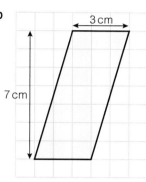
3 cm
7 cm

Q5a hint

Imagine making the parallelogram into a rectangle by moving part of the shape to the other side.

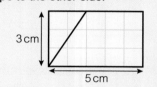
3 cm
5 cm

6 Sketch these trapeziums.

a 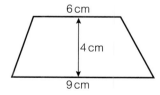 **b** 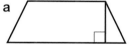 **c**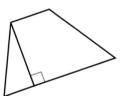

Label the parallel sides a and b and the perpendicular height h.

Q6a hint

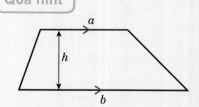
a
h
b

7 Copy and complete the working to find the area of this trapezium.

6 cm
4 cm
9 cm

Area = $\frac{1}{2}(a + b)h$
= $\frac{1}{2} \times (□ + □) \times □$
= $\frac{1}{2} \times □ \times □$
= $□$ cm^2

$a = 6$
$h = 4$
$b = 9$

8 Find the area of each trapezium.

a
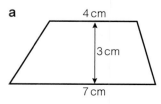
4 cm
3 cm
7 cm

b
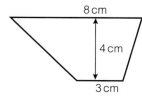
8 cm
4 cm
3 cm

Q8 hint

Use the method in Q7.

Working with 3D solids

1 a Look at this cuboid.
Choose the correct words to make these sentences true.

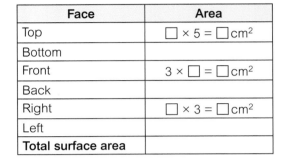

   back   left-hand side   bottom

   i The area of the top face is the same as the area of the _____ face.

   ii The area of the front face is the same as the area of the _____ face.

   iii The area of the right-hand side face is the same as the area of the _____ face

b Copy and complete the table to find the surface area of the cuboid.

Face	Area
Top	$\square \times 5 = \square \, cm^2$
Bottom	
Front	$3 \times \square = \square \, cm^2$
Back	
Right	$\square \times 3 = \square \, cm^2$
Left	
Total surface area	

2 Work out the surface area of the cuboid.

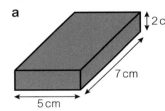

> **Q2 hint**
>
> Use a table.

3 These cuboids are made from 1 cm cubes.

A 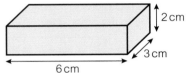   **B** 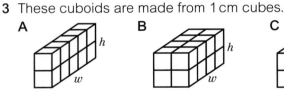   **C**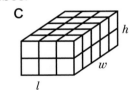

a For each cuboid write $l = \square\,cm$, $w = \square\,cm$, $h = \square\,cm$.

b Find each volume.

c Check your answers by counting cubes.

> **Q3b hint**
>
> Volume of a cuboid
> = length × width × height
> = $l \times w \times h = \square \, cm^3$

4 Calculate the volume of each cuboid.

a 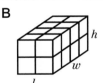 2 cm   7 cm   5 cm

b 1 cm   7 cm   5 cm

c 3 cm   3 cm   3 cm

Measures of area and volume

1 These squares are the same size.

a Work out the area of each square.

b Copy and complete this number line for converting cm² to mm² areas.

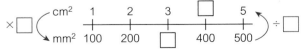

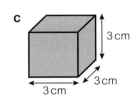 **A**   1 cm   1 cm

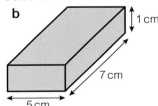 **B**   10 mm   10 mm

2 Work out the area of each shape in cm². Then convert it to mm².

a 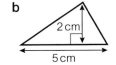 3 cm   4 cm

b 2 cm   5 cm

> **Q2 hint**
>
> Use your number line from Q1 to help you.

3 Work out each area in mm². Then convert it to cm².

a
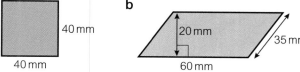
40 mm
40 mm

b

20 mm
35 mm
60 mm

4 These squares are the same size.
   a Work out the area of each square.
   b Copy and complete this number line for converting m² to cm² areas.

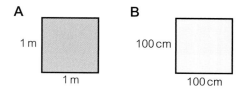

A 1 m × 1 m

B 100 cm × 100 cm

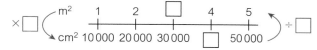

$\times \square$ ⟨ m² 1   2 $\square$ 4   5
   cm² 10 000 20 000 30 000 $\square$ 50 000 ⟩ $\div \square$

5 Copy and complete these conversions.
   a $2.05\,m^2 = 2.05 \times \square = \square\,cm^2$ **b** $0.07\,m^2 = \square\,cm^2$
   c $\square\,m^2 = 8600\,cm^2$

6 These cubes have the same volume.
   a Work out the volume of each cube.
   b Copy and complete this number line for converting cm³ to mm³ volumes.

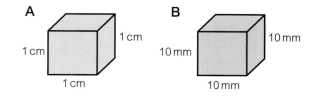

A 1 cm, 1 cm, 1 cm

B 10 mm, 10 mm, 10 mm

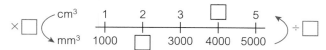

$\times \square$ ⟨ cm³ 1   2   3 $\square$ 5
   mm³ 1000 $\square$ 3000 4000 5000 ⟩ $\div \square$

7 Copy and complete these conversions.
   a **i** $6\,cm^3 = \square\,mm^3$ **ii** $0.012\,cm^3 = \square\,mm^3$
   iii $\square\,cm^3 = 15\,800\,mm^3$
   b **i** $0.04\,m^3 = \square\,cm^3$ **ii** $12.7\,m^3 = \square\,cm^3$
   iii $\square\,m^3 = 1.4$ million cm³

> **Q7 hint**
>
> Use your number line from Q6 to help. Draw a similar one for converting cm³ to m³ volumes.

Enrichment

1 Problem-solving Jo wants to grow vegetables.
   She buys 16 raised beds measuring 1 m by 4 m by 0.5 m.
   a Calculate the volume of one raised bed.
   b Write its dimensions in centimetres.
   c Calculate the volume in cubic centimetres.
   A 40-litre bag of soil costs £2.50.
   d How many 40-litre bags of soil will Jo need for each raised bed?
   e How much will soil cost for one raised bed?
   f How much will she spend on soil in total?

> **Q1 hint**
>
> 1 litre = 1000 cm³

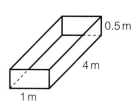
0.5 m
4 m
1 m

2 Reflect In this unit you have had to do lots of different things to find the answers to questions.
   Write these in order, from the one you found easiest to the one you found hardest:
   A Knowing which is the perpendicular height in a shape
   B Using a formula to find the area of a shape
   C Working out what the net of a 3D solid will look like
   D Finding the surface area of a cuboid
   E Knowing when to multiply and when to divide when converting measures.
   Write a hint, in your own words, for the one you found the hardest.

Reflect

9 Extend

You will:
• Extend your understanding with problem-solving.

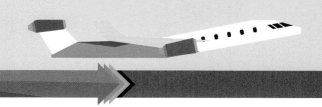

1 The diagram shows a pentagonal prism.
This solid has faces in the shape of 2 pentagons and 5 rectangles. It has 7 faces, 15 edges and 10 vertices.

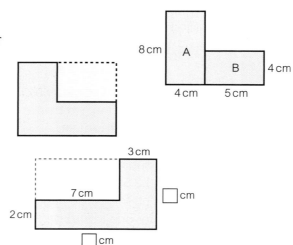

  a What shapes are the faces of these 3D solids:
    i a hexagonal prism
    ii a heptagonal prism
    iii a decagonal prism?

> **Q1a hint**
> heptagon – 7 sides
> decagon – 10 sides

  b Copy and complete this table for the solid in the diagram and described in part **a**.

Solid	Faces	Edges	Vertices	Check: F + V = E + 2
Pentagonal prism	7	15	10	□ + □ = □ + 2 = □
Hexagonal prism				

  c A prism has 8 rectangles and 2 end shapes.
    What is the name of this prism?

2 **Reasoning**
  a Find the area of this shape by adding together the areas of A and B.
  b Find the area of the same shape again, by finding the area of the whole rectangle and subtracting the shaded area.
  Discussion Which method do you prefer? Why?

3 **Problem-solving** The area of this L shape is 32 cm².
Find its perimeter.

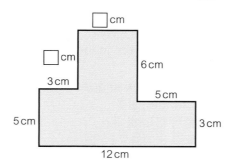

4 For this shape work out
  a the perimeter
  b the area.

Topic links: Prisms, Range, Percentages, Rounding, Properties of 2D shapes, Ratio and proportion

5 Reasoning Show why these statements are wrong.
  a When the length and the width of a rectangle are doubled, the area is also doubled.
  b Ignoring the units, the area and the perimeter of a square are always different.

6 Problem-solving / Modelling A container ship carries goods around the world. A standard container is 40 ft long, 8 ft wide and 8 ft 6 inches high.
  a Convert these measurements into centimetres.
  b Calculate the volume of the container in cubic centimetres.
  The deck of a large ship measures 1200 ft long and 160 ft wide.
  c Approximately how many containers can fit into this area?
  d The ship can carry approximately 7500 containers. How high will the containers be stacked?

7 Problem-solving The volume of water in a fish tank is 84 000 cm³. The fish tank has length 60 cm and width 35 cm.
  The water comes to 10 cm from the top of the tank.
  Calculate the height of the tank.

8 Barry has a freezer with a capacity of 18 cubic feet.
  a Write possible dimensions for the freezer in
    i feet
    ii centimetres.
  b Calculate the volume of the freezer in cubic centimetres.

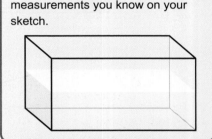

9 Write an expression for the area of each parallelogram. Write each answer in its simplest form.

a
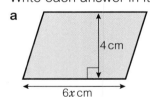
4 cm
6x cm

b
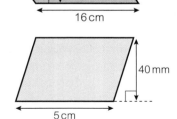
0.25y cm
16 cm

10 Work out the area of this shape in square centimetres.

40 mm
5 cm

11 Work out the area of each rectangle.
  Give your answers in the units shown on each rectangle.

a
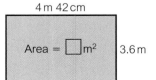
4 m 42 cm
Area = ☐ m²   3.6 m

b
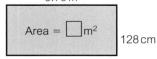
3.75 m
Area = ☐ m²   128 cm

Give your answers to parts **c** and **d** to 2 decimal places.

c
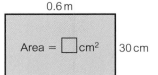
0.6 m
Area = ☐ cm²   30 cm

d
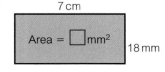
7 cm
Area = ☐ mm²   18 mm

Q5 hint
Sketch some shapes. Try different lengths and widths. Show working or an example for each statement that proves it is wrong.

Q6 hint
1 ft = 12 inches ≈ 30 cm

Q7 hint
Sketch the water in the tank. Put the measurements you know on your sketch.

12 a Work out the area of A and B.

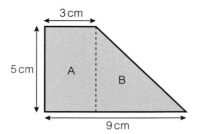

b What is the total area?

c How else could you have worked out the total area?

13 Work out the shaded area of each shape.

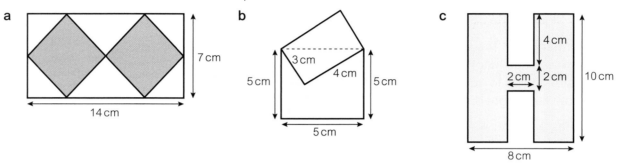

a 14 cm, 7 cm

b 5 cm, 3 cm, 4 cm, 5 cm, 5 cm

c 4 cm, 2 cm, 2 cm, 10 cm, 8 cm

Investigation   Real / Reasoning

These boxes have the same volume.

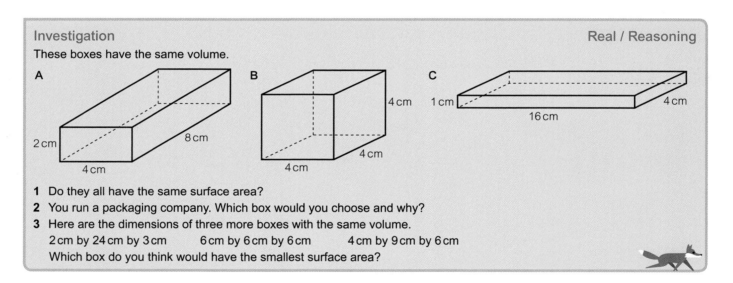

A 2 cm, 4 cm, 8 cm

B 4 cm, 4 cm, 4 cm

C 1 cm, 16 cm, 4 cm

1 Do they all have the same surface area?

2 You run a packaging company. Which box would you choose and why?

3 Here are the dimensions of three more boxes with the same volume.
   2 cm by 24 cm by 3 cm   6 cm by 6 cm by 6 cm   4 cm by 9 cm by 6 cm
   Which box do you think would have the smallest surface area?

---

14 Reasoning Look at this cuboid.

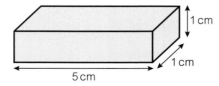

1 cm, 1 cm, 5 cm

a Calculate the volume of the cuboid.

b Calculate the surface area of the cuboid.

c John has six of these cuboids.
   How can he put them together to make a cuboid with
   i the smallest surface area
   ii the largest surface area?

15 Calculate the volume of each solid.

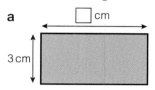
a

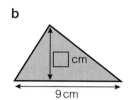
b

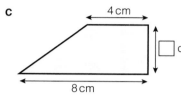
c

Q15 hint

First calculate any missing lengths. Then divide the shape into cuboids and work out the volume of each cuboid separately.

16 Each of these shapes has an area of 18 cm².
Find the missing numbers.

a

b

c

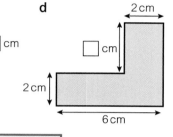
d

17 **Real** An Olympic-size swimming pool measures 50 m by 25 m and has a depth of 3 m.
   a Calculate the volume of the pool in
      i m³   **ii** cm³
   b How many litres of water can the pool hold?

Q17 hint

1 litre = 1000 cm³

18 Copy and complete the working to calculate the surface area of this triangular prism.

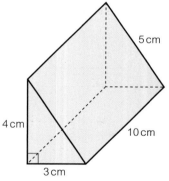

A triangular prism has ☐ faces. There are ☐ triangles and ☐ rectangles.

Area of triangle A = $\frac{1}{2}$ × ☐ × ☐ = ☐ cm²
Area of triangle B = $\frac{1}{2}$ × ☐ × ☐ = ☐ cm²
Area of rectangle C = ☐ × ☐ = ☐ cm²
Area of rectangle D = ☐ × ☐ = ☐ cm²
Area of rectangle E = ☐ × ☐ = ☐ cm²
Surface area = ☐ + ☐ + ☐ + ☐ + ☐ = ☐ cm²

19 **Reflect** Look back at Q5. It asked you to show why some statements were wrong.
What methods did you use to show that they were wrong?
In what sort of situation might you need to prove that a statement is untrue?

Master
P207

Check
P223

Strengthen
P225

Extend
P229

TEST

9 Unit test

Log how you did on your
Student Progression Chart.

1 For this shape work out
  a the perimeter
  b the area.

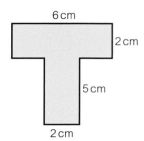

6 cm

2 cm

5 cm

2 cm

2 For each solid work out
  a the volume
  b the surface area.

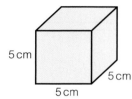

5 cm

5 cm

5 cm

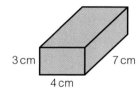

3 cm

7 cm

4 cm

3 Work out the area of each shape.

  a

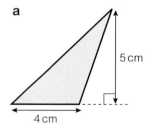

5 cm

4 cm

  b

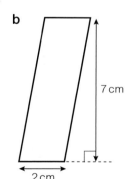

7 cm

2 cm

4 Calculate the shaded area of each shape.

  a

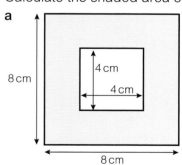

8 cm

4 cm

4 cm

8 cm

  b

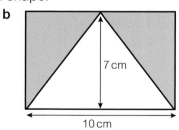

7 cm

10 cm

5 The square and the rectangle have the same area.
  Work out
  a the area of the square in cm²
  b the area of the square in m²
  c the length marked ☐

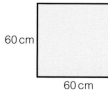

60 cm

60 cm

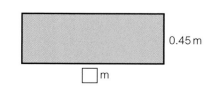

0.45 m

☐ m

6 Work out the volume of this solid.

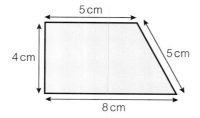

7 Work out the area of this trapezium.

5 cm
4 cm
5 cm
8 cm

8 Copy and complete these conversions.

a $4.3\,m^3 = \square\,cm^3$ **b** $\square\,cm^3 = 8500\,mm^3$ **c** $540\,ml = \square\,cm^3$

Challenge

9 This is a tangram puzzle.

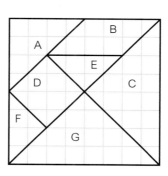

a Name the shapes that make up the puzzle.
b The total area of the puzzle is $64\,cm^2$.
Find the area of each shape in the puzzle.
c Gary tries to put the shapes back in a square by
placing the two largest triangles opposite each other.

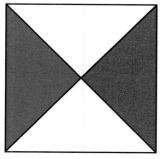

Can he fit in the remaining pieces?
Explain your answer.

10 Reflect Write a heading, 'Five important things about perimeter, area
and volume'.
Now look back at the work you have done in this unit, and list the five
most important things you think you have learned.
You could include
• formulae
• conversions
• methods for working things out
• mistakes to avoid (with tips on how to avoid them in future).

10.1 Sequences

You will learn to:
- Work out the terms of an arithmetic sequence using the term-to-term rule
- Work out a given term in a simple arithmetic sequence.

CONFIDENCE

Why learn this?
Economists spot patterns and sequences when they are predicting trends in business growth.

Fluency
What are the first five multiples of
- 3
- 8?
What is the number halfway between
- 18 and 26
- 24 and 38?

Explore
How long will it take you to count in 2s up to 1 million?

Exercise 10.1

Warm up

1 Write the next three **terms** in each **sequence**.
  a 4, 8, 12, 16, □, □, □
  b 0.5, 1, 1.5, 2, 2.5, □, □, □
  c 3.1, 3.3, 3.5, 3.7, □, □, □
  d 1.8, 1.5, 1.2, 0.9, □, □, □

2 Write the missing terms in each sequence.
  a 12, 15, □, 21, 24, □
  b 1, 2, 4, □, 16, 32, □, 128
  c 1, □, 5, 7, □, 11
  d 30, □, □, 15, 10, 5

3 Look at the sequences in Q2.
  Which ones are **ascending**?

4 Are these sequences **finite** or **infinite**?
  a integers
  b positive multiples of 10 up to 100
  c prime numbers
  d square numbers smaller than 200
  e multiples of 5

5 Describe each sequence by giving the **1st term** and the **term-to-term rule**.
  a 5, 7, 9, 11, 13, ...
  b 100, 90, 80, 70, 60, ...
  c 15, 21, 27, 33, 39, ...
  d 20, 15, 10, 5, 0, ...

6 Which of these sequences are **arithmetic**?
  a 18, 17, 16, 15, 14, ...
  b 1, 3, 9, 27, 81, ...
  c 5, 8, 11, 14, 17, ...
  d −12, −7, −2, 3, 8, ...
  e 1, 0, 1, 0, 1, ...
  f 1, 2, 4, 7, 11, ...

Key point
Numbers in a **sequence** are called **terms**.

Key point
Numbers *increase* in **ascending** sequences.
Numbers *decrease* in **descending** sequences.
A **finite** sequence has a fixed number of terms.
An **infinite** sequence goes on forever.

Key point
You can describe a sequence by giving the **1st term** and the **term-to-term rule**. The term-to-term rule tells you how to get from one term to the next.

Key point
An **arithmetic sequence** goes up or down in equal steps. This step is called the **common difference**.

Q6 hint
Do you get to the next term each time by adding (or subtracting) the same amount?

Topic links: Negative numbers, Types of number

7 Work out the first five terms of each arithmetic sequence.

  a 1st term = 9   **common difference** = 5

  b 1st term = 15   common difference = −3

  c 1st term = −50   common difference = −5

  d 1st term = 0   common difference = 4

  e 1st term = 9.5   common difference = 0.2

  f 1st term = −12   common difference = 0.3

Q7a hint

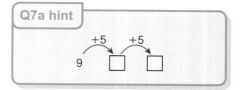

  Discussion What type of sequence do you get from a positive common difference? … a negative common difference?

8 Describe each arithmetic sequence by writing the 1st term and the common difference.

  a 9, 18, 27, 36, …   **b** 20, 30, 40, 50, …

  c 3, 5, 7, 9, 11, …   **d** 30, 25, 20, 15, 10, …

  e 9, 11, 13, 15, 17, …   **f** 100, 89, 78, 67, 56, …

9 A computer virus affects two more computers each day it is running.

  a Copy and continue the sequence to show how many computers will be affected up to 10 days after the start of the virus.

    1, 3, 5, …

  b How many days will it be before the virus has infected more than 40 computers?

  Discussion How did you work out the answer to part **b**? Is there a quick way to work out the answer?

10 The first five terms of a sequence are 3, 6, 9, 12, 15

  What is the

  a 10th term

  b 50th term

  c 100th term?

11 **Modelling / Reasoning** The table shows the UK population in 1950 and 2000.

Year	UK population (to the nearest million)
1950	51 000 000
2000	59 000 000

  a Assuming that the population growth is an arithmetic sequence, what will the population be in 2050?

  b Do you think it is sensible to predict the population like this? Explain your answer.

  c The population in 2010 was actually 62 000 000

    Does this change your prediction for the population in 2050?

12 **Explore** How long will it take you to count in 2s up to 1 million? Look back at the maths you have learned in this lesson. How can you use it to answer this question?

13 **Reflect** Think carefully about your work on sequences. How would you define a sequence in your own words? Write down your definition. Compare your definition with someone else in your class.

Explore

Reflect

10.2 The nth term

You will learn to:

- Work out and use expressions for the nth term in an arithmetic sequence.

Why learn this?
Surveyors need a general rule to work out the materials needed for different heights of building.

Fluency
What is the 10th term of the sequence of multiples of
- 2
- 4
- 9?

Explore
How many windows do you need for a row of 100 beach huts?

Exercise 10.2

1 What is the term-to-term rule for each sequence?

  a 6, 11, 16, 21, 26, …

  b 10, 7, 4, 1, −2, …

2 When $n = 3$, work out the value of

  a $2n$ **b** $3n + 2$ **c** $5n - 4$

3 Solve these equations.

  a $8n = 96$ **b** $2n + 1 = 15$

> **Key point**
>
> n is the **term number**.
> 1st   2nd   3rd   4th…
> n is always a positive integer.
> You can describe a sequence by giving the **general term** (or nth term). The general term relates the term number, n, to the term.

Worked example

The **general term** of a sequence is $n + 12$

a Write the first five terms of the sequence.

1st term: $1 + 12 = 13$ — 1st term: $n = 1$

2nd term: $2 + 12 = 14$ — 2nd term: $n = 2$

3rd term: $3 + 12 = 15$

4th term: $4 + 12 = 16$ Replace n with the term number each time, to work out the rest of the terms in the sequence.

5th term: $5 + 12 = 17$

The sequence is 13, 14, 15, 16, 17, …

b Work out the value of the 12th term.

12th term: $12 + 12 = 24$ — 12th term: $n = 12$

4 The general term of a sequence is $4n$.

  a Write the first five terms in the sequence.

  b Work out the 15th term.

5 Work out the first five terms of the sequence for each general term.

  a $5n$ **b** $7n$ **c** $12n$

  Discussion How else could you describe these sequences?

Topic links: Negative numbers, Multiples

6 Reasoning Work out
   a the 10th term in the sequence with general term $n - 3$
   b the 22nd term in the sequence with general term $2n$
   c the 50th term in the sequence $n - 20$
   Discussion Is it easier to find a term of a sequence using the general term of a sequence or the 1st term and the term-to-term rule? Explain your answer.

7 Find the general term of each sequence.
   a 3, 6, 9, 12, 15, …   **b** 2, 4, 6, 8, 10, …
   c 10, 20, 30, 40, 50, …   **d** 11, 22, 33, 44, 55, 66, …

Q7 hint
Look at your answers to Q5. Can you see a pattern?

8 a Work out the first five terms of the sequence for each general term.
     i $n + 10$ **ii** $n - 7$ **iii** $n + 12$ **iv** $n - 1$
   b Describe each sequence by giving the 1st term and the common difference.

9 The first four terms of a sequence are 3, 4, 5, 6
   Alice compares each term to its term number in the sequence.

Term number  1   2   3   4   … n
Term   +☐   3   4   5   6   … $n +$ ☐   +☐

   What is the general term of the sequence?

Q9 hint
What do you do to the term number to get the term?

10 Find the general term of each sequence.
   a 5, 6, 7, 8, 9, …   **b** 0, 1, 2, 3, 4, 5, …
   c 10, 11, 12, 13, 14, … **d** 21, 22, 23, 24, 25, …

Q10 hint
Use the method from Q9.

11 Work out the first five terms of the sequence for each general term.
   a $3n + 4$ **b** $2n + 5$ **c** $4n - 2$
   d $n + 12$ **e** $5n - 3$
   Discussion How does the common difference relate to the general term in each sequence?

12 Work out the first five terms of the sequence for each general term.
   a $n - 12$ **b** $2n - 15$ **c** $n - 8$ **d** $10n - 50$

Worked example

Work out the general term of the sequence
5, 7, 9, 11, 13, …

5   7   9   11   13   …
+2 +2 +2 +2 +2

First work out the common difference.

+3 ⟨ 2   4   6   8   10 ⟩ +3
     5   7   9   11   13

The common difference is 2, so compare it to the multiples of 2. (The general term for multiples of 2 is $2n$)

From multiples of 2 add 3 to get the sequence.

General term: $2n + 3$

13 Work out the general term of each sequence.
   a 4, 7, 10, 13, 16, …   **b** 7, 9, 11, 13, 15, …
   c 12, 17, 22, 27, 32, …   **d** 8, 18, 28, 38, 48, …
   e 24, 36, 48, 60, …   **f** 8, 17, 26, 35, 44, …
   g 9, 19, 29, 39, 49, …

14 Reasoning The general term of a sequence is $10n$.

   a Is 35 a term in this sequence?
     Explain your answer.
   b Which term number has the value 60?
   c Which term will be the first one larger than 105?

15 a Solve the equation $2n + 1 = 11$
   b Joe says the 5th term of a sequence with general term $2n + 1$ is 11
     Is he right?
   c What position is 23 in the sequence with general term $2n + 1$?

Q15b hint

Look at part **a**.

16 The general term of a sequence is $5n - 3$
   Which term number is
   a 22   **b** 47   **c** 112?

17 Problem-solving / Reasoning Solve the equation $4n + 7 = 17$
   Is 17 a term in the sequence $4n + 7$?
   Explain your answer.

18 Which of the terms in the cloud are in
   sequences with these general terms?
   a $2n - 3$
   b $5n - 8$

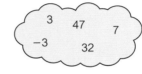
3   47   7
−3   32

   Discussion Which terms are in both sequences?

19 Reasoning / Modelling The number of people reading a blog
   increases by 100 each day.
   a On the first day 300 people read the blog.
     How many will be reading it after 28 days?
   b Is this a good model for predicting the number of blog readers
     over time?

Q19a hint

Work out the general term for the
sequence of the number of people
reading the blog each day.

20 For an arithmetic sequence with a 1st term of -12 and a common
   difference of 5, work out
   a the nth term
   b the term number of the first term greater than 200

21 **Explore** How many windows do you need for a row of 100 beach
   huts?
   Look back at the maths you have learned in this lesson.
   How can you use it to answer this question?

22 **Reflect** After this lesson Karen says, 'I can work out any number in
   a sequence using the general term.' Fiona says, 'I can tell whether
   a number will be part of a sequence using the general term.'
   Look back at the work you did this lesson.
   Which questions could Karen be talking about?
   Which questions could Fiona be talking about?

Explore

Reflect

10.3 Pattern sequences

You will learn to:
- Generate sequences and predict how they will continue
- Recognise geometric sequences and work out the term-to-term rule.

Why learn this?
Identifying patterns in nature can help biologists detect population growth or decline in the animal kingdom.

Fluency
- What is the term-to-term rule for 2, 4, 6, 8?
- Is this an arithmetic sequence?
- What is $2n^2$ when $n = 3$?

Explore
What is the half-life of a radioactive substance?

Exercise 10.3

1 Draw the next two patterns in this sequence.

2 a Draw the next two patterns in this sequence.
b Write the next three terms in this sequence.
1, 4, 9, 16, ☐, ☐, ☐
c What is the name for the numbers in part **b**?
d Look at the difference between the terms in the sequence. What do you notice?

3 This is the start of the sequence of triangular numbers.
a Draw the next two patterns in the sequence.
b Look at the difference between the terms in the sequence. What do you notice?
c Work out the 10th triangular number.

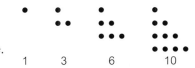

1   3   6   10

4 For each sequence in parts **a** and **b**
  i draw the next two patterns
  ii copy and complete the table
  iii write the 1st term and the term-to-term rule.

a

Term number	1	2	3	4	5
Number of lines	6	11			

b

Term number	1	2	3	4	5	6
Number of dots	2	6	12			

Warm up

5 The 1st term of a sequence is 2. The term-to-term rule is 'double the previous term'.
Write the first six terms in the sequence.

6 Describe each sequence by giving the 1st term and the term-to-term rule.
  a 1, 3, 9, 27, …
  b 10, 100, 1000, 10 000, …
  c 1, 0.5, 0.25, 0.125, …
  Discussion Is the sequence in part **c** geometric?

> **Key point**
>
> In a **geometric sequence**, the term-to-term rule is 'multiply by ☐'.
> You find each term by multiplying the previous term in the sequence by a constant value.

7 Decide whether each sequence is arithmetic or geometric.
  a 2, 5, 8, 11, 14, …
  b 5, 50, 500, 5000, …
  c 128, 64, 32, 16, …
  d 0.1, 0.2, 0.4, 0.8, 1.6, …
  e 0.5, 0.3, 0.1, −0.1, …

8 For each geometric sequence in parts **a** to **d**
  i describe the sequence by giving the 1st term and the term-to-term rule
  ii write the next two terms.
  a 1, 2, 4, 8, 16, …
  b 200, 100, 50, 25, …
  c 5, 25, 125, 625, …
  d $1, \frac{1}{2}, \frac{1}{4}, \frac{1}{8}, \ldots$

9 Work out the first three terms of the sequence for each general term.
  a $3n^2$
  b $n^2 + 4$
  c $\dfrac{n^2}{2}$

10 In the Fibonacci sequence you find each term by adding the previous two terms together.
1, 1, 2, 3, 5, …
  a Work out the next two terms in the Fibonacci sequence.
  b Look at the differences between terms in the Fibonacci sequence. What do you notice?

> **Q10 Literacy hint**
>
> The **Fibonacci sequence** is named after the Italian mathematician Leonardo Fibonacci.

Investigation   *Modelling / Problem-solving*

A robotic rabbit is in a field. It is lonely.
It learns how to make a new robotic rabbit when it is 2 months old.
From then on, it can produce one new robotic rabbit each month.
Each new robotic rabbit works the same way, and can produce a new one when it is 2 months old.
The robotic rabbits never die.
How many robotic rabbits will there be in one year?

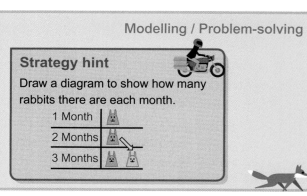

> **Strategy hint**
>
> Draw a diagram to show how many rabbits there are each month.
>
> | 1 Month | 🐰 |
> | 2 Months | 🐰 |
> | 3 Months | 🐰 🐰 |

11 Explore What is the half-life of a radioactive substance?
Is it easier to explore this question now you have completed the lesson?
What further information do you need to be able to answer this?

12 Reflect Narayani and Uzma are discussing sequences. Narayani says, 'Geometric sequences get bigger more quickly than arithmetic sequences.' Uzma says, 'Not always.'
Write down a geometric and an arithmetic sequence that Narayani could have been thinking of.
Write down a geometric and an arithmetic sequence that Uzma could have been thinking of.

10.4 Coordinates and line segments

You will learn to:
- Use positive and negative coordinates
- Work out the midpoint of a line segment.

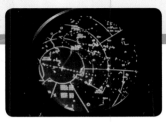

Why learn this?
Air traffic controllers use the coordinates of aircraft and plot their journeys to ensure there are no accidents.

Fluency

Work out half of
- 16
- 13
- 19

Work out
- −3 + 5
- 8 + −2
- $\dfrac{-3 + 8}{2}$

Explore
How do you tell a computer to display graphics in the bottom left corner of the screen?

Exercise 10.4

1 a Write the coordinates of points A, B and C.
b D is the point (4, 1).
c What is the name of shape ABDC?

2 The length of the **line segment** AB is 4 units.
Work out the length of the line CD.

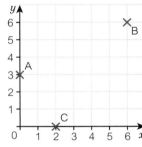

3 Work out the distance between each pair of coordinates.
a (0, 4) and (5, 4)   **b** (4, 8) and (4, 0)   **c** (3, 7) and (5, 7)
Discussion How could you find the distance between (2, 7) and (2, 3) without plotting them? Does this work for (3, 1) and (5, 6)?

4 Write the coordinates of points A, B, C and D.

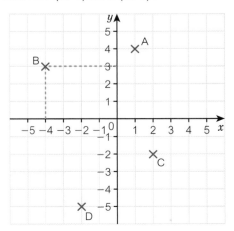

Key point
A **line segment** is part of a line.
It has a beginning and an end point.

Q3 Strategy hint
Draw a pair of axes, plot the points and join them together.

Key point
The x- and y-axes extend below 0, so you can plot points with negative x- and y-coordinates.
The point (0, 0) is called the **origin**.

Q4 hint
Look at point B. Read off the coordinate from the x-axis and then the y-axis.

5 Draw a grid with x- and y-axes from −5 to 5

   a Plot and label these points.

      A (3, 0)   B (2, 2)   C (0, 3)   D (−2, 2)

      E (−3, 0)   F (−2, −2)   G (0, −3)   H (2, −2)

   b Join the points in alphabetical order.
      What shape have you made?

6 Work out the coordinates of the midpoint of each line segment.
The first one has been done for you.

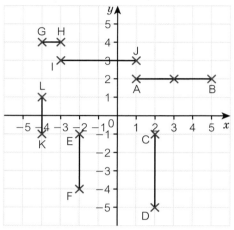

Midpoint of AB = (3, 2)

Q6 hint

Find the point halfway between A and B. Write its coordinates.

7 Work out the midpoint of each line segment.

   a A (2, 2)   B (4, 2)   **b** C (1, −2)   D (1, 4)

   c E (1, 4)   F (−5, 4)   **d** G (−5, 1)   H (−5, −4)

   Discussion How could you find the midpoint of a line without
plotting the coordinates?

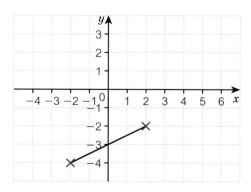

Q7 Strategy hint

Plot each pair of points and join them. Then mark on the midpoints.

8 Find the midpoint of the line segment joining each pair of points.

   a A (2, 4)   B (2, 12)   **b** X (11, 4)   Y (5, 4)

   c M (2, 5)   N (6, 9)   **d** P (6, −2)   Q (4, 4)

   e G (−5, 2)   H (−1, −4)   **f** V (20, −10)   W (−3, 1)

9 Explore How do you tell a computer to display graphics in the
bottom left corner of the screen?
Is it easier to explore this question now you have completed the
lesson?
What further information do you need to be able to answer this?

10 Reflect Freya, Noah and Stef are talking about this line:
Freya says, 'One end is at the point: (2, −2)'
Noah says, 'The midpoint is at: (−3, 0)'
Stef says, 'The other end is at the point: (2, 2)'

   a Who is right and who is wrong?

   b Write a hint on reading coordinates, in your own words,
to help the students who are wrong.
Check your hint. Will it stop them making their mistakes?

Topic links: Negative numbers   _Active_ Learn   Delta 1, Section 10.4

10.5 Graphs

You will learn to:
- Draw straight-line graphs
- Recognise straight-line graphs parallel to the axes
- Recognise graphs of $y = x$ and $y = -x$.

Why learn this?
Meteorologists plot graphs to show trends in data and predict future weather.

Fluency
Work out
- -2×4
- $-3 \times 5 + 3$
- $8 \times -2 - 7$

Explore
Do two straight lines always cross? Can they cross more than once?

Exercise 10.5

1 Work out the output from each function machine.

a
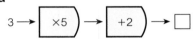
$3 \rightarrow [\times 5] \rightarrow [+2] \rightarrow \square$

b
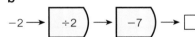
$-2 \rightarrow [\div 2] \rightarrow [-7] \rightarrow \square$

2 a $y = 3x$
   Work out the value of y when
   i $x = 7$
   ii $x = -4$

b $y = 2x - 3$
   Work out the value of y when
   i $x = 3$
   ii $x = -2$

3 a Write the coordinates of all the points on line A.
  b What do you notice about the x-coordinates?
  c Copy and complete these statements.
     i The **equation** of line A is $x = \ldots$
     ii The equation of line B is $x = \ldots$
     iii The equation of line C is $y = \ldots$

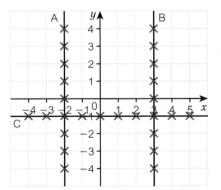

> **Key point**
>
> A line on a coordinate grid is called a **graph**. You can describe it by giving the **equation** of the line.

4 Look at these points.
  P (5, 2)   Q (12, 5)   R (5, −3)   S (5, 0)   T (−2, 5)
  Which of them are on the line
  a $x = 5$ **b** $y = 5$?
  Discussion Which axis is the **graph** of $x = 6$ parallel to?

5 Draw a grid with x- and y-axes from −5 to 5
  Draw and label these graphs.
  a $x = 4$ **b** $y = 2$ **c** $y = -3$ **d** $x = -3$
  Discussion Which axis is the graph of $y = 2$ parallel to?

> **Q5 hint**
>
> When you draw a graph it should go to the edge of the grid.

Warm up

6 a Copy and complete the table of values for the equation $y = 2x$

x	0	1	2	3	4
y	$2 \times 0 = 0$				

Q6a hint

Substitute each value of x into the equation $y = 2x$

b Write down the coordinate pairs from the table.
The first one has been done for you.

(O, O)

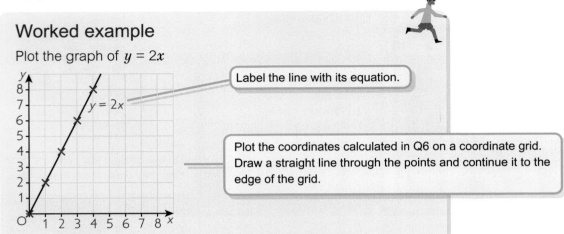

Worked example

Plot the graph of $y = 2x$

Label the line with its equation.

$y = 2x$

Plot the coordinates calculated in Q6 on a coordinate grid.
Draw a straight line through the points and continue it to the edge of the grid.

7 a Copy and complete the table of values for the equation $y = x + 3$

x	0	1	2	3	4
y					

Q7 hint

Label your graph.

b Write the coordinates.
c Draw a grid with x- and y-axes from 0 to 8. Plot the graph of $y = x + 3$

8 a Copy and complete the table of values for the equation $y = 2x - 1$

x	1	2	3	4	5
y	$2 \times 1 - 1$ $= \square - 1$ $= \square$				

b What is the highest y-value in your table?
c Draw a pair of axes up to this y-value. Plot the graph of $y = 2x - 1$

9 a Copy and complete the table of values for the equation $y = 3x + 2$

x	−2	−1	0	1	2
y					

b Draw a pair of axes and plot the graph of $y = 3x + 2$

10 a Copy and complete the table of values for the equation $y = 4x - 3$

x	−1	0	1	2	3
y					

Q11c hint

Draw a line from $y = -7$ across to your graph and then up to the x-axis.

b Draw a pair of axes and plot the graph of $y = 4x - 3$

11 a Copy and complete the table of values for the equation $y = 3 + 2x$

x	−6	−4	−2	0	2
y					

b Plot the graph of $y = 3 + 2x$
c Use your graph to find the value of x when $y = -7$

Topic links: Negative numbers

Investigation

Reasoning

1 Make a table of values for each graph. Use the x-values 0, 1, 2, 3, 4
   a $y = x$
   b $y = 2x$
   c $y = 3x$
2 For each table, complete the statement
   'When the x-value increases by 1, the y-value increases by ▢'
3 a Predict what you think will happen in the table for $y = 4x$
   b Check your answer by making the table of values.
4 a Plot all the graphs from part **1** on the same pair of axes.
   b Which graph is steepest?
5 Look at these tables of values.

too sim. to Core 9.2 Q5?

Graph A

x	−1	0	1
y	−6	0	6

Graph B

x	−1	0	1
y	−5	0	5

   a Which graph is steepest, A or B?
   b Plot the graphs to check your answer.

12 Draw a grid with x- and y-axes from −5 to 5
   a Plot the graph of $y = x$
   b Plot the graph of $y = -x$
   c What is the angle between the two graphs?

13 Match the equations of the graphs to the lines.

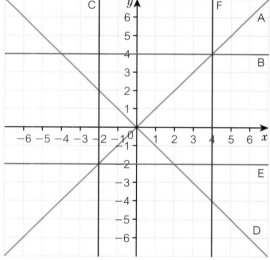

$x = -2$

$y = x$

$y = 4$

$y = -x$

$y = -2$

$x = 4$

Q12a hint

The y-coordinate will always be the same as the x-coordinate, for example (3, 3).

Q12b hint

The y-coordinate will always be equal to the x-coordinate, but with the opposite sign, for example (2, −2) or (−2, 2).

14 **Explore** Do two straight lines always cross?
   Can they cross more than once?
   Look back at the maths you have learned in this lesson.
   How can you use it to answer this question?

15 **Reflect** Here are three things you have done in this lesson:
   A Completed a table of coordinate pairs.
   B Drawn a straight-line graph.
   C Read coordinates from a straight-line graph.
   Which of these things did you find easiest? What made it easy?
   Which of these things did you find most difficult? What made it difficult?
   Do you think you need more practice on any of these things? If so, which one(s)?

Explore

Reflect

10 Check up

Log how you did on your Student Progression Chart.

Sequences

1 Describe each sequence by writing the 1st term and the term-to-term rule.

   a 3, 5, 7, 9, …

   b 2, 20, 200, 2000, …

   c 20, 17, 14, 11, …

2 For this sequence

  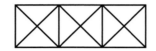

   a sketch the next two patterns

   b copy and complete the table

   c write the 1st term and the term-to-term rule.

Term number	1	2	3	4	5
Number of lines	6	11			

3 The first few terms of an arithmetic sequence are 7, 14, 21, 28, …
What is the 11th term in the sequence?

4 Work out the first five terms of each arithmetic sequence.

   a 1st term = 12   common difference = 5

   b 1st term = 8   common difference = −6

5 Work out the first three terms and the 6th term of the sequence for each general term.

   a $3n$

   b $n + 7$

   c $5n - 3$

6 Work out the general term of each arithmetic sequence.

   a 5, 10, 15, 20, …

   b 4, 5, 6, 7, 8, …

   c 3, 5, 7, 9, 11, …

7 Is each sequence arithmetic or geometric?

   a 1, 2, 4, 8, 16, …

   b 1, 3, 5, 7, 9, …

   c 20, 10, 0, −10, −20, …

   d 240, 120, 60, 30, 15, …

8 A geometric sequence starts 1, 5, 25, …

   a What is the term-to-term rule?

   b Work out the 4th term.

Graphs

9 Write the coordinates of the points
A, B, C, D, E, F.

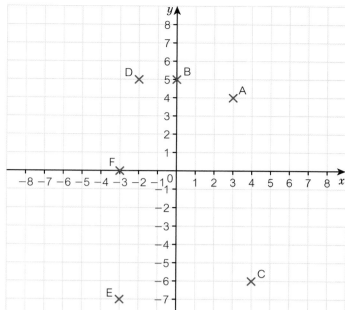

10 Write the equations of the graphs A, B, C and D.

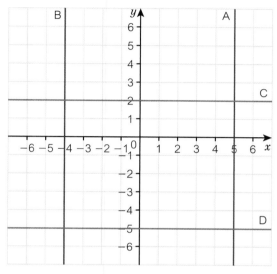

11 a Copy and complete the table of values for the
graph of $y = x + 2$
b Write five pairs of coordinates from the table.

x	0	1	2	3	4
y					

12 a Copy and complete the table of values for the
graph of $y = 2x - 3$
b Draw a grid with x- and y-axes from −10 to 10.
Plot the graph of $y = 2x - 3$

x	−2	0	2	4	6
y					

13 Work out the midpoint of the line segment joining
a (1, 5) and (1, 9)   **b** (3, 5) and (7, 1)   **c** (−2, 3) and (6, −5)

14 Draw a grid with x- and y-axes from −5 to 5
Draw and label the graphs of $y = x$ and $y = -x$

15 How sure are you of your answers? Were you mostly
😖 **Just guessing**   😐 **Feeling doubtful**   🙂 **Confident**
What next? Use your results to decide whether to strengthen or extend your learning.

Challenge

16 a Work out the first three terms of the sequence with a general term of $7 - n$.
b How many positive terms are in the sequence?

17 The general term of a sequence is n^2.
How many terms in the sequence are less than 100?

18 Write the equation of a graph that goes through the point (3, 3).
Can you find more than one?

Reflect

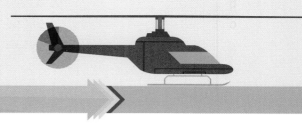

10 Strengthen

You will:

- Strengthen your understanding with practice.

Sequences

1 a An arithmetic sequence starts 4, 6, 8, 10, …
  - **i** What is the common difference?
  - **ii** Work out the next two terms.

b Another arithmetic sequence starts 49, 43, 37, 31, 25, …
  - **i** What is the common difference?
  - **ii** Work out the next two terms.

2 a Work out the next three terms of each sequence.
  - **i** 6, 11, 16, 21, …
  - **ii** 50, 43, 36, 29, …
  - **iii** 30, 41, 52, 63, …

b For each sequence, is it **ascending** or **descending**?

3 Look at this sequence made of blocks.

a Draw the next pattern in the sequence.

b Copy and complete the table.

Pattern number	1	2	3	4
Number of blocks	2	4		

c Work out the number of blocks in pattern number 5.

4 Which of these are arithmetic sequences?

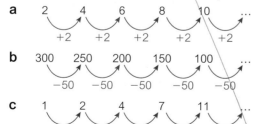

5 The 1st term of an arithmetic sequence is 3.
The common difference is 4.
Copy and complete the table to find the first five terms of this sequence.

Term number	1st	2nd	3rd	4th	5th
Term	3	3 + 4 = 7	7 + ☐ = ☐	☐ + ☐ = ☐	

Q1ai hint

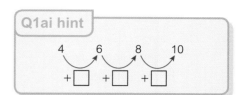

Q1bi hint

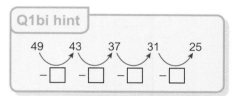

Q2b Literacy hint

Ascending numbers get bigger.
Descending numbers get smaller.

Q3c hint

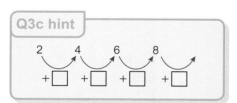

Q4 hint

In an arithmetic sequence you add or subtract the *same* number each time.

6 Find the next two terms for each arithmetic sequence.

   a 1st term = 5   common difference = 4

   b 1st term = 18   common difference = −2

   c 1st term = −10   common difference = 2

   d 1st term = 3   common difference = −3

7 Look at the sequence 5, 10, 15, 20, 25, …

   a These are multiples of □.

   b What is the 12th term?

   c Copy and complete this statement.
      'The general term is □n'

Q7 hint

1st term: 1 × □ = 5
2nd term: 2 × □ = 10
…
12th term: 12 × □ = □

8 For each sequence in parts **a** to **d**, work out

  i the general term.

  ii the 10th term

   a 4, 8, 12, 16, …

   b 11, 22, 33, 44, 55, …

   c 3, 6, 9, 12, 15, …

   d 12, 24, 36, 48, …

Q8a hint

These are multiples of □.
Use the method from Q7.

9 Look at the sequence in the table.

Term number	1 ⟩+□	2 ⟩+□	3 ⟩+□	4 ⟩+□	5 ⟩+□	n ⟩+□
Term	3	4	5	6	7	…

   a What do you add to the term number each time to get the term?
      Is it the same for every term?

   b Write the general term of the sequence.

Q9b hint

n + □

10 Work out the general term of each sequence.

  a

Term number	1	2	3	4	5
Term	10	11	12	13	14

Q10a hint

Use the method from Q9.

  b

Term number	1	2	3	4	5
Term	0	1	2	3	4

Q10b hint

n − □

   c 15, 16, 17, 18, …

   d −3, −2, −1, 0, 1, …

Q10c hint

Draw a table to help you.

11 The general term (nth term) of a sequence is $n + 5$
    Work out the first five terms.

Q11 hint

1st term: 1 + 5 = □
2nd term: 2 + □ = □

12 Work out the first five terms of the sequence with nth term $2n − 1$
    The first one has been done for you.

   nth term: 2 × n − 1

   1st term: ②×①− 1 = 2 − 1 = 1

Q12 hint

2nd term: 2 × □ − 1 = □
3rd term: 2 × □ − 1 = □

13 The general term of a sequence is $2n − 7$
    Work out the first five terms.

Q13 hint

Substitute $n = 1$, $n = 2$, $n = 3$, $n = 4$, $n = 5$ into $2n − 7$

14 These two sequences have the same common difference.

Sequence A   3, 6, 9, 12, 15, …

Sequence B   5, 8, 11, 14, 18, …

  a Work out the general term of sequence A.

  b What do you add to each term in sequence A to get the terms in sequence B?

  c Copy and complete the general term of sequence B.

    $3n + \square$

Q14a hint

Sequence A is multiples of $\square$.

Q14b hint

15 Work out the general term of each sequence.

  a 11, 21, 31, 41, 51, …

  b 7, 10, 13, 16, 19, …

  c 7, 12, 17, 22, 27, …

Q15a hint

The common difference is 10, so compare this sequence to the multiples of 10 (10, 20, 30, 40, 50, …).

16 Which sequence in each set is a geometric sequence?

  a **A** 2, 4, 8, 16, …   **B** 2, 4, 7, 11, …   **C** 2, 8, 14, 20, …

  b **D** 32, 28, 24, 20, …   **E** 32, 8, 2, 0.5, …   **F** 32, 16, 0, −16, …

Q16 hint

In a geometric sequence the term-to-term rule is to multiply or divide by the same number each time.

17 a Work out the term-to-term rule in this geometric sequence.

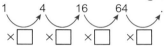

  b Work out the next two terms in the sequence.

Q17a hint

Check that the multiplier is the same each time.

 18 For each sequence in parts **a** to **e**, work out

  i the term-to-term rule

  ii the next two terms in the sequence.

  a 1, 10, 100, 1000, …

  b 2, 7, 12, 17, …

  c 3, 6, 12, 24, …

  d $\frac{1}{6}$, 1, 6, 36, …

  e 50, 45, 40, 35, …

Q18 hint

For ascending sequences try + $\square$ and × $\square$

For descending sequences try − $\square$ and ÷ $\square$

Graphs

1 a Copy this grid with x- and y-axes from −5 to 5.

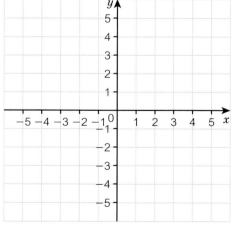

  b Plot the points (1, 2), (1, 3), (1, −5), (1, −3), (1, 0). Draw a line through all the points.

  c What do you notice about the x-coordinate of all the points?

  d Copy and complete

    'The equation of the line is $x = \square$. It is parallel to the __-axis.'

Q1b hint

To plot the point (1, −5) move 1 to the right along the x-axis and 5 down the y-axis.

2 a Copy the grid from Q1.

b Plot the points (2, −3), (4, −3), (−2, −3), (−5, −3), (0, −3).
Draw a line through all the points.

c What do you notice about the y-coordinate of all the points?

d Copy and complete
'The equation of the line is $y = \square$. It is parallel to the __-axis.'

3 Write the coordinates of five points that lie on the graph of

a $y = 3$

b $x = -2$

c $y = -1$

d $x = 14$

4 a Copy and complete the table of values for the equation $y = x + 2$

x	0	1	2	3	4	5
y	2					

b Write each pair of coordinates from the table.
The first one has been done for you.

(O, 2)　　(1, □),(2, □),(3, □),…
↑↖
x　y

c Copy this coordinate grid.
Plot the points.
The first one has been done for you.

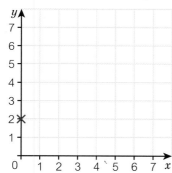

d Join the points with a straight line.
Label the graph, $y = x + 2$

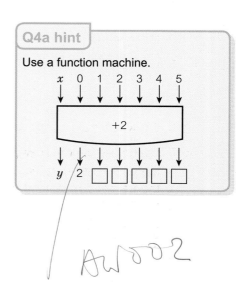

AW002

AW003

5 a Copy and complete the table of values for the equation $y = 3x$

x	0	1	2	3	4
y	0				

b Draw a grid with x- and y-axes from 0 to 12
Plot the points.

c Join the points with a straight line.
Label the graph, $y = 3x$

AW 004

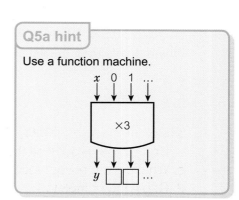

6 Copy and complete the table of values for the equation $y = 2x + 3$.

x	0	1	2	3	4
y	3				

Q6 hint

Use a function machine.

x 0 1 ...

×2

+3

y ☐ ☐ ...

7 Copy this grid with x- and y-axes from -10 to 10.

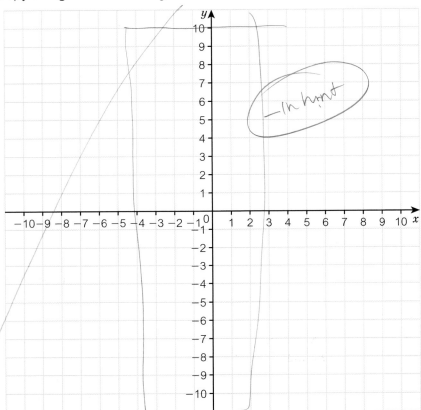

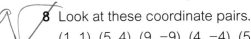
Plot the points from Q6 and join them with a straight line to draw the graph.
Label the graph, $y = 2x + 3$

8 Look at these coordinate pairs.

$(1, 1)$, $(5, 4)$, $(9, -9)$, $(4, -4)$, $(5, -5)$, $(2, 2)$, $(-3, -3)$, $(-6, 6)$

Which points from the list lie on the graph

a $y = x$

b $y = -x$?

Q8a hint

Read the equation of the graph aloud, 'y equals x'. This means that the x- and y-coordinates are the same.

Q8b hint

Read the equation of the graph aloud, 'y equals minus x'. This means that the y-coordinate is the negative of the x-coordinate.

9 a What number is halfway between

   i 1 and 5

   ii 2 and 4?

b Use your answers to help you find the midpoint of this line.

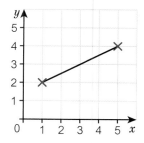

Q9a hint

The midpoint of a line segment is the point halfway between the two ends. Add the values together and divide by 2

10 Work out the midpoint of the line segments joining

   a (3, 5) and (11, 15)

   b (2, 7) and (6, 13)

   c (9, 4) and (3, 10)

Q10a hint

Find the number halfway between 3 and 11, and the number halfway between 5 and 15

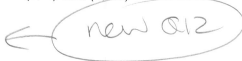

Enrichment

1 a Write five coordinate pairs that are on the graphs of

   i $y = x$

   ii $y = -x$

b Are there any that are on both graphs?

2 An ancient tale tells of an emperor offering a reward to a wise man. The wise man could choose his own reward and he asked for:
'… one grain of rice on the first square of a chessboard. Then two grains on the next square, and four on the one after that. Then double the number of grains again on every square until the board is full.'

   a A bowl of rice for one person holds about 3000 grains. Starting at the first square, how many squares does he need to take rice from to fill one bowl?

   b How many squares does he need to take rice from to fill six bowls?

Q2a hint

1 square: 1 grain of rice
2 squares: 1 + 2 grains of rice
3 squares: 1 + 2 + 4 grains of rice

Q2b hint

You could use a spreadsheet to work out the total for each number of squares.

3 Reflect Elsa says, 'The words 'term' and 'coordinates' are used a lot in these lessons. These must be important words for understanding sequences and graphs'.
Write down a definition, in your own words, for 'term' and 'coordinates'.

Reflect

10 Extend

You will:
• Extend your understanding with problem-solving.

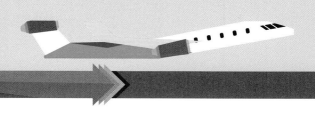

1 **Modelling** A finance director looks at the profit her company has made over the last three years.

Year	2012	2013	2014
Profit	£1500	£2000	£2500

Assume that the profit is an arithmetic sequence.
How much profit will the company make in
a 2015 **b** 2020 **c** 2050?
Discussion Are these predictions sensible?

2 A car hire company offers a special six-month deal. For the first month it costs £300 to hire the car. For the next five months the cost reduces by £50 each month.
How much will it cost to hire the car in
a the 3rd month **b** the 6th month?
Discussion Why is the deal for only six months?

3 **a** Draw a grid with x- and y-axes from −5 to 5
Draw the graphs of
i $x = 4$
ii $x = -2$
iii $y = 1$
iv $y = -1$
b Work out the area of the rectangle enclosed by the four lines.

> **Q3b hint**
> The area will be in 'square units'.

4 **Problem-solving** Two of the corners of an isosceles triangle are the points (−4, 1) and (2, 1).
List as many possible coordinates for the third corner as possible.

> **Q4 hint**
> Plot the two points first.

5 **Reasoning** Use a spreadsheet to follow these steps and answer the questions.
Step 1: Type a number into cell **A1**
Step 2: In cell **A2**, type the formula **=(A1+10)/2**. Press **Enter**.
Step 3: Click and drag cell **A2** down using its bottom right-hand corner, so the formula repeats itself.
a Describe in words what the formula does.
b What do you notice about the numbers in the sequence?
c What happens if you change the number in cell **A1**?
d Repeat this process with a different formula, replacing the **2** with a different number. What happens?
e Use the spreadsheet to plot a graph of the sequence generated in part **d**. Write a sentence about the shape of the graph.

6 a Copy and complete the table of values for the equation $y = 2x - 3$

x	−2	0	2	4	6
y					

  b Draw a grid with x- and y-axes from −10 to 10 and plot the graph of $y = 2x - 3$

  c Copy and complete the table of values for the equation $y = 6 - x$

x	−3	−1	0	5	10
y					

  d Plot the graph of $y = 6 - x$ on your grid from part **b**.

  e Write the coordinates of the point where the two graphs **intersect**.

← new Q6 f, g

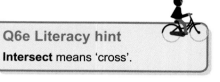

> **Q6e Literacy hint**
>
> **Intersect** means 'cross'.

7 Problem-solving / STEM In a physics experiment, Simon measures and records how much a spring stretches by, when different forces are used.

Force, F (N)	0	0.5	1	1.5	2
Extension, p (cm)	0	2.5	5	7.5	10

  a Plot the graph of F against p. Put F on the vertical axis and p on the horizontal axis.
  Hooke's law says that $F = $ (a **constant**) $\times (p)$.

  b Work out the value of the constant.
  The constant for a second spring is 0.5, so $F = 0.5p$

  c Plot the graph of $F = 0.5p$ on the same axes as in part **a**.

> **Q7a Literacy hint**
>
> A **constant** is a value that doesn't change.

> **Q7b hint**
>
> How much does F change by for 1 unit change in p?

8 STEM / Real A manufacturer claims that a car does 60 miles to the gallon.

  a Draw the graph of $d = 60f$ where $f = $ fuel used and $d = $ distance travelled.

  b Use the graph to work out
    i how much fuel is needed for a journey of 150 miles
    ii how far a car can travel on 3.5 gallons.

9 Reasoning / Real A restaurant has square tables, and 4 people can sit at each one.
When 2 tables are put together, 6 people can sit at them.

  a How many people can sit at 3 tables put together?

  b Copy and complete this table of values.

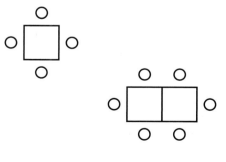

Number of tables	1	2	3	4	5
Number of seats	4	6			

  c How many people can sit at 10 tables?

  d How many extra seats are made each time a table is added?

  e Anya says the general term for the number of seats for n tables put together is $4n$, since four people can sit at each table.
  Is she right?
  Explain your answer.

  f Work out the general term for the number of seats for n tables.

  g How many tables are needed for 30 people?

10 Reasoning Write the equation of the line that goes through the points

   a A, B and C

   b D, E and F

   c B, G and H.

   Discussion Does the graph in part **c** go through point D? Explain your answer.

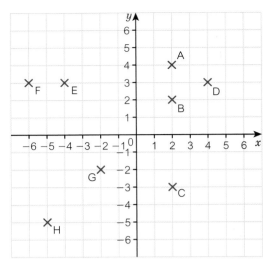

11 a Work out the midpoint of the line segment joining (1, 5) and (−4, −2).

   b A line segment RS has midpoint, M, at (7, 10). R is the point (5, 3).

   What are the coordinates of S?

12 The diagram shows three corners of a parallelogram ABCD.

   a What are the coordinates of point D?

   b Work out the coordinates of the midpoints of

     i AB   **ii** CD   **iii** BC   **iv** AD   **v** AC

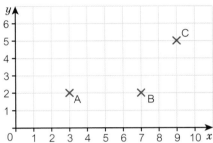

13 a Draw a grid with x- and y-axes from 0 to 5 and draw the graphs of

     i $y = x$ **ii** $x = 5$

   b **Problem-solving** Work out the area of the triangle enclosed by the lines and the x-axis.

14 Reasoning The general term of a sequence is $9n + 5$

   a Which of these numbers are in the sequence? Explain your answers.

     i 14   **ii** 99   **iii** 860   **iv** −4

   b Which number term has the value 383?

   c Which term is the first term greater than 1000?

15 Problem-solving The general term of a sequence is $-2.5n - 15$

   a Is the sequence finite or infinite?

   b Which term has the highest value? What is this value?

16 Work out the next two terms in each sequence.

   a 2, 6, 12, 20, 30, …   **b** 1, 2, 3, 5, 8, 13, …

   c 1, 2, 5, 10, 17, …   **d** 0, $\frac{1}{2}$, $1\frac{1}{2}$, 3, 5, $7\frac{1}{2}$, …

17 Work out the next two terms in each sequence.

   a 1, −1, 1, −1, 1, …

   b 2, −4, 6, −8, 10, …

   c 1, $-\frac{1}{2}$, $\frac{1}{4}$, $-\frac{1}{8}$, $\frac{1}{16}$, …

   Discussion Which of these sequences are geometric?

18 Describe each geometric sequence by giving the 1st term and the term-to-term rule.

   a 1, 4, 16, 64, …

   b 1, 10, 100, 1000, 10 000, …

   c 200, 100, 50, 25, …

   d 81, 27, 9, 3, 1, …

Topic links: Properties of polygons, Area, Algebraic manipulation

Subject links: ICT (Q5, Q21, Investigation), Science (Q7, Q8)

19 Work out the missing terms in each sequence.

    a 1, ☐, 9, 27, ☐   **b** 0, 2, 6, 12, ☐, 30

    c 10, 10, 20, 30, ..., 80, 130

Q19 Strategy hint

Look for a pattern between the terms. Test whether your pattern works for all the terms in the sequence.

20 The first two terms of a sequence are 1 and 3.
The sequence could be arithmetic *or* geometric.

    a For an arithmetic sequence starting 1, 3, ...

        i write the next two terms

        ii work out the nth term.

    b For a geometric sequence starting 1, 3, ...

        i write the next two terms

        ii describe the sequence giving the 1st term and the term-to-term rule.

21 **Reasoning**

    a Use a computer graph-sketching package to draw the graphs of

        i $y = x$ **ii** $y = x + 1$ **iii** $y = x + 2$ **iv** $y = x - 1$

    b Write the coordinates where each graph crosses the y-axis.

    c Predict where these graphs will cross the y-axis.

        i $y = x - 5$ **ii** $y = x + 12$

    Check your predictions on the graph-sketching package.

amended

22 **Reasoning** The first four terms of a geometric sequence are 2, 4, 8, 16, ...

    a Write the 5th term in the sequence.

    b Copy and complete the table.

1st term	2nd term	3rd term	4th term	5th term
2	2×2 $= 2^2$	$2 \times 2 \times 2$ $= 2^\square$	... $= 2^\square$	... $= 2^\square$

    c Work out the 10th term of the sequence.

    d Write the general term of the sequence.

Investigation   **Reasoning**

1 Create this spreadsheet to work out the first six terms of the sequence where the general term is n^2.
Click and drag the bottom right corner of cell **D2** across, so the formula repeats itself.

◢	A	B	C	D	E	F	G
1	Term number	1	2	3	4	5	6
2	Term	=B1*B1	=C1*C1	=D1*D1			

2 Add and complete this next row to work out the differences between consecutive terms for each sequence in step 1.
This is called the 1st difference.

3	1st difference		=C2–B2	=D2–C2			

3 Add and complete this next row to work out the differences between consecutive 1st differences.
This is called the 2nd difference. What do you notice?

4	2nd difference			=D3–C3			

4 Modify your spreadsheet to work out the 1st and 2nd differences for the sequences

    a $n^2 + 1$ **b** $2n^2$ **c** $3n^2$

What patterns can you see?

Now try working out the 3rd differences for n^3

---

23 **Reflect** Jacob says, 'Sequences and straight line graphs are all about following patterns.'

Look back at the work you have done in this unit. Write three sentences that describe how what you have learned is all about 'following patterns'.

Master
P235

Check
P247

Strengthen
P249

Extend
P255

TEST

10 Unit test

Log how you did on your Student Progression Chart.

1 For each sequence in parts **a** and **b**
   i draw the next two terms
   ii copy and complete the table

a

Term number	1	2	3	4	5	6
Number of dots	2	6	12			

b

Term number	1	2	3	4	5	6
Number of dots	36	25				

2 The 1st term of a sequence is 64. The term-to-term rule is 'divide by 2'.
   Write the first five terms of the sequence.

3 The first five terms of a sequence are 6, 12, 18, 24, 30, …
   What is the 9th term?

4 Work out the first four terms of these arithmetic sequences.
   a 1st term = 7   common difference = 8
   b 1st term = 10   common difference = −6

5 **a** Draw a grid with x- and y-axes from −5 to 5
   b Plot and label these points.
      A (1, 3)   B (0, 5)   C (−3, 4)   D (−5, −1)   E (2, −3)   F(−3, 0)
   c Draw and label the graphs of
      i $x = 4$ **ii** $y = −3$

6 **a** Copy and complete the table of values for the equation $y = x + 3$
   b Draw a grid with x- and y-axes from 0 to 6.
      Plot the graph of $y = x + 3$

x	0	1	2	3
y				

7 **a** Copy and complete the table of values for $y = 2x + 1$
   b Draw a grid with x- and y-axes from −10 to 10.
      Plot the graph of $y = 2x + 1$

x	−4	−2	0	2	4
y					

8 Work out the first three terms of these sequences.
   a $2n + 5$ **b** $5n − 10$

9 Decide whether each sequence is arithmetic or geometric.
   a 1, 2, 4, 8, 16, …   **b** 1, 2, 3, 4, 5, …
   c 9, 7, 5, 3, 1, …   **d** 2, 6, 18, 54, …

10 Work out the general term of each sequence.
   a 9, 18, 27, 36, …
   b 7, 8, 9, 10, …
   c 6, 11, 16, 21, 26, …

11 Calculate the midpoints of the line segments shown on the right.

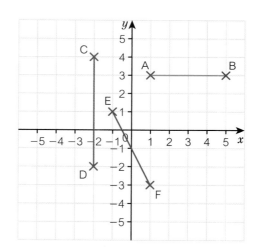

12 The diagram shows four graphs.
   a Write the letter of the graph with equation $y = -x$
   b What are the coordinates of the points where lines B and C intersect?

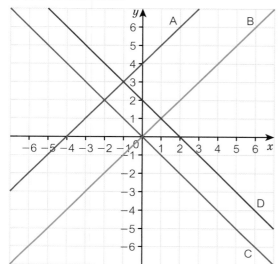

13 A geometric sequence starts 3, 9, 27, …
   a Write the 4th and 5th terms of the sequence.
   b What is the general term?

Challenge

14 Dominic makes a tile pattern from a square of red tiles surrounded by a border of blue tiles.

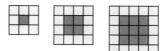

   a Copy and complete the table for the number of tiles in each pattern in the sequence.
   b Work out the general term for
      i the number of red tiles
      ii the number of blue tiles
      iii the total number of tiles.
   c Investigate similar patterns using rectangles.

	1	2	3	4	5	6
Red tiles	1					
Blue tiles	8					
Total number of tiles	9					

15 Reflect Write a heading 'Five important things about sequences and graphs'.
Now look back at the work you have done in this unit, and list the five most important things you think you have learned.
For example, you might include:
• words (with their definitions)
• methods for working things out
• mistakes you made (with tips on how to avoid them in future).